THE IROQUOIS AND THE NEW DEAL

An Iroquois Book

THE IROQUOIS

and

THE NEW DEAL

Laurence M. Hauptman

SYRACUSE UNIVERSITY PRESS 1981

Chapter 1 is reprinted by permission of the Museum of Natural History, Smithsonian Institution.

Chapter 3 is copyright © 1979 by the American Indian Historical Society, all rights reserved, and is reprinted with permission.

Chapter 4 is reprinted by permission of the Department of Anthropology, Franklin Pierce College and by the Editor of *Man in the Northwest, Occasional Publications in Northeastern Anthropology.*

Chapter 8 is reprinted by permission of the New York State Historical Association.

Library of Congress Cataloging in Publication Data

Hauptman, Laurence M.
    The Iroquois and the New Deal
    (An Iroquois book)
    Bibliography: p.
    Includes index.
1. Iroquois Indians — Government relations.
2. Indians of North America — Government relations —
1934–   I. Title.   II. Series.
E99.I7H33   323.1′197   81-21198
ISBN 0-8156-2247-3   AACR2

For Ruth

LAURENCE M. HAUPTMAN is Associate Professor of History, State University of New York College at New Paltz. He is the author of numerous articles on the Iroquois, co-editor of *Neighbors and Intruders: An Ethnohistorical Exploration of the Indians of Hudson's River,* and a contributor to *American Indian Environments: Ecological Issues in Native American History.*

CONTENTS

PREFACE

> Perhaps the first thing is to clarify the history of the respective reservations as they entered the New Deal era to determine exactly how they looked upon that whole program which Collier put into effect.
>
> Vine Deloria, Jr.
> *Red Men and Hat Wearers:*
> *Viewpoints in Indian History*

UNTIL THE LATE 1960s, scholars acclaimed the New Deal era as a model of Indian administration. Indeed, John Collier's tenure as commissioner of Indian affairs was truly remarkable in both its achievements and duration. In twelve years in office Collier and his staff were responsible for some of the most far-reaching legislation in Indian history, including the Indian Reorganization Act (1934), the Johnson O'Malley Act (1934), the Indian Arts and Crafts Board Act (1935), the Oklahoma Indian Welfare Act (1936), and the Alaska Reorganization Act (1936). The Indian New Deal formally ended the allotment policies of the past, encouraged Indian arts and the study of Indian cultures and languages, added acreage to some tribes' land bases, instituted the codification of Indian law, supported the idea of a future Indian Claims Commission, and pushed for tribal political reorganization as well as intertribal organization.

Historians in recent years have tended to qualify praise of Indian policy and policy-makers of the period. They emphasize that good intentions on the part of Commissioner Collier were undermined by his paternalistic attitude toward Indians, his naive and often romantic perceptions, his abrasive and

authoritarian personality, and even by his general lack of understanding of
Native Americans, their cultures and their diversity. Consequently, historians now view the Indian New Deal, although still praising more than
condemning it, as a period of missed opportunities in building trust between
Indian and non-Indian and in providing long-lasting economic betterment.[1]

In the process of re-evaluating the Indian New Deal, historians have
finally begun to take the significant Indian criticism of Collier and his
policies more seriously than in the past. Although the commissioner won
praise from many Indians, from the time of the passage of the Indian
Reorganization Act (IRA) in 1934 through the present day, other Native
Americans have looked askance at the political legacy of the Collier years.
Long before the take-over of Wounded Knee in 1973, bitter political battles
raged on reservations between traditional leadership and the elected systems
created under the IRA. To many Native Americans today, the New Deal
years thus mark an era of increased discord and factionalism as well as
non-Indian tampering with existing tribal political systems.[2] Native Americans have also questioned the economic importance of Indian New Deal
policies. Holding this view, the recent report of the American Indian Policy
Review Commission chastises government policy-makers from 1934 onward
for failing to promote aggressive land acquisition for tribes under the IRA
and for failing to protect even the existing Indian land base. From 1934 to
1974, under section 5 of the act, only 595,157 acres were purchased for tribal
use. In the same period, government agencies condemned 1,811,010 acres of
Indian land.[3] Although a large share of the blame for the failure of
repurchase rests with budget-minded congressmen who did not allocate the
necessary funds for implementation of the act, the rhetoric of the Indian
New Deal often exceeded administrators' abilities to accomplish the promises made.

The Iroquois population found in Ontario and Quebec in Canada and
New York, Oklahoma, and Wisconsin in the United States provides the
opportunities for studying New Deal policies and American Indian responses that few peoples offer. Historians, unlike anthropologists, have
devoted surprisingly little attention to the Six Nations in the twentieth
century.[4] Moreover, New York tribesmen overwhelmingly rejected tribal
reorganization while Iroquois in Oklahoma and Wisconsin accepted it.
Because of this marked contrast in attitudes, the Iroquois appear to be the
ideal case study to determine the successes as well as limitations of federal
governmental policies.

The New Deal era left a significant legacy of achievements behind in

Iroquoia. The Oneidas of Wisconsin and the Seneca-Cayugas of Oklahoma accepted new tribal political structures under the provisions of the Indian Reorganization Act and the Oklahoma Indian Welfare Act, governments that still operate today. In both the East and the West, Iroquois participated in innovative work-relief programs —especially those under Works Progress Administration auspices—that have left a positive mark on Indian life. These programs included the Seneca Arts Project that stimulated a fluorescence of Iroquois culture; the Oneida Language and Folklore Project that collected a rich record of Indian history and lifeways while laying the basis for modern language programs; and the construction of the Tonawanda Community House, the first center built for Iroquois use that still serves as a focal point of Seneca life. During the time of the country's worst depression, the Iroquois also survived through employment that took the form of Works Progress Administration-sponsored road building, Civilian Conservation Corps-Indian Division drainage projects, and National Youth Administration-sponsored Indian camp counselor programs. However temporary the programs were, the Iroquois New Deal was marked by community building efforts, both in a symbolic and literal sense. The Iroquois, under a myriad of government programs, reconstructed tribal governments, added to tribal land bases, constructed buildings, community centers, drainage ditches, homes, roads, and wells, revived arts, began an effort to breathe life into the fading Iroquoian languages, and inculcated the young and old with increased pride in being Iroquois.

New leadership also emerged as a result of, or in reaction to, governmental policies of the New Deal. These leaders continued to play a prominent role well into the 1960s and 1970s. Oscar Archiquette emerged as the major political force at Oneida, Wisconsin, under the new IRA tribal structure. Louis R. Bruce, Jr.'s NYA experience afforded him an early administrative opportunity and contributed to his becoming a viable candidate for commissioner of Indian affairs in the future. Alice Lee Jemison, the New Deal's harshest critic among the Iroquois, became one of the most prominent activists of her generation, testifying before Congress from the early 1930s through the 1950s, as a harbinger of Red Power militance.

Despite these achievements, the Iroquois New Deal era also left a less beneficial heritage behind. Throughout the decade prior to John Collier's administration, the Iroquois push for land claims achieved a new intensity and reached new heights. Although this movement was sidetracked by a sizeable amount of tribal factionalism and corruption on the part of some Iroquois leaders, the Indian Bureau throughout the 1930s and 1940s showed indifference to this concern paramount in the minds of many Iroquois. Moreover, because of the severity of the Great Depression and the dire need for federal programs, the land claims movement was dissipated and Iroquois leadership to a large degree was co-opted in favor of cooperation with federal officials.

The New Deal was also marked by a new aggressive thrust in Indian policy. The attempt to push through tribal reorganization on reservations in New York was seen by these Indians as unwarranted interference with their internal political systems and a threat to their concepts of sovereignty. Collier, a small, slender, slightly stooped man from Georgia who often wore baggy suits or beat-up green sweaters, appeared to many casual observers as the epitome of a mild-mannered liberal academic. Nevertheless, his emotional attachment to causes combined with his extreme self-assuredness to produce an individual that was frequently inflexible and vindictive. Although he was among the ablest of commissioners, he tolerated dissent neither from his staff nor from the Indians themselves. As the New Deal Great White Father, he thought he knew what was best for them. Overbearingly paternalistic, he antagonized many Iroquois, especially in New York, by his condescending approach to their affairs. Moreover, his spiritual infatuation with Northern Pueblo lifeways in part blinded him to the different realities of other Indians' needs. Collier's activist administration of Indian affairs also did not win friends by its rejection of Iroquois definitions of sovereignty, by acceding to the damming and flooding of Iroquois lands in Oklahoma, and by placing Iroquois, viewed as "obstructionist," under surveillance through the use of Indian informants and the Federal Bureau of Investigation.

The Iroquois New Deal was larger than the efforts of the Indian Bureau at tribal reorganization. Collier also helped set the tone, with his fervent insistence on Indian cultural retention, for policies set in motion by other governmental agencies such as WPA and NYA, encouraged community building through the employment of an applied anthropologist in the field among the Iroquois and gave his polite cooperation to efforts at constructing an Indian center at Tonawanda. He dealt head-on with the near-starvation conditions of western Iroquois who had lost their landed birthright and their political cohesion under the assault upon tribalism policies of the Dawes Act. These initiatives along with bureau-run CCC-ID work-relief projects contributed to community and reservation improvements. Just as he had made efforts at community building among diverse immigrant groups on New York's Lower East Side during the Progressive Era, Collier recreated this experience as commissioner of Indian affairs during the New Deal years.

As the present study clearly shows, much of the success of New Deal programs can be attributed to anthropologists and their work among the Iroquois. William N. Fenton, Floyd Lounsbury, Morris Swadesh, and especially Arthur C. Parker contributed their expertise in making the Indian New Deal a significant venture in community building. The artistic and language revivals that were encouraged helped to save the distinct Iroquois cultural pattern of life. Moreover, Parker's ideas about the role of museums and their responsibilities to communities has also affected the Iroquois. Today Ray Fadden, strongly influenced by Parker's example, directs the Six Nations' Museum at Onchiota; while Ernest Benedict, one of Fadden's former NYA camp counselors, founded the North American Travelling College at St. Regis to foster a better understanding and appreciation of Native American cultures through Parker-styled educational outreach programs.

Unlike most studies of the period whose authors chose to base their conclusions primarily on their analysis of documents in government archives, I decided to supplement my archival research by visiting and conducting interviews in every Iroquois community in the United States. Benjamin S. Cohn of the University of Chicago has recently pointed out that "history can become more historical in becoming more anthropological."[5] The historian, if possible, should proceed beyond the documents, since the past exists not only in archival form but also in the material culture left behind to observe. To Cohn: "The historian needs the direct experience of another culture through systematic fieldwork. It is not just the idea of the exotic, but the sense one gets that other systems work, that there are such things as cultural logics, that there is as much rationality in other societies as in our own, even though they flow from other principles."[6] Nevertheless, the employment of field work techniques by historians should not lead them to overly rely on oral history, itself fraught with inherent dangers and limitations. Furthermore, as Cohn insists, historians should not neglect archival research. They should learn, however, "how the particular documents being used were produced as well as test them for reliability."[7] Documents must be read not only for the facts but for the meanings intended, and in this respect, field work helps a historian uncover the subtleties of the written word.

Recent Native American history offers the historian unique chances to meet older tribal leaders who had been involved in the decision-making process in the 1930s and 1940s. As Vine Deloria, Jr., the noted Native American writer, has observed: "Even the people who were young during the first days of the Indian Reorganization Act are now in their fifties and sixties and would have valuable information that should be preserved."[8] As a result of the generosity of Native Americans in New York, Oklahoma, and Wisconsin and the encouragement of colleagues in the State University of New York, I concluded that the present was the optimum time to carry out the research since Indian participants were still alive and yet separated sufficiently from the events and turmoil of the 1930s to give cogent descriptions.

The Iroquois in New York, Oklahoma, Wisconsin, and Canada as well are often viewed as being distinct from each other in their culture, history, and institutions since the late eighteenth and first half of the nineteenth century. In reality, as will be subsequently shown, there were and are many common threads tying these individual communities, reservations, and reserves together: ceremonials, conservatism, kinship, land claims assertions, language, reaffirmations of historic federal-Iroquois treaty relationships, religion and religious revitalization movements, and views of Washington and Indian Service officialdom. Significantly, each community was never isolated entirely from another despite the separation by sizeable distances. The movement of ideas back and forth reinforced their common historic memory bank to make them Iroquois in identity and in outlook.

This study does not attempt to give equal treatment to all the Iroquois people. The Iroquois experience across the border during the interwar years, a vital period in Canadian-Six Nations history, is itself deserving of a book-length study and is only briefly mentioned in Chapter 1 of this book. Because the largest number of Iroquois reside in New York, and the East is the historic center as well as the mother culture of Iroquois existence, the Oklahoma Seneca-Cayugas and the Wisconsin Oneidas receive somewhat less attention.

The present study shows both the successes and limitations of the Indian New Deal in Iroquoia. Where the federal government was indirectly involved, had community-based support, worked slowly to cultivate the backing of prominent leaders, or offered land for the homeless or federal recognition for those Iroquois whose identity had been suppressed, policies succeeded. When the Iroquois — people suspicious of experimenters, new solutions or any changes in existing federal-Six Nations relations — perceived the Collier administration as arbitrarily imposing uniform legislation from distant Washington, the Indian New Deal was less successful.

By focusing on the New Deal, generally recognized as being somewhat more enlightened in its administration of Indian affairs, one can clearly see the need to work closely with local Indian communities in order to design satisfactory Indian policies. Perhaps through this analysis of Iroquois reactions to policies, future policy-makers may also better understand these unique Native American peoples. In so doing, they may come to appreciate the Iroquois and their cultural resilience, conservative outlook, legalistic nature, and views of sovereignty which they have maintained and espoused since the coming of the white man to North America.

My obligations to people who aided in my research are many. I should like to thank the numerous Iroquois people who aided in my research. The following were especially helpful in understanding the modern Iroquois: Chief James Allen, Marilyn Anderson, Ray Fadden, Jeanne Marie Jemison, Francis and Winifred Kettle, Beulah Rickard Lillvick, Gordie McLester, and Pauline Seneca. Five of my colleagues in the State University of New York system also deserve special thanks. Dr. William N. Fenton, formerly Research Professor of Anthropology at the State University of New York at Albany, and currently co-director of the Documentary History of the Iroquois Project sponsored by the Newberry Library and National Endowment for the Humanities, made many important suggestions, opened his extensive files, and offered encouragement to me throughout the writing of the book. Professor Jack Campisi of the State University of New York at Albany taught me the value of ethnohistory, especially the need to go beyond the documents by undertaking field work to gain a clearer understanding of the Iroquois. Professors William T. Hagan, State University of New York College at Fredonia, and Robert Venables formerly of the State University of New York College at Oswego, and presently with the Museum of the American Indian, were both helpful in the preparation of the manuscript by their critical reading of select chapters. My earlier collaboration with Professor Ronald G. Knapp of the State University of New York College at New Paltz on a series of articles on aboriginal peoples and the frontier process in Asia and America helped show me the full value of employing the comparative historical approach in my research. In addition to my colleagues at the State University of New York, I should like to thank Professor Barbara Graymont of Nyack College for encouraging my work at its initial stage.

As the bibliography of sources suggests, the book owes a considerable debt to the many fine archivists and librarians throughout the country who are too numerous to personally thank in print. Moreover, grants from the Research Foundation of the State University of New York, the National Endowment for the Humanities, and the American Philosophical Society and a sabbatic leave awarded me by the State University of New York

College at New Paltz provided in part the necessary funding and release time to hasten the completion of the study. Portions of this book have appeared elsewhere in preliminary form: *New York History* (July 1979); *The Indian Historian* (Summer 1979); *Studies on Iroquoian Culture,* ed. Nancy Bonvillain (Rindge, New Hampshire: *Occasional Publications in Northeastern Anthropology,* published by *Man in the Northeast,* 1980); and the forthcoming (Smithsonian) *Handbook of North American Indians* (Washington, D.C.), II. The author gratefully acknowledges permission granted him by these editors to publish copyrighted materials.

Most importantly, I should like to acknowledge the work of my wife Ruth whose skillful and numerous editorial suggestions vastly improved the book.

New Paltz, New York   Laurence M. Hauptman
Winter 1980

THE IROQUOIS AND THE NEW DEAL

EASTERN IROQUOIS

SETTLEMENTS

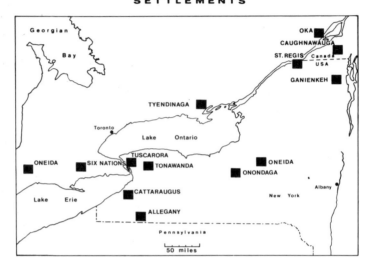

WESTERN IROQUOIS

SETTLEMENTS

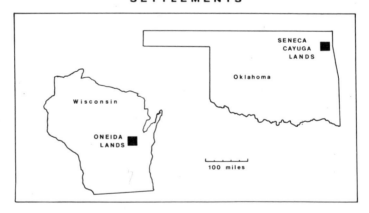

Iroquois settlements, 1981. Map by Jo Margaret Mano.

1

IROQUOIS CONCEPTS OF SOVEREIGNTY

The Past as a Present Reality

Many wonder why we hold to our reservation so tenaciously. They advise us to stop our weak struggling and give in to the State and National governments and lose our racial identity in competition with the outside world. We answer that one cannot do that so easily. Why does not the United States join itself with the Soviet Republic whose numbers and territory are greater than its own? Because Americans feel that their social system is so much superior to that of Russia. Similarly, we Six Nations Indians feel we have potentially a superior social system to that of the United States. If only we were left alone, we could redevelop our society to part of its original form which was old in democracy when Europe knew only monarchs. In it was the real equality for all, and Religion had the strength of daily practice. At one time, the great nations awaited with anxiety the decisions of the Six Nations councils, today our death cries are lost in the clamor for power.

Ernest Benedict (Mohawk)
Letter to American Civil
Liberties Union, March 27, 1941

I felt that I had visited a world as different from the United States as any foreign country, and I began to see upstate New York, all my life so familiar to me, in a new and larger perspective.

Edmund Wilson
Apologies to the Iroquois

The issue here at Wounded Knee is the recognition of the treaties

1

between the United States Government and the sovereign nations. ...
Sovereignty is freedom of a people to act and conduct affairs of its own
nation. We, the Hotinonsonni, the Six Nations, have our sovereignty. We
conduct on our territories and we act for our people. And so we have the
Oglala Sioux, who should be conducting their affairs here because this is
their territory, but who now have its government interfered with and who
now have another form from another power acting within their territory.

Chief Oren Lyons (Onondaga)
Voices from Wounded Knee

A NY UNDERSTANDING of the Iroquois must begin with their unique
concepts of their own sovereignty. Two definitions of Indian
sovereignty, one from Iroquoia and the other from Washington, came
head-on after 1933, resulting in tensions and conflicts over the direction of
Indian policy. These battles characterized the entire New Deal era and made
it impossible for federal officials to completely achieve what they desired for
these Indians.

The Iroquois, as six individual nations — Mohawks, Oneidas, Onondagas, Cayugas, Tuscaroras, and Senecas — have beliefs about their
sovereignty based upon their unique perceptions of their long history. In
addition to their individual separate insistence on tribal sovereignty, there
exists a collective belief in a body called a "league." Today two Iroquois
leagues continue to function, one centered at Onondaga near Syracuse, New
York, and the other at the Six Nations Reserve near Brantford, Ontario.
Despite this second supralevel affirmation of Iroquois sovereignty, non-
Indian officials in the United States historically have recognized that
Iroquois sovereignty rests only in the existence of tribal governments, in
certain tribal judicial authority such as the Peacemakers' Court of the
Seneca Nation, and in the acceptance of some features of tribal customary
law.[1] Since the American Revolution, the concept of collective Iroquois
League sovereignty has been rejected repeatedly by the non-Indian world,
prompting these North American Indians to frequently challenge United
States and Canadian policies.

Important to understanding these Native Americans, the Iroquois share
a common belief in the Code of Handsome Lake and its more ancient
antecedents. The *Gaiwiio*, the "good word" or the Code of Handsome Lake,
is a Native American religion that is still practiced by a small but nevertheless influential minority of Iroquois people on their reservations in the
United States and Canada. After the defeat, demoralization, and despair of

the Iroquois during and after the American Revolution, a Seneca prophet named Handsome Lake arose in 1799 in this spiritual vacuum to revitalize these communities with a message that was essentially an amalgam of ancient traditions and his own innovations received during a series of visions. Although the Old Way of Handsome Lake is a non-Christian religion, it includes some elements that were borrowed from Christianity.[2] This Longhouse religion, as it is more often called, which varies in influence and number of members from reservation to reservation, is a most important bond holding these, however diverse and dissimilar, Iroquois communities together.

The two leagues in Canada and in the United States trace the source of their sovereignty to the period 1784– 94 and define their world as far different and distinct from other Indian nations. Although today the Iroquois recognize Onondaga as the historic and primary capital, the League is nonetheless a "two-headed organism,"[3] which cooperates on occasion while still maintaining a studied autonomy from each other. In the United States, the League of the Iroquois, or, as it is more often called, "the Six Nations Confederacy," affirms that it is a sovereign entity with the sole right to speak for all Iroquois tribes, even those not represented in council at Onondaga, in matters involving all dealings with the United States, New York and other state governments, as well as other tribes. This self-assertion is based upon four historical factors: the long-established practice of colonial governments and their rulers in England, France, and Holland to negotiate with tribal representatives of the Iroquois Confederacy in council, and the three major treaties consummated after the American Revolution — Fort Stanwix (1784), Jay (1794), and Canandaigua (1794).

These treaties are the key to any understanding of the twentieth-century Iroquois — Christian and Longhouse — as well as the Confederacy and its political ideology. To Iroquois leaders, the Treaty of Fort Stanwix of 1784, confirmed at Fort Harmar five years later, not only ended the hostility between the Six Nations and the United States but also gave recognition to the collective sovereign status of the Iroquois Confederacy for the future. The Six Nations also point to the Jay Treaty of 1794 made between the United States and Great Britain, which assures free passage and unrestricted trade to all Iroquois dwelling on both sides of the United States-Canadian border. Most important to Indian interpretation, the Treaty of Canandaigua between the United States and the Iroquois recognized the Confederacy's sovereign claim. Both parties exchanged assurances of perpetual friendship while the United States gave a guarantee of territorial integrity. The treaty also stipulated that difficulties arising between the parties were to be resolved by the president of the United States or his agent. The federal government agreed to give the constituent tribes residing within the United States a $4,500 annuity, a payment that continues today and which reaffirms Iroquois sovereignty in their eyes. In the later context of fighting the building of the Kinzua Dam that broke the Treaty of Canandaigua in the 1960s, George Heron, former president of the Seneca Nation of Indians, expressed in clear terms the Iroquois interpretation of the treaty's meaning: "To us it is more than a contract, more than a symbol; to us, the 1794 Treaty is a way of life."[4]

Throughout the twentieth century, the Six Nations drew on these historic negotiations to counter perceived threats to their existence. Viewing themselves as a pocket in the midst of unfriendly, insensitive, or unknowing intruders, the Iroquois have often been on the defensive insuring beliefs in sovereignty, taking on diverse opponents —federal and state Indian policy-makers, immigration officials, the New York State Power Authority, the New York State Departments of Environmental Conservation and Transportation, the United States Selective Service System, and the Army Corps of Engineers. One noted anthropologist has observed that the "survival into the present century of the mechanisms of the Iroquois League is one of the phenomena of ethnology."[5] Perhaps more phenomenal has been the persistence of Iroquois beliefs about sovereignty up to the present day. They have clung dogmatically to these beliefs, before, during, and since the New Deal; through sit-down demonstrations and border-crossing celebrations on bridges connecting the United States and Canada; through dramatic appeals made to international organizations such as the League of Nations, the United Nations, or convocations dealing with aboriginal, human and/or treaty rights; through draft resistance, rejection of legislation emanating from Albany and Washington, assertion of land claims, sending of Confederacy delegates to the take-over of Wounded Knee in 1973, as well as through their own forced occupations of contested areas, including Ft. Hunter, and most recently, Ganienkeh.

Threats to Iroquois beliefs in sovereignty were not new and did not suddenly arise during World War I. In the sixty years after the American Revolution, the Iroquois were nearly dispossessed of their entire land base in New York. Through the legal, extra-legal, or outright fraudulent methods employed by Joseph Ellicott, Nathaniel Gorham, Robert and Thomas Morris, David Ogden, Oliver Phelps, and others, the Iroquois were stripped of their lands. Right through the negotiations at the Treaty of Buffalo Creek in 1838, land sharks in the guise of the Holland and Ogden land companies bribed chiefs with whiskey and money, threatened lives, and misrepresented facts to steal Indian lands in central and western New York.[6] The threat of land loss continued throughout the second half of the nineteenth and early years of the twentieth centuries in the pressures for allotment of Iroquois lands, especially those of the Senecas and Onondagas. However, because of unresolved questions relating to the preemptive claims of the Ogden Land Company to Iroquois lands and other factors, the Six Nations were able to repel these efforts.[7] In the process of countering these diverse pressures, the Six Nations, peoples with a strong reverence for tradition and legality, insisted that their sovereignty as guaranteed by their treaties of the 1780s and 1790s was being violated.

Many Iroquois, faced with these overwhelming pressures, chose not to remain in New York. After the American Revolution, some of these Indians became Loyalist refugees in the Canadian wilderness. Still others, at the urging of missionaries, government agents, and land speculators, chose Wisconsin and Indian Territory (Kansas) as their red zion. Those Iroquois that made the trek westward — the ancestors of the present Oneidas of Wisconsin and Seneca-Cayugas of Oklahoma — because of their new environment, their lengthy separation from their ancient homeland, and their diverse experiences over the past 150 years, developed somewhat different attitudes about sovereignty, a uniqueness that will be analyzed in two subsequent chapters. Tribal sovereignty concepts in the West were especially undermined by United States governmental policies of allotment that broke down the reservation concept and substituted land-in-severalty in its place. The Dawes General Allotment Act of 1887 resulted in the shattering of general communal land patterns, and eventually, the loss of most of Iroquois lands.

A series of major issues arose from World War I onward to challenge Iroquois self-assertions about tribal and Confederacy sovereignty: federal legislation such as the Indian Citizenship Act of 1924, the Seneca Conservation Act of 1927, the Snell Bill of 1930, the Indian Reorganization Act of 1934, and the Selective Service Act of 1940. The Iroquois in New York claim they are not and have never been part of the United States or Canada but are a separate people who are citizens of their own nations of the League. Despite this belief, Congress in 1924 extended citizenship and suffrage to American Indians. Many Iroquois rejected the act, arguing that participating in non-Indian society would be a denial of their cherished separate status which they insisted was guaranteed by treaties. After all, they argued, how could one be beholden to more than one sovereign at the same time. The maintenance of their belief in their own sovereignty requires these Indians, right up to the present day, to have only Iroquois citizenship and deny the existence of any federal and state authority over their lives.[8] One prominent Mohawk, pointing to treaty guarantees, emphatically maintained just prior to World War II: "The law of 1924 cannot then apply to Indians [Iroquois] ... since they are independent nations. Congress may as well pass a law making Mexicans citizens."[9]

Since making Indians citizens was an assimilationist goal from the early days of the American Republic and was often identified with policies tied to land-in-severalty, taxation of allotment, land frauds, and a shrinking Indian land base, many Iroquois, perhaps more historically and legally minded than other Indians, saw citizenship and participation in non-Indian elections as the first steps in the loss of their remaining lands. Although there were enrolled Iroquois in New York who voted in general off-reservation elections, the practice was scorned by the majority of these New York Indians. In one instance in 1931, the chiefs at Onondaga threatened to throw these voters off the reservation.[10] Chief William Rockwell, a New York Oneida, explained the Iroquois position on this matter in 1919 at a meeting in Syracuse: "The idea is when an Indian [Iroquois] votes, the contention of the lawyers and the people who are interested in the destruction of such a nation will say, 'He is a citizen and there is his land. Go and tax it.' You want us to become citizens in order to reap the benefits of your work."[11] Rockwell concluded that the Indians should be given the choice of whether to accept or reject United States citizenship. Chief Clinton Rickard, a Tuscarora, later elaborated on the reasons for Iroquois rejection of the Indian Citizenship Act:

> United States citizenship was just another way of absorbing us and destroying our customs and our government. How could these Europeans come over and tell us we were citizens in our country? We had our own citizenship. We feared citizenship would also put our treaty status in jeopardy and bring taxes upon our land. How can a citizen have a treaty with his own government? To us, it seemed that the United States government was just trying to get rid of its treaty obligations and make us into taxpaying citizens who could sell their homelands and finally end up in the city slums... The Citizenship Act did pass in 1924 despite our strong opposition. By its provisions all Indians were automatically made United States citizens whether they wanted to be so or not. This was a violation of

our sovereignty. Our citizenship was in our own nations. We had a great attachment to our style of government. We wished to remain treaty Indians and preserve our ancient rights. There was no great rush among my people to go out and vote in white man's elections. Anyone who did so was denied the privilege of becoming a chief or a clan mother in our nation.[12]

The Iroquois asserted their concepts of sovereignty in their repeated attempts to win recognition for their fishing and hunting rights on their lands. Despite Iroquois insistence that they did not need a license to fish or hunt on their own lands because of federal treaty guarantees, New York State fish and game wardens from 1896 onward barged onto reservations and arrested Indians for failure to purchase licenses. In October 1915, the United States District Court for the Western District of New York formally recognized Seneca fishing rights on Cattaraugus Reservation, maintaining that these Indians did not require a state license. As if this decision had not been rendered, New York State fish and game wardens continued to arrest Indians as "poachers" on their own reservations and attempted to regulate the time of fishing, the size of hooks, and the methods of taking and the kinds of fish and game caught.[13]

In 1927, the Congress, with the cooperation of a corrupt Seneca Council, passed the Seneca Conservation Act that allowed New York the power to apply the state's fish and game laws on the Allegany, Cattaraugus, and Oil Spring reservations. In return, the congressional law allowed the Seneca Nation Council the right to issue and sell licenses to non-Indians wishing to fish or hunt on reservation lands. The law proved unworkable. Indians continued to be arrested and fined, while state conservation officers insisted they had no authority to enforce the new Indian license requirements on non-Indian sportsmen on the reservations. As a result of the failure to repeal the act after serious lobbying efforts, this issue of sovereignty remained a volatile concern, especially for the Senecas during the early years of the New Deal. Indians continued to be arrested on their reservations under the state fishing laws which applied to their streams until the 1970s.[14]

Iroquois sovereignty was further manifested in attempts to prevent other jurisdictional changes in its relationship with the non-Indian world. According to the late Felix Cohen, the foremost authority on Indian law, the treaties of the 1780s and 1790s "had the effect of placing the tribes and their reservations beyond the operation and effect of general state laws."[15] Nevertheless, New York State legislators and representatives in Congress, inspired by assimilationist goals, myopic philanthropy, a need for legal order, or less than noble motives of land and resource acquisition, sought increasing control over Indian affairs in the last quarter of the nineteenth century until the mid-twentieth century. In 1888, 1906, 1915, and 1930, the Iroquois successfully fought off efforts seeking this change.[16] The battle over the so-called Snell Bill of 1930, which provided that the "laws of the United States shall not apply to Indians and Indian Reservations in New York or be inconsistent with the exercise of New York State authority," clearly illustrated Iroquois thinking on this matter.[17] Although the bill provided for a formal recognition of property rights guaranteed by treaties, it was opposed vehemently by the Council of the Six Nations Confederacy on the ground that it was a "contravention of treaty rights"[18] and that it would result in throwing "the Iroquois into the turmoil of State politics beyond redemption of any obligation on the part of the Government of the United States."[19] Speaking on behalf of the Six Nations Council, Chief Aaron Poodry, a Tonawanda Seneca, insisted that if the United States-Iroquois historic treaty relationship had become inadequate, then the two parties should consider amending it rather than abandoning it altogether.[20] Hence, sovereignty to the Iroquois required them to reject jurisdictional changes which they believed subvert treaties no matter what formal assurances they received to the contrary.

A major blow to New York State's attempts to win jurisdiction was a United States Court of Appeals for the Second Circuit's decision in 1942 involving leases of Indian lands at Salamanca which in part held that the "Indians are not subject to state laws and the process of its courts."[21] Despite the continued rejection of any jurisdictional changes by the Council of the Six Nations Confederacy, Congress finally awarded New York courts criminal jurisdiction over the Indians in 1948. Two years later, civil jurisdiction was also turned over to the state courts.[22]

Some Iroquois, choosing to ignore Supreme Court decisions to the contrary, have clung to the belief that Congress has no right whatsoever to legislate for them. They have been outspoken in rejecting all federal legislative efforts insisting they are sovereign bodies. Iroquois reaction in New York to the Indian Reorganization Act of 1934 (IRA), one of the most comprehensive pieces of legislation ever passed by Congress, illustrated this point. The act, as will be discussed fully in a subsequent chapter, included provisions for the establishment of educational and financial loan programs, a cultural encouragement of Indian higher education as well as the establishment of tribal elections, constitutions, and corporations. Despite many worthwhile features, the IRA was overwhelmingly rejected in New York. There were many factors leading to the act's rejection, including the age-old Iroquois distrust of the non-Indian world, dislike of Commissioner Collier, suspicions about the act's strange voting procedures, and the Iroquois view that the act was mass legislation having too many new and cumbersome regulations that were primarily intended for western tribes. Yet, the uniquely Iroquois opinion of sovereignty was also behind the Confederacy's rejection of the IRA. One leader of the Confederacy insisted that the United States government under treaty obligations had to deal with the League as a whole, not individual tribes, and that "no white man has any right to introduce any bills without the consent of the Confederate League of Indians."[23] This view was reiterated in separate but similar appeals made by other leading Iroquois leaders of the period.[24]

The Iroquois concern for maintaining its position on sovereignty was further reflected in their reactions to foreign wars. During World War I, the Confederacy separately declared war against Germany. This declaration was no token act but a means to reaffirm their belief in their independent status as free nations. The Iroquois reaction to World War II was considerably different. Although a faction led by a Confederacy Subchief Jesse Lyons declared war on the Axis in June 1942, and Iroquois willingly enlisted in the United States armed forces,[25] the Six Nations Council rejected compulsory service and the Selective Service Act's application to them.[26] According to Chief Clinton Rickard, a veteran of the Spanish-American War: "We had absolutely no objection to our young men serving in the armed forces, but we did object to a violation of our national sovereignty and a brushing aside of our treaties as well as the governments' legislating for us."[27] Consequently, the Confederacy brought a test case in 1941 arguing that the Indian Citizenship Act of 1924 was unconstitutional; that the Iroquois were foreign nations; that Congress had no right to make laws affecting them, particularly without their consent, and thus they were ineligible for the draft, not being United States citizens. The United States Court of Appeals for the Second Circuit later rejected these contentions. Despite this setback, Iroquois challenges to Selective Service jurisdiction continued sporadically right through the Vietnam War.[28]

The assertion of sovereignty over land from which they were dispossessed is but another way the Iroquois express their cultural uniqueness. Throughout the interwar period, the Iroquois, collectively through the Confederacy and individually through several of the Six Nations, made claim to large tracts of land in New York State, land from which they were

Chief Jesse Lyons and one faction of the Iroquois declaring war against the Axis at the Capitol, Washington, D.C., June 1942. Photograph courtesy of the National Archives.

dispossessed in the fifty years following the American Revolution. To the more conservative caretakers of the League tradition at Onondaga, the president of the United States and the Six Nations Council are on an equal footing under the Treaty of Canandaigua and must together and alone work out any and all treaty violations that have led to Iroquois land loss. The Confederacy Council's view is that the League as a whole, not individual nations, still own, despite the reality of white encroachment, half of the acreage of New York State. Nevertheless, this Confederacy view often runs counter to the arguments and actions made by the separate Iroquois nations.[29]

The Confederacy's claim to lands gained increasing support among the Iroquois during the 1920s as a consequence of two important factors: firstly, the Everett Commission, a New York State Assembly committee formed in 1919 to examine "the history, the affairs and transactions had by the people of the state of New York with the Indian tribes resident in the state and to report to the legislature the status of the American Indian residing in said state of New York"[30] and secondly, the activities of Laura "Minnie" Cornelius Kellogg, a controversial Oneida Indian from Wisconsin, who pressed for the final settlement of the Confederacy's land claims. The Everett Commission, headed by St. Lawrence County Assemblyman Edward A. Everett of Potsdam, grew out of a meeting held at Syracuse in March 1919, under the auspices of the Onondaga Historical Association. The meeting focused on the general conditions of the Indians of New York and called for the state legislature to improve the Indians' social and political status. On March 3, 1920, the United States Circuit Court of Appeals for the Second Circuit, in an ejectment proceeding involving the removal of Oneidas living on a thirty-two-acre tract of land and the partition of it to non-Indians, found that these Indians were a federally recognized tribe and that New York State courts had no jurisdiction disposing of the Indians' property without the consent of the United States. Because of the confusion caused by the decision and the ambiguous line between federal and state jurisdiction, the Everett Commission, like so many previous and subsequent official investigations, attempted to demarcate the ill-defined responsibilities of Washington and Albany to these Indians.[31]

With a chairman sympathetic to the Indians, the commission, from August 1920 onward, held hearings on every Iroquois reservation in New York State as well as at the Six Nations Reserve near Brantford, Ontario. The members of the commission included the New York State attorney general, three members of the state senate, five members of the state assembly, one representative each from the state Departments of Health, Education, and Charities, and Iroquois Chief David R. Hill. Despite Everett's urgings, the New York State Legislature refused to pay for a second on-site visit of each reservation and for payment for Indian delegates to commission conferences in Albany. On April 22, 1922, the report was presented to the assembly, signed only by Chairman Everett. The assembly did not accept it nor did it bother to print and distribute its findings.[32] Despite the obvious lack of support within the commission,[33] Everett concluded that the Iroquois were legally entitled to 6 million acres of New York State:

> the Indians of the State of New York are entitled to all of the territory ceded to them by the treaty made with the Colonial Government prior to the Revolutionary War, relative to the territory that should be ceded to the Indians for their loyalty to said colonies and by the treaty of 1784 by which said promise by the colonists was consummated by the new Republic known as the United States of America and in a speech by General Washington to the conference of Indians comprising the Six Nations and recognizing the Indians as a Nation.[34]

To Everett, the Iroquois Confederacy collectively as a nation still had fee simple title of the territory ceded to the Indians by the United States at Fort Stanwix in 1784. It is significant to note that Everett, after being defeated for reelection, went on to become one of the attorneys for the Iroquois in a land claims case in 1927.[35]

Everett's report helped rekindle a movement among the Iroquois to assert their claims. Unfortunately, not all of the land claims activists were honest nor did they all have a completely beneficial or positive impact. Minnie Kellogg was the most influential of these individuals, having the intellectual qualities and educational training for great leadership. She had been born on the Oneida Indian Reservation near Green Bay on September 10, 1880. Her education included attendance at a boarding school at Fond du Lac, Wisconsin, and later Stanford, Barnard, and the School of Philanthropy at Columbia University. In 1912, she married Orrin Joseph Kellogg, a non-Indian attorney from St. Paul, Minnesota. By that time, she had already become a politically active leader in Indian affairs as a vocal member of the Society of American Indians and as a writer.[36]

By 1916, she was among the leading critics of the Indian Bureau. Her attacks included her plan, the Lolomi Policy, to abolish the bureau and to substitute for it a nonpolitical trust headed by individuals of national and international reputation to administer Indian affairs. Her basic critique of the administration of Indian policy was clearly set forth in a later interview:

> There is nothing but degradation and inevitable vagrancy under the present system of Indian relations in the United States. The Bureau of Indian Affairs surpasses every form of bureaucracy in the world, because it has such control of their property. ... The United States Government

made treaties with the American Indians and in almost every instance the right to self-government was expressed or implied. Subsequently, a policy of intentional centralization possessed the United States and they scorned their own contracts with the Indians because his self-government made him too formidable, because he occupied too vast an estate and owned too much wealth.[37]

By 1920, she published her book, *Our Democracy and the American Indian*, that expanded her criticism of the bureau to include the entire framework of Indian policy in the United States, especially the Indian boarding school educational system.[38]

In 1923, Kellogg presented her grand design to the Six Nations Confederacy Council at Onondaga, namely the pursuit of Iroquois claims to land taken illegally. She, her husband, and her many followers collected money in every Iroquois community—in New York, Oklahoma, Wisconsin, Ontario, and Quebec—with the intention of using it for a massive Iroquois claim to 18 million acres of land in New York and Pennsylvania. Much of the money collected, a considerable sum especially from economically hard-pressed Indians, never went for the intended purpose and was never returned to the contributors. The Indians were also told that if they did not contribute, they would not be eligible for the claims when awarded.[39] It is evident that Minnie Kellogg's success in securing money was directly related to her keen ability to articulate the traditional Iroquois belief in their sovereignty based upon treaties. In testimony before a senate committee in Washington in March 1929, she clearly set forth this view:

> Here are a group of Indians, 16,000 in all, occupying some 78,000 acres in reservations in New York or colonized in small groups in western states and in Canada. Their legal status is peculiar to Indian relations. They have a treaty with the United States Government which gives them the status of an independent protectorate of the United States under this treaty of 1784, confirmed and added to in the treaty of 1789. They are a protected autonomy, with the title of original territory vested in them. In specific language, the U.S. ceded all right and title to them to territory they reserved to themselves out of their Iroquois domain in return for their ceding all right and title in the Ohio Valley to the United States Government.[40]

By the mid to late 1920s, the Kelloggs had helped factionalize every

Iroquois reservation between those who supported their efforts and those who rejected them. Moreover, the Kellogg Party, as it was called, actually began referring to themselves in correspondence as the official voice of the Six Nations Confederacy, raising new chiefs on several of the reservations.[41] In October 1927, the Kelloggs were arrested in Canada, indicted on the criminal charges of conspiracy to defraud and of obtaining money under false pretenses. A week later, one of the land cases supported by the Kelloggs, seeking redress for the violation of the Treaty of Fort Stanwix of 1784 by the return of a parcel of land one mile square in St. Lawrence and Franklin counties, was dismissed by the United States District Court because of the court's lack of jurisdiction in the matter. On November 14, 1927, the Kelloggs were cleared of all charges by the Canadian court. Despite their release, the Kelloggs' influence slowly waned when the size of their embezzlement scheme was revealed. Yet, as late as the mid-1930s, the federal government was repeatedly warning the Iroquois about the activities of the Kellogg Party.[42]

The Kelloggs, despite their chicanery, kept the belief in the validity of the Confederacy's land claims alive. Yet, several of the individual Iroquois nations themselves pressed for their own claims. The Cayugas, landless in New York and living on the Seneca's Cattaraugus Reservation, pursued the dream of land on the northern end of Cayuga Lake in the interwar period. Through persistent efforts, the Cayugas from Six Nations Reserve in Ontario won an arbitrational award of $100,000 in 1926 for the United States' failure to pay annuities on treaties made between 1789 and 1814. Moreover, during the late 1930s, the Seneca Nation of Indians pushed its claims to lands lost along the Niagara frontier.[43]

Perhaps most determined of all were the Oneidas in the pursuit of their land claims. The Oneidas were repeatedly told by state and federal officials that they had no case, that they had no tribal status, that the federal government was powerless to help, and that Congress would ratify any illegal land sales even if the Indians won in court. Despite the frequent dismissal of their claims, the Oneidas, one faction led by the self-styled Wisconsin attorney Chief "Willie Fat" Skenandore, sent legal memoranda and even a formal brief to Washington, arguing their case. In New York, the constant efforts of Mary Winder, an Oneida living on the Onondaga Reservation, helped keep the cause alive. Until 1974, the Oneida claim seemed only a quixotic dream until the historic United States Supreme Court decision that allowed these Indians the right to sue New York State in federal courts. The maintenance of the belief in these claims for nearly two centuries, another manifestation of asserting their sovereignty, permitted these Indians to cling determinedly to a culturally separate and distinct way of life.[44]

Despite the focus of this analysis of the Iroquois on the American side of the border, the Six Nations in Canada cannot be completely ignored in any study. The Six Nations Confederacy in Canada was established at the end of the American Revolution. A portion of the Iroquois loyal to the Crown settled on a reserve of land along the Grand River in Ontario in 1784 under the provisions of the Haldimand Patent. Included in the migration were individuals from the Six Nations from New York and a number of allied Indian groups. Under the leadership of Joseph Brant, the Mohawk war chief, the Iroquois emigrés reconstituted the League which then became the governing body of the reserve. In time the separate political structures of the tribes atrophied, and the Confederacy Council became the sole governmental unit. Almost from its inception, Crown and Confederacy conflicted over the nature of the Confederacy's sovereignty.

From World War I onward, the Canadian government became increasingly involved in reservation affairs at Grand River, much to the anger of the Confederacy Council. Ottawa's application of the Soldier's Settlement Act, legislation designed to encourage World War I veterans to take up farming by advancing them local interest loans, only increased tensions. The Iroquois hereditary leadership believed the act would lead to land loss through tax foreclosures for nonpayment of these obligations and promote the growing trend toward assimilation, citizenship, and elected systems. Because of increased disturbances between supporters and opponents of the Confederacy council, the Dominion government in 1923 appointed a special commissioner to investigate the political and social conditions on the reserve. At the recommendation of this special commissioner, an elected council was imposed by Ottawa without any determination if the Grand River Iroquois desired the proposed change. On October 21, 1924, the first election of twelve councilors was held under the watchful eyes of the Royal Canadian Mounted Police brought onto the reserve without prior Confederacy permission. In a move still largely resented and resisted by a majority of these Iroquois, Canadian government officials, working with a minority of Iroquois supporters and under an armed escort, read an order excluding the hereditary chiefs from the Council house at Brantford and replacing them with the elective council. Ten years later this episode was repeated at Oneida, another Iroquois reserve along the Thames River in Ontario. To the present day, the Canadian-imposed elected systems are a source of bitter factionalist activity on the Six Nations Reserve.[45]

In reaction to these policies, an Iroquois leader emerged from 1917 onward who had a significant impact on the Six Nations in Canada and in the United States both in his ideas on sovereignty and the means employed to assert it. In 1920 and 1923, Levi General or Deskaheh, a spellbinding Cayuga sachem from Six Nations Reserve, travelled to Europe as a delegate of the Confederacy Council at Grand River in an attempt to counter Canadian policies. Accompanied by George P. Decker, the attorney for the Six Nations, and travelling under an Iroquois-issued passport, Deskaheh tried to bring the Indian case before the British secretary of state of the Colonial Office and King George V, in addition to the League of Nations in Geneva. In these appeals, which proved fruitless except in their deeper meaning to the Iroquois themselves, Deskaheh insisted that the Iroquois Confederacy had never relinquished sovereignty, citing as support for his position the historic alliance known as the Covenant Chain established in the colonial period between the English and the Indians. He added that his contention was also based on treaties and land patents made between the British Crown and the Iroquois after the American Revolution.[46] Prior to his death in 1925, Deskaheh, in a radio address from Rochester, compared Canadian and American policies insisting that "in Ottawa, they call that policy 'Indian advancement.' Over in Washington, they call it 'Assimilation.' We who would be the helpless victims say it is tyranny." He added by explaining the Iroquois concept of sovereignty: "If this must go on to the bitter end, we would rather that you come with your guns and get rid of us that way. Do it openly and above board. Do away with the pretense that you have the right to subjugate us to your will. Your governments do that by enforcing your alien laws upon us. That is an underhanded way. They can subjugate us if they will through the use of your law courts. But how would you like to be dragged down to Mexico, to be tried by Mexicans and jailed under Mexican law for what you did at home?"[47]

The Canadian policy of imposing elected systems had an impact on the Six Nations' reactions in New York to the New Deal, since it came at a time when Commissioner Collier advocated the Indian Reorganization Act that promoted western-styled political models for the Indians of the United States. The activities of Deskaheh, in his globe-trotting efforts on behalf of the Iroquois, had won many admirers on the American side of the border and had forewarned the Indians to the possibilities that similar governmental actions could take place in New York. Moreover, since the nineteenth century New York State had imposed an elected system of chiefs at St. Regis Reservation, a fact resented by a large number of these Indians right up to the present day. To many New York Iroquois, except for the Seneca Nation who also have an elected system, these officials have less standing than the traditional hereditary systems still operating on other reservations.

Deskaheh's activities and the Iroquois crisis in Canada influenced the Six Nations living in the United States in other areas. The Iroquois, as in the land claims issue, became more politically assertive in maintaining their treaty rights in the period. The border question was one area that became a testing ground for this new assertiveness. As self-proclaimed Iroquois citizens distinct from either Canada or the United States, they repeatedly refused to recognize a border drawn by a foreign people through their lands. With the growth of stricter immigration policies arising in both countries and increasing harassment of Iroquois by immigration agents after World War I, Clinton Rickard, a Tuscarora chief, and David Hill, a Mohawk from Six Nations Reserve, founded the Indian Defense League of America in 1926. Inspired by Deskaheh's example, these Iroquois reacted to what they interpreted as the erosion of the right of free and unlimited passage guaranteed to them under the provisions of the Jay Treaty and the Treaty of Ghent. Although the Iroquois contentions were upheld in federal courts and confirmed by an act of Congress in 1928, the issue remained alive.[48] As late as 1941, the Iroquois, especially the St. Regis Mohawks whose reservation straddles the United States-Canadian border, continued to complain about seizures of their property as contraband, indiscriminate arrests and flagrant disregard of rules by customs and immigration officials. One Mohawk described the situation: "In late years there have been cases too numerous to mention wherein the Indians have had to pay either a prohibitive duty on baskets of their own manufacture, or had property taken away from them because they attempted to cross the border within the reservation without reporting to the customs office."[49] This issue continued to irritate the Iroquois until more recent times, especially after the imposition of an $8.00 Canadian head tax in the late 1960s.[50] To this day, the Indian Defense League holds its annual celebration of the Jay Treaty every July with a parade across the International Bridge connecting Niagara Falls, Ontario, to Niagara Falls, New York.

Consequently, two worlds, each self-assured as to its own righteousness and its own definitions of Indian sovereignty, were to face each other and come into conflict during the Indian New Deal, 1933–41. The Iroquois view would be based in sum on a conviction that they were still sovereign, autonomous entities. Yet, Commissioner Collier, specifically referring to the Iroquois, insisted in February 1935, that the United States through the

"Congress can extend its sovereignty at will over any of these nations, no matter how sovereign they were made by treaties." He added that "insofar as an Indian tribe continues to exercise sovereignty it does so because Congress has not legislated to take away that sovereignty."[51] Although Collier was correct according to the technical definitions of American law set down in decisions of the United States Supreme Court,[52] the Iroquois, working from a completely distinct belief system and based on their need to maintain themselves as culturally separate peoples, totally rejected this interpretation and attempted to aggressively assert their special definition of sovereignty throughout the New Deal era.

2

JOHN COLLIER AND THE IROQUOIS

Indian affairs can be viewed not only as of significance in themselves; they can also be seen as an ethnic laboratory of universal meaning.

John Collier
Indians of the Americas

Self-proclaimed friends of the Indian all too often would help their objects of philanthropy according to their image of the Indian rather than through any understanding of Native Americans as people(s). Both countercul-turists and assimilationists, therefore, share the urge to reform the Indian according to their desires rather than to help Native Americans on their own terms.

Robert F. Berkhofer, Jr.
The White Man's Indian

COMMISSIONER JOHN COLLIER was an industrious social engineer with a strong humanitarian bent who accomplished significant changes in his twelve years in office. Nevertheless, his true concern for helping Native Americans was more often than not negated by the conditions he found among Indian nations in the period, the poorly managed operations that he inherited in the Bureau of Indian Affairs (BIA), and his frequent and bitter clashes with Congress, especially after 1937, over the direction of Indian policy. Equally important in retarding his efforts, especially among New York tribesmen, was Collier's inability on occasions to adjust his own strong will, idealism, and romanticism to the reality of a situation.

John Collier, commissioner of Indian affairs, 1933–45. Photograph courtesy of the National Archives.

The magnitude of the problems that Indians faced was the major impediment to Collier's efforts at making a noticeable improvement. The

Indian land base had shrunk by 91 million acres since the passage of the Dawes General Allotment Act of 1887. By 1933, Indians retained approximately 48 million acres, much of it arid, unusable land. Moreover, 49 percent of Indians on allotted reservations were landless.[1] Five years earlier, the Meriam Report on Indian administration prepared by the Institute for Government Research, a private "think-tank," observed about past allotment policies: "It almost seems as if the government assumed that some magic in individual ownership would in itself prove an educational civilizing factor, but unfortunately this policy has for the most part operated in the opposite direction."[2] Even before the onset of the Great Depression, the Meriam Report indicated that 96 percent of all Indians earned wages less than $200 per year and that only 2 percent had a per capita income greater than $500 per year.[3] When the Great Depression finally hit in force, these crisis conditions were further aggravated by a "back to the reservation" movement by urban Indians thrown out of work by the economic downturn of the nation.

The extent of Indian poverty and the failures of past policies were reflected in other areas. The Meriam Report severely criticized bureau health care delivery to the Indians who suffered from much higher rates of infant mortality, trachoma, and tuberculosis than other Americans. The report was especially critical of bureau efforts in educating Indian children at boarding schools, pointing out the overcrowded conditions, the lack of qualified school personnel, uniformity of curriculum as well as the improper diet, poor medical care, and harsh discipline accorded students. It added that the overall quality of Indian service employees was lower than in other governmental agencies and that they showed little empathy for the people they were serving.[4] Because of past failures, the report insisted: "Indians are entitled to unfailing courtesy and consideration from all government employees. They should not be subjected to arbitrary action."[5]

Although there had been some improvements from 1929 onward, primarily in Indian education and increased congressional appropriations under the reformist administration headed by Secretary of the Interior Ray Wilbur and Commissioner of Indian Affairs Charles Rhoads, Collier faced a Herculean task when he entered office in 1933. D'Arcy McNickle, Collier's close friend and member of the Indian Service during the New Deal, summarized these problems:

Collier began his commissionership at a time when law and policy extending back 100 years had wrought incalculable damage to Indians, their property and their societies. Tribes had been moved about like livestock until, in some cases, the original homeland was no more than a legend in the minds of old men and women. Children had been forcefully removed from the family and kept in close custody until they lost their mother language and all knowledge of who they were — while parents often did not know where the children had been taken or whether they even lived. Tribal religious practices when they were not proscribed outright were treated as obscenities. Land losses ... were catastrophic, while the failure of government to provide economic tools and the training for proper land use left the land untenable or put out to white farmers at starvation rates. The bureaucratic apparatus had penetrated the entire fabric of Indian life, usurping the tribal decision-making function, obtruding into the family, demeaning local leadership — and yet was totally oblivious of its inadequacies and its inhumanity.[6]

The problems Collier faced in attempting to help the Iroquois were no less challenging. The Oneidas of Wisconsin, with the possible exception of the Winnebagos, suffered more from the abuses and failures of allotment policies than any other Indian nation. Their land was almost totally lost through alienation of fee patent allotments from the late 1880s onward. The Seneca-Cayugas of Oklahoma were not far behind in this dubious distinction.[7]

In New York, where the Dawes Act had not been applied, the Iroquois were relatively better off,[8] even though their educational, health and housing conditions were substandard. One Seneca from New York described the poor conditions at Tonawanda Reservation in 1930: "I believe there are some unfortunate Indians on this reservation who will have a hard struggle this coming winter. Even today I know of one family who sometimes have nothing but string beans to eat. I dread to think of this winter. Our potatoes did not do so well on account of the long hot and dry spell we had. Babies have succumbed in the last couple of months and there will be a funeral today or tomorrow for the last death."[9]

The federal government's involvement in New York was minimalized by the presence of an unobtrusive agent at Salamanca. The only thing that the United States seemed to provide to the New York Iroquois on a regular basis was the annual distribution of "treaty cloth," a symbolic gesture to abide by the Treaty of Canandaigua. The treaty cloth was in lieu of a payment of an annuity of $4,500 for the Six Nations in the form of clothing, animals, and farm utensils. Until the New Deal era, federal officials, despite their frequent assertions of paramount jurisdiction over the Iroquois, rarely intervened in New York or interfered with the trend toward increased state involvement in Indian affairs.[10] In 1929, former Assistant Commissioner Edgar Meritt testified before a senate hearing that the federal government spent only $8,380.02 on these Iroquois during the previous years, since he insisted that "we have practically nothing to do with the handling of the affairs of the New York Indians."[11]

Despite appeals for federal support for improved educational opportunities and legal defense for destitute Indians, the Iroquois received little attention. Bureau inaction led some Iroquois leaders to reluctantly turn to state agencies for aid during periods of crisis.[12] Equally important, federal neglect had reinforced the belief among the New York Iroquois that they were still independent sovereign nations outside the scope of all non-Indian jurisdiction. Unlike their western relatives in Wisconsin and Oklahoma who had all-too-frequent experiences with the federal bureaucracy in such areas as removal, allotment, and historically corrupt and powerful Indian agents, the New York tribesmen were less directly affected by the Indian Bureau.

Collier had to face other factors that were beyond his control. Iroquois political divisions in the interwar period were especially evident. Among the Seneca Nation, the nearly forty-year reign of political boss William C. Hoag had produced sharp schisms and a rival council by the mid-1920s. Although Hoag died in 1927, these divisions remained just below the political surface. At Onondaga, George Thomas and Joshua Jones, two rival "Tadodahos," or spiritual leaders of the Six Nations vied for power from the mid-1920s through the New Deal. This rivalry was largely accentuated by the Kellogg claims movement. At St. Regis Reservation, Mohawk traditionalists and elected officials battled for political influence as well as outside recognition. In Wisconsin, factionalism reached new heights and created the most complicated political situation of any Iroquois community. By 1933, each of four separate factions that maintained separate political leadership and rival councils insisted that it was the legitimate government of the Oneida Indians.[13]

Commissioner Collier was not totally unaware of the Iroquois and their problems when he assumed office. Throughout the 1920s, he had written speeches attacking the Indian Bureau for Wisconsin Congressmen James Frear and Robert LaFollette, Jr., and had worked closely with Senator William H. King of Utah who had championed the Iroquois cause in the border crossing controversy. On November 25, 1929, Collier was present at a senate subcommittee hearing at Salamanca investigating Iroquois conditions in New York. Working closely with subcommittee members in his capacity as executive secretary of the American Indian Defense Association, Collier drafted some of the questions asked at the meeting. The Indians testified, among other things, about the history of the Ogden Land Company's preemptive claim to their lands, their undervalued leases, and their criticism about the Seneca Conservation Law of 1927.[14]

Although Collier gained some understanding of the Iroquois from this hearing, his ability to deal with them and their problems was somewhat limited, given his personality and several of his life experiences. Part of the problem of understanding Collier was his constant search for larger meanings to define his actions. To Collier, the American industrial order had produced a morally bankrupt leadership that was incapable of working for the greater good. Perhaps naively, he sought answers in the mystical qualities of Indian tribal life which he believed would someday be the example for the transformation of American society as a whole.[15] D'Arcy McNickle observed: "Because he could not temper the quality of his conceptual grasp, Collier was dismissed as a visionary, an impractical intellectual." McNickle added that Collier "wrote or talked in a prose style that often dazzled and confounded his audience."[16] Writing about the Iroquois, Collier clearly confirmed McNickle's interpretation and revealed his own need to search the Native American experience for answers to greater human concerns:

I think of the Six Nations League of the Iroquois, a chapter in human greatness, and a forerunner of our federal constitution and of the League of Nations. Very early after the first white-man contact, there came to these warring Iroquois a passion, from the same mystic and nameless region of the spirit which spoke through Lao-Tse, Buddha, Socrates, Christ, and St. Francis. This message from the placeless center of the human moral life came as a new law superceding all earlier laws. The new law was that of peace, not of peace as a mere ceasing of war, but of peace as a means to, and a function of, a whole life. This whole life was life of body, soul, and group. It was a seeking of justice. Possibly it was the first complete seeking of equal opportunity for women. I venture the proposition that no great social-religious movement of history has united the mystical with the practical, and the conception of life as an art, and of the individual achievement of intense excellence, with social and political codes and institutions, in a balance and synthesis more perfect and more consciously intended, than did the Six Nations League. To indicate the place that the Iroquois vision has in our present world, I only note the principle governing the relations of the tribes within the League. That principle, which the Iroquois knew to be worldwide, was that world society must be a collaboration of different and differing groups, cooperating to intensify their significant individualities.[17]

Despite his eloquent and often romantic rhetoric, Collier was not merely an ethereal do-gooder. His record of accomplishment on a nationwide scale indicates that he was not just a dreamer. In his first four years in office, his legislative achievements were impressive: the Indian Reorganization Act, the Johnson-O'Malley Act, the Indian Arts and Craft Board Act, the Oklahoma Indian Welfare Act, the Alaska Reorganization Act. Yet Collier's romanticism and his own background limited his effective dealing with Indian policy in certain other areas.

Collier was a product of the Progressive reform tradition. As a socially minded reformer committed to helping American Indians since the early 1920s, his humanitarian bent led him to go well beyond past commissioners' efforts on behalf of Indians. On the other hand, as head of one of the most historically corrupt, mismanaged agencies of the federal government, the BIA, he sought order, efficiency, honesty, and uniformity in policy directives. Thus the problem of reconciling these two Progressive ideals — social justice and managerial efficiency — was a major dilemma he faced in his twelve years as commissioner.

Collier was equally affected by the post–World War I intellectual setting with its emhasis on the decay of western values, its cynicism, and its attempt to seek answers in so-called "primitive cultures." The activities of the Taos salon of Mabel Dodge Luhan and the sojourn of D. H. Lawrence to the Southwest are clear examples of this trend of searching for the primitive. Both Luhan and Lawrence were neighbors of Collier in New Mexico in this period. The romantic inflation of the Southwest was to grip Collier as it had affected early Pueblophiles such as Charles F. Lummis and Edgar L. Hewett.[18]

Collier's path to involvement in Indian policy reform was influenced by three major events: a tragic home life, an early career as a social worker among immigrants, and his personal discovery of the Pueblo Indians at Taos. The deaths of his parents — his mother from drug addiction and his father from suicide — before the age of sixteen turned him away from the materialistic pursuits which he blamed for his parents' tragic ruin. Collier was also influenced greatly by a stint as a social worker from 1907 to 1919 among New York City's bustling immigrant community. He served as secretary for the People's Institute in Manhattan, an organization devoted to promoting through educational efforts: a sense of brotherhood to the immigrant masses in their local neighborhoods; a peaceful reorganization of society by providing a political and social alternative to socialism on the one hand or to Tammany Hall on the other; and the advance of democracy through the alliance of working class and intellectuals. He encouraged immigrants to be proud of their past through lectures and pageants; sponsored political awareness talks on local, state, and national affairs; and attempted to change immigrant attitudes by regulating what they saw in nickelodeons and movies, what they read in his Institute's *Civic Journal*, or heard in the lyceum at Cooper Union.[19] The "greater meaning" of the People's Institute was set forth by Collier in his autobiography: "The People's Institute was seeking to bring to the common folk of New York, as we now in retrospect realize, what is known as the *gemeinschaft* mode of life (the sufficing brotherhood, within innumerable local communities which are moved by *shared* purposes), but that effort and, for the 'modern western world,' that mode of life, faded before the scorching onset of the *gesellschaft* mode of life — before the shattering aggressive drive toward competitive utility."[20]

It is clear that what Collier formulated as commissioner of Indian affairs was a direct outgrowth of his experience in New York among immigrants. His attempt to reestablish a sense of ethnic community and his desire to use the immigrant experience for larger purposes in breathing new life into a morally bankrupt America predated his similar concerns with Indians. In the period before and during World War I, he reacted to Social Darwinism and to the increasing problems caused by rapid urbanization and industrialization. At the People's Institute, he drew upon the social sciences to manipulate the environment in the way he thought best for the immigrant. In the 1930s, reacting to the past inefficiency, insensitivity, and mismanagment of the BIA as well as to its overdependence on religious sects, he introduced, based on what he believed workable and scientific principles, the British colonial policy of indirect rule with its reliance on social scientists.[21] Collier's biographer, Kenneth Philp, has perceptively evaluated the impact of these years in New York:

> Like those other middle class settlement workers, his efforts to close the gap that existed between the urban lower classes and the rest of society through various techniques of social control were marred by internal contradictions. Collier found it impossible to apply his mystical vision of classless agrarian community, where people discovered meaning and spiritual values in their work, to the social chaos of New York City. He

failed to establish a new system of primary group relationships in the unstable tenement neighborhoods because of the confusion produced by the great variety of nationalities. This frequently caused him to abandon the democratic goals of the People's Institute and impose coercive measures to secure his reforms. He discovered that it was often easier for an elite to direct the immigrants rather than listen to their aspirations.[22]

The third and perhaps most important experience that helped shape his future course was Collier's visit to Taos, New Mexico, in November 1920. Invited by Mabel Dodge Luhan, a friend from New York City whose previous prewar Greenwich Village salon was a center of avant-garde activity, Collier was to find his "Red Atlantis," the tribal communitarian ideal that he believed had been long lost by western man.[23] After contrasting this experience with an earlier awakening of "cosmic consciousness" [Collier's words], Collier described the personal meaning of his visit to Taos:

> But here, at Taos, a whole race of men before my eyes, passed into ecstasy through a willed discipline, splendid and fierce, yet structural, an objectively impassioned discipline which was a thousand or ten thousand years old and as near to the day of first creation as it had been at its prime. Here was a reaching to the fire-fountain of life through a deliberate social action employing a complexity of many arts. Here was the psychical wonder-working we think we find in Christ. And here it was a whole community which entered into the experience and knew it as a fact. These were unsentimental men who could neither read nor write, poor men who lived by hard work, men who were told every day in all kinds of unsympathetic ways that all they believed and cared for had to die, and who never answered back. For these men were one with their gods.[24]

To Collier, Northern Pueblo culture had the secret to redeeming American society. The Pueblos, as he saw them, repudiated materialism, secularism, and the increased automization of western industrial society by their continuing emphasis on human relationships, the supernatural, land, and their environment.[25] As Robert Berkhofer, Jr., has observed, Collier "romanticized the heritage of these folk societies as part of his alienation from his own 'sick' times, and the Pueblos became his own personal countercultural utopia."[26] The nirvana that Collier had hoped could be built in the slums of New York for the world to learn from had now been transferred to a tribal New World culture in New Mexico:

The discovery that came to me there, in that tiny group of a few hundred Indians, was of personality-forming institutions, even now unweakened, which had survived repeated and immense historical shocks, and which were going right on in the production of states of mind, attitudes of mind, earth-loyalties and human loyalties, amid a context of beauty which suffused all the life of the group.... Yet, it might be that only the Indians, among the people of this hemisphere at least, were still the possessors and users of the fundamental secret of human life — the secret of building great personality through the instrumentality of social institutions. And it might be, as well, that the Indian life would not survive.[27]

As a result of this experience, Collier devoted the next years to the Pueblos, who, at that time, were being threatened by the loss of their lands in Congress by the so-called Bursum Bill. It was Collier, through his writings and organizing ability, who brought the Pueblo situation before the nation. Collier's championing of the Pueblo's interests was so intense that D. H. Lawrence feared that Collier's "benevolent volition" on behalf of the Indians might go too far in subverting their ways through interference.[28] In the process of winning the battle to save Pueblo lands, Collier formed and became executive secretary of the American Indian Defense Association, a full-time position held until he was appointed commissioner in 1933.

Collier's Taos years had shaped his outlook both toward the Indian and non-Indian worlds as a whole. Moreover, it proved to be a difficult transition for him when he assumed power as commissioner after his highly vocal attacks on the Indian Bureau in the 1920s and early 1930s. One year before his appointment, a Department of the Interior press release described Collier as a "fanatical Indian enthusiast with good intentions, but so charged with personal bias and the desire to get a victim every so often, that he does much more harm than good." It added: "His statements cannot be depended upon to be either fair, factual or complete. He presents facts the way the curved mirrors make the people look who attend the chamber of horrors of the side show. He has developed a high nuisance value in connection with the handling of Indian problems. Since all money and legislation for the Indians has to be passed through Congress, Mr. Collier's methods have not led to satisfactory results."[29] According to McNickle, Collier had to "turn around and win the confidence of the Indian people as chief of the bureau he had vilified. It was an awkward situation to be in and he never entirely succeeded in extricating himself."[30] As a former hard-nosed agitator with numerous enemies inside and outside of government service, Collier believed his tenure as commissioner would be short, resulting in his efforts to package reforms in large and lengthy pieces of legislation such as the IRA. It is apparent that the uniformity of his approach to Indian policy reform was also in part a manifestation of this political necessity.

Collier's early perceptions of the Pueblos determined much of his approach to other vastly different Indian nations. Despite his work for the national American Indian Defense Association, where he was exposed to the problems of most Indians, Collier was stubbornly southwestern oriented. In this respect, his romanticism was glaringly apparent. Few Indians were as untouched by white encroachment and retentive of language and ceremonials as were the Pueblos. Consequently, to Collier, other Native Americans were somehow less "Indian." After all, how could others match the splendid isolation of the Pueblos pristine existence. As Berkhofer has observed: "In this sense, all Indians became Pueblos in his vision, regardless of Collier's belief that his program allowed for the multiplicity of tribal cultures and conditions."[31] Hence, Collier's efforts were seen as condescendingly rehabilitational to those who could not match his Pueblo ideal.

Collier's approach to the Iroquois was consciously and subconsciously affected by his own real experiences and self-inflated perceptions of southwestern Indians. As in the manner of his Pueblo fight against the Bursum Bill, he fiercely defended the Iroquois from threats of land loss. His stand against the building of a dam at the Cornplanter tract was strong and forthright throughout his commissionership. Moreover, he supported the Seneca Nation in its efforts in the Forness case to challenge the legality of underassessed leasing arrangements at Salamanca. He was especially explicit in his warnings to the Six Nations in New York and Wisconsin about the activities of Minnie Kellogg, her husband, and other smooth-talking political operators and financial swindlers who promised quick solutions to thorny legal problems such as land claims. Iroquois rights, as he defined them, had to be protected not only for the Indians' sake but for all humanity who needed the Native American to learn from. Just as he "saved" the Pueblos, Collier was determined to do so for all Indians because of his need to see Indian affairs "as an ethnic laboratory of universal meaning."[32]

Despite his good intentions and significant accomplishments, Collier largely did not understand the Iroquois. Collier especially did not comprehend the Iroquois' overriding concern with legality as well as with the real and symbolic reaffirmation of treaty rights.[33] Onondaga Chief George Thomas, reacting to Collier's announcement of the coming of an Indian New Deal, was hardly impressed since to him "so far as treaties and laws are concerned, America still has a bad mess of old deals to clear up."[34] Largely unaware that every Iroquois prides himself on his ability to interpret the meaning of treaties made with the federal government, Collier gave short shrift to these overriding legal concerns in an interview in 1933: "I'm not a lawyer, so I don't know anything about the legal status of the Iroquois; but what's more I don't think anybody else knows either and I do know that the federal government has a moral responsibility, if not a legal one, and I am here to exercise it if I can."[35]

Collier's major concern had to be relief for over 100,000 landless Indians, mostly in the Plains and Great Lakes states, a fact not lost on the New York Iroquois. According to Collier, these Indians had been "ruined economically and pauperized spiritually" by the loss of two-thirds of their landed heritage since 1887 under the Dawes Act.[36] After allotment, the remaining acreage was usually checkerboarded with white holdings and often too small to support the Indian family and tribal needs. Although the Indians affected by past allotment policies included Iroquois in Oklahoma and Wisconsin, Collier had little understanding of the age-old New York Iroquois differentiation of themselves from western Indians, including their own relatives. At a special Iroquois gathering in 1934 at Niagara Falls, Collier's ignorance of this fact was manifest in his policy address: "I believe that the Federal policy toward New York Indians [the Iroquois] should become exactly what that policy is toward the Blackfeet, the Sioux, the Papagos, the Pueblos, or the Navajos."[37] In addition, by bringing a western Indian, the noted Winnebago educator Henry Roe Cloud to New York State, to speak on behalf of federal legislation, Collier failed to comprehend both the scope and importance of Iroquois pride and nationalism.

Collier also did not fully grasp the full meaning of how the New York Iroquois defined their world. As people of conservative persuasion, many viewed Collier's plans with apprehension and as a threat to the status quo. One prominent Onondaga insisted that the best program would be to "leave us alone."[38] The Iroquois were especially skeptical of Collier's promises. Nearly every commissioner upon coming into office had made similar pledges, but, in the end, they had promoted forced assimilation, pushed for allotment of reservation lands, did little to protect tribal resources, or urged Indian acceptance of American citizenship. President Hoover and his reform-minded Department of Interior leadership had committed themselves in 1929 to improving Indian policy, but by 1933, these assurances seemed like largely empty promises. Consequently, one Onondaga affirmed in 1933: "We don't want new deals — the raw deals of past years are too sharp in our memory."[39]

Charles J. Rhoads and J. Henry Scattergood, commissioner and assistant commissioner of Indian affairs, 1929–33. Photograph courtesy of the National Archives.

By 1933, the Iroquois in New York were also resentful of the swelling federal Indian bureaucracy which to them contributed so little to improvement at the reservation level. Although commissioner Rhoads and his assistant J. Henry Scattergood, both active members of the Indian Rights Association, had begun the reorganization of the Indian Bureau and initiated other reform measures, little money trickled to reservation communities. When Collier assumed office and announced his intentions for further reorganization and suggested that the Indian agent to the Iroquois be replaced by a large staff of experts, the Iroquois in New York interpreted these moves as "business as usual," namely the further strengthening and expansion of the bureaucracy of Indian administration. To them, new reformers and reform organizations in office meant a continuity, not a break, with an ineffective past.[40]

Collier's own writing also reveals another reason for his inability to deal effectively with the Iroquois in New York. Unlike his often expressed views about the grandeur of contemporary Pueblo life, Collier in his speeches and his writings frequently alluded to the Iroquois' significance but always in the past tense. In his book, *The Indians of the Americas*, written after he left office, Collier devoted half a chapter to the Iroquois, considerably more attention than his treatment of most other Indian nations.[41] He hailed their past Confederacy as the "most important Indian grouping on the continent, north of Mexico" until after the American Revolution. With typical romantic abandon, he insisted that the Confederacy was the greatest institutional achievement of mankind "accepting the limits of its time and place."[42] Ignoring the violent intertribal warfare of Iroquois history in the seventeenth and eighteenth centuries, Collier naively maintained that the Confederacy was a pacifist organization devoted to peaceful aims. Stressing the workability of its political structure, Collier saw it as a near perfect representative democracy which others should follow as a successful historical model.[43]

Although the Iroquois example had some ambiguous but real influence on the founding fathers, Collier's romanticism blinded him to realities. One could easily point to the lesser political roles of the Oneidas and Cayugas and the less-than-equal political status of the Tuscaroras in the Confederacy to challenge Collier's generalizations. Yet, Collier's Iroquois with their ancient grandeur had to be restored wherever possible as a lesson for mankind today. He firmly believed that "the mighty generations of these eastern tribes [Iroquois] are among the dead, but the present can still do its duty to the extent of practical possibilities."[44]

Collier's basic presumption was that the Iroquois and other tribes were less "Indian" than the Pueblos whom he had first encountered. This assumption of lost identity was not entirely an outgrowth of his southwestern experience. His knowledge of the Iroquois was in part conditioned by his overreliance on experts. Instead of direct personal contact with the leaders of the Six Nations, Collier worked closely with Bureau of American Ethnology personnel, especially William Duncan Strong and J. N. B. Hewitt, the foremost specialist on Iroquois culture.[45] Unfortunately, both of these distinguished scholars were captives of much of the anthropological thought of the time. D'Arcy McNickle has written that Indians "were, in fact, more tribal and communal in outlook than administrators, missionaries, legislators, or social scientists of the period recognized." He added that the "popular belief was that native custom no longer functioned, and therefore structures and institutions adapted to the white man's experience would be readily accepted by all such tribes."[46] Strong, upon Collier's urging, attempted to ascertain from field anthropologists whether there was "enough of the Indian left anthropologically speaking, to make it worthwhile to make the [legislative] effort."[47] Hewitt, a man frequently quoted by Collier, was asked a similar question by one of the commissioner's assistants. He replied that "there is nothing of the [Iroquois] old life left worth saving, and so it would be better to make a complete change in economic and civil relations."[48] Although of Tuscarora ancestry himself, Hewitt had a limited social vision and was strongly resented by many Iroquois leaders of the period.[49] After first suggesting an assimilationist course for the Iroquois, Hewitt gave his full support to the IRA and to Collier's entire program, claiming that the proposed new elected systems would prevent the tyranny and corruption of the traditional chiefs and end "the despoliation by those [meaning the Kelloggs] whose sole object in life has been to enrich themselves at the expense of the Indian."[50]

William N. Fenton, Hewitt's successor at the Bureau of American Ethnology, has written: "The prophet who would succeed among the Iroquois must speak in ancient tongues, he must use the old words, and he must relate to old ways. He is a conservator at the same time that he is a reformer."[51] This statement, although written in the far different context of Iroquois leadership, describes why Collier had limited success among the Iroquois in New York. Wanting to do good, he was, nevertheless, handicapped by his inability, based upon his background and temperament, to understand them as distinct, fiercely proud Native American peoples. Not comprehending the symbols and style of Iroquois culture and diplomacy with its emphasis on treaty language and patience of approach, he alienated a considerable number of Iroquois in New York who still had land intact and who were fearful of any changes in federal-Indian relations. Romantic notions and good intentions were insufficient to win the day in New York. In Wisconsin and Oklahoma, however, where the Iroquois were largely landless and removed from much of the conservative cultural trappings of Iroquois existence, Collier succeeded in political reorganization of tribal government. His greatest failure to understand the Iroquois on their own terms, their culture, politics, and world-view, can be seen in his attempt to "sell" his program, the Indian Reorganization Act, in New York in 1934 and 1935. Even before Collier could initiate other programs among the Iroquois, the commissioner had to contend with a vocal group of militant Iroquois demanding greater federal recognition of their unique view of sovereignty and the abolition of the Bureau of Indian Affairs itself.

3

THE ONLY GOOD INDIAN BUREAU
IS A DEAD INDIAN BUREAU

Alice Lee Jemison, Seneca Political Activist

In behalf of our people, with the spirit of Moses, I ask this — THE
UNITED STATES OF AMERICA — LET MY PEOPLE GO.

> Carlos Montezuma, M.D.
> *Let My People Go*

The Six Nations have no desire to see the United States repudiate the
Treaty of Canandaigua which has been kept intact and which has protected the New York Indians from the ravages of Bureau [BIA] control
and the loss of land which other Indians have suffered through the
mal-administration of the Indian Bureau.

> Alice Lee Jemison (Seneca)
> Letter to the President
> Franklin D. Roosevelt,
> June 20, 1935

Who says the Government takes care of the Indians???? The Indians
take care of the Government employees.

> Alice Lee Jemison
> *The First American,*
> July 1, 1937

A check of the Attorney General's List and that of the House Committee
on Un-American Activities fails to indicate that the American Indian
Federation has been cited by either of them as subversive.

> Guy Hottel to Director
> FBI, June 4, 1948

AMONG THE IROQUOIS, Alice Lee Jemison was the major critic of both John Collier and the Indian New Deal. Jemison, a Seneca Indian, waged war relentlessly against the Indian Bureau throughout the 1930s and remained committed to its abolition until her death on March 6, 1964.[1] Long before the federal government was concerned about the activities of the Red Power Movement, the Interior Department felt the prod of Jemison and her disparate and controversial organization, the American Indian Federation. In retaliation for her attacks, which were frequently overblown but nonetheless scathing, the Roosevelt administration used its influence and power to disparage her efforts and even attempted to silence her. She was labeled by government officials in press conferences and before congressional committees as "Bundist," "Communist," "Fascist," "Nazi," and "Silver Shirt"; put under governmental surveillance and spied on by Indian informants; condemned by Commissioner Collier and Secretary of the Interior Harold Ickes as a crook, a traitor to her race, and as a spy in the pay of Nazi Germany. The FBI kept Jemison under surveillance from 1938 through 1948. All of her alleged Nazi connections were based on hearsay or other unsupported evidence. Mrs. Jemison's FBI file, released in 1978, reveals that the FBI viewed the American Indian Federation as nonsubversive and that most of the information accusing her of subversion came directly from Ickes and Collier themselves.[2]

Despite these calumnies, Jemison in reality was a true representative voice of a considerable segment of Iroquois opinion. In sharp contrast to the usual historical interpretation of Jemison, based both on interviews of Senecas and non-Indian associates and by a more careful reading of governmental records and congressional testimony and the release of her FBI file heretofore closed, she emerges as a hardworking and earnest critic of the BIA, working on behalf of Native Americans. Her close collaboration with and her support by the Seneca Council and her lobbying activities in support of California, Cherokee, Seneca, and Sioux Indians show another side of her career, not revealed in simply reading Collier's and Ickes' diatribes against her.

Born in 1901 and raised in Silver Creek, New York, just off the Cattaraugus Indian Reservation, Jemison was representative of a new leadership class of highly articulate Indians that emerged to dominate Native American politics from the 1880s onward. Although a product of two worlds —the non-Indian world of conservative western New York and the deeply rooted tribal life of the Seneca Indian community on Cattaraugus—she saw herself primarily as an Iroquois woman living in the modern world of the twentieth century. As the daughter of a Seneca mother and a Cherokee

Harold Ickes, secretary of the interior. Photograph courtesy of the National Archives.

father, both of whom were educated at the Hampton Normal and Agricultural Institute, she reflected the influence of her parents' teachers and teachings.[3] The Puritan work ethic instilled by her parents' boarding school training combined with Jemison's own pride in her Seneca heritage to produce an individual who was extremely industrious, confident of her abilities, and capable of strong leadership qualities among her people. Raised in the matrilineal society of the Senecas, with its ancient traditions of women's behind-the-scenes political participation, she had the self-

Alice Lee Jemison, mid-1930s. Photograph courtesy of Jeanne Marie Jemison.

assurance that became the cornerstone of her later political crusades. It was Jemison's conservative Seneca background with its suspicion of all non-Indian governmental authority and the right-of-center political attitudes of western New York with its historic distrust of Washington-directed policies that molded her into a leading Indian opponent of the New Deal.

Poverty plagued Jemison and her family throughout much of their lives. Although her goal had been to become an attorney, her formal education was limited because of family financial exigencies. She was graduated from Silver Creek High School in 1919, and on December 6 of that year, she married Le Verne Leonard Jemison, a Seneca steelworker. They had two children before the marriage ended in separation in December 1928. From that time onward, because of severe economic pressures, Jemison worked at various jobs to support her two children and her mother: beautician, Bureau of the Census employee, clerk, confectionary store manager, dressmaker, factory worker, farmer, free-lance journalist, housekeeper, para-legal researcher, peddler, political lobbyist, practical nurse, secretary, and theatre usher. Poverty continued to plague her throughout the 1930s and proved to be a major influence in her acceptance of money from political groups, however extreme, who were attempting to discredit the Roosevelt administration during the New Deal era.[4]

Jemison's background on and off the reservation helped make her a formidable opponent of the Indian Bureau. Since she had been born and educated off the reservation, her world was not solely limited to that of the Cattaraugus Reservation. She had lived in Buffalo for several years, working for E. Claudia Handley, the Erie County Woman's Democratic Party leader and executive secretary of the Cosmopolitan Association. Ironically, it was Hanley's candidate Roosevelt that Jemison attacked politically throughout the 1930s. This firsthand exposure to the workings of non-Indian politics broadened her perspectives of the non-Indian world and gave her insights into how to organize and shape political campaigns to bring her points across. This experience merged with her earlier training in debating and journalism while in high school and her later employment in law offices to sharpen her skills to deal effectively in combative situations.[5]

Her proximity to the seat of power in Seneca Nation politics unquestionably influenced the direction of her life. She first became involved in tribal politics in the late 1920s and early 1930s as a result of *Woodin v. Seeley,* a case involving an Indian and his non-Indian wife who were thrown off the Cattaraugus Reservation. As a part-time "girl-friday" to Seneca President Ray Jimerson in the early 1930s, she continued to actively serve the nation: she worked as a legal researcher; wrote invaluable articles for Buffalo newspapers improving the image of the nation in western New York; campaigned actively for the Six Nations' choice for commissioner—Joseph Latimer; and lobbied against the Seneca Conservation Act and the Indian Reorganization Act. Along with the Six Nations Confederacy Council, she led Seneca resistance to the Selective Service Act prior to World War II and was closely tied to the political leadership of the Seneca Nation well into the 1940s. Importantly, her highly respected uncle, Cornelius Seneca, was elected to the presidency of the Seneca Nation, a post which he held several times. As a result of her work for the Senecas, she was nominated by the tribal council for positions in the Indian service on at least two occasions.[6] President Jimerson, lauding her past work, recommended her to Congressman James Mead on January 28, 1933:

Personally I take pleasure in recommending Alice Lee Jemison for such a position. I have known her all of her life and she is a fine representative of the highest development of our Senecas. Although her actual school education is limited to high school and business training, she is exceptionally well qualified for such a position through practical experience, a sympathetic understanding and power to see both sides of a question *and particularly because she retains the high esteem and absolute faith of all the Senecas, regarding Indian questions, regardless of political party or religious lines.* [emphasis mine]. Her capacity for hard work is amazing. Her personal life has been one of hardships, against almost insurmountable difficulties. Her school education was obtained under most discouraging conditions. For the past four years she has been supporting herself, her two children and her mother and still continuing her own education, hoping some day to become an attorney. Through all of this struggle, she has maintained a cheerful optimistic outlook on life, has given much time in loyal service promoting the welfare of her race and has developed a poise and dignity well beyond her years.[7]

The Marchand Murder case was the turning point in the political awakening of Alice Lee Jemison. Two Indian women from Cattaraugus, Lila Jimerson and Nancy Bowen, were accused of murdering Clothilde Marchand, the artist wife of the internationally renowned sculptor Henri Marchand. Although the murder occurred in Buffalo, the two women were arrested by New York State authorities on Cattaraugus Reservation. Guy Moore, the Republican District Attorney of Erie County, hoping to use the case as a political springboard for higher office, had within two and a half weeks of the murder in March 1930, arrested, indicted, and helped select a jury for the murder trial of the two women. A carnival atmosphere surrounded the proceedings with pervasive anti-Indian publicity. Because Jimerson admitted her love for the victim's husband and Bowen, a deranged individual, told of her use of a ouija board, Moore made frequent references to what he claimed was the immorality of all Indian women and superstitious nature of Indian life as a whole. The case, which received national attention, was viewed by Indians nationwide as totally offensive, especially to those from Cattaraugus, the home reservation of Bowen and Jimerson. During the trial, a fictitious diary revealing Jimerson's amorous affairs was publicized. To make matters worse, Jimerson collapsed during the first trial after contracting tuberculosis.[8]

The Iroquois resented the pervasive anti-Indian publicity accorded the defendants by the press, the hesitant response of the United States attorney's office in Buffalo to represent the two women, and the slow wheels of white justice that allowed the women to languish in jail. Moreover, many Indians viewed the case as a clear example of two-sided white justice since they saw the middle-aged Henri Marchand, the man who had hired Lila Jimerson to be his model, as the culprit. Marchand was never prosecuted and soon after married his wife's teenage niece.[9]

Working closely with Chief Clinton Rickard and Ray Jimerson, Jemison was an important cog in the defense of Lila Jimerson. They attempted to obtain the services of Clarence Darrow, but Darrow's attorney fees and expenses were too high for the Indians. They then appealed both directly and indirectly to major non-Indian political leaders. Using the arguments that the arrests of the two women by state police on Indian land were illegal and that the United States attorney in western New York was empowered to come to the aid of the Indians under the Treaty of Canandaigua, the defense committee, with the aid of Jemison's friend and patron, Mrs. Handley of Buffalo, began to get results. Their letters, especially to Charles Curtis, vice-president of the United States and one-quarter Indian himself, resulted in federal intervention in the case, slowed down the lynchlike qualities of the proceedings, and allowed time for the ugly publicity to dissipate.[10] Eventually, in her second trial, Jimerson was acquitted while Bowen, who had pleaded guilty to first degree manslaughter, was released after spending more than a year in prison.

Jemison's appeal also took the form of writing articles for the Buffalo newspapers attempting to influence public opinion favorably about Jimerson and about Indians in general. Writing in the *Buffalo Evening Times* on March 23, 1930, she insisted, in an article entitled "Present Crime Poor Example of True Indian," that the "Indian today is not murderous."[11] It was this involvement in the legal defense of the two Indian women that familiarized Jemison with both the techniques of political lobbying and leading journalists in the country. It also contributed to her securing a syndicated column from the North American Newspaper Alliance. It is also quite clear, from her later numerous newspaper and newsletter writings devoted to improving the image of the Indian, that her concern stemmed in part from her activities in the turbulent Marchand murder case.[12]

The Seneca activist was also influenced by the writings and ideas of Dr. Carlos Montezuma, the leading Pan-Indian writer and critic of the BIA in the first decades of the twentieth century. Montezuma, a Yavapai Indian and a former physician in the Indian Service, in evangelical abolitionist fashion, believed in one fundamental tenet and worked in the last decade of his life to accomplish it: the abolition of the BIA. Giving up a career in the Indian Health Service after seeing what he considered to be the colonial nature of the relationship of Indian and white, Montezuma, from his Chicago-based home, created a national network devoted to exposing the conditions on the reservations, improving the life of Native Americans, and destroying the bureaucracy that he believed enshackled his people. He published the *Wassaja: Freedom's Signal for the Indian* which repeatedly chastised the political patronage, corruption, insensitivity, bureaucratic framework, racism, and general incompetence of the BIA. Besides the employees of the BIA, his targets were missionaries, philanthropists, anthropologists, sociologists, psychologists, archeologists, artists, novelists — everyone whom he alleged exploited the Indians. Moreover, he had little sympathy for Native American employees in the BIA or those reformers, Indian or non-Indian, who attempted to correct the system by working within it.[13] What is most important for a knowledge of Jemison is to realize that Montezuma understood reform only meant the strengthening, not the diminishing, of bureaucratic control in the lives of American Indians. Montezuma insisted that reorganization "means to strengthen and to improve, [and that] no amount of reorganization of the Indian Bureau will abolish the Indian Bureau. Without much thought one can see that his reorganization business of the Indian Bureau will strengthen and enlarge the Indian Bureau."[14]

Although Montezuma died in 1923, to a whole generation of Native American intellectuals, his words ignited a movement that is still alive today. Although Montezuma's message was tinged with assimilationist ideas, he remains a key in understanding not only Jemison but also much of Indian criticism of the BIA since 1923.[15]

In New York, Montezuma's message was spread throughout the 1920s and 1930s by his former secretary and confidant, attorney Joseph W.

Carlos Montezuma, M.D., 1896. Photograph courtesy of the National Anthropological Archives, Smithsonian Institution.

Latimer. In Latimer's newsletter *Bureaucracy à la Mode,* he continued Montezuma's assault. Using Montezuma's slogan "Abolish the Indian Bureau and Let My People Go," as his newsletter's masthead, he became known in New York State as a thorn in the administrative side of the BIA. By 1932, his own slogan "The Only Good Bureau is a Dead Bureau" appears to have converted Jemison to Latimer's candidacy for commissioner of Indian affairs.[16]

What is also important to note is that a magazine, *The Six Nations*, with a similar perspective, although somewhat less radical than Montezuma and Latimer, was being published in the late 1920s on Jemison's Cattaraugus Indian Reservation. *The Six Nations* carried articles denouncing the BIA as well as New York State for their failure to live up to treaty agreements, to educate Iroquois, to provide decent health care, and to protect Indian mineral rights in Oklahoma.[17] In one article written in 1926, the magazine concluded that bureau-controlled Indians were "essentially slaves" and that the Iroquois were fortunate not to be as rich as the Osage in Oklahoma, for if they did have wealth the "Federal Indian Bureau would soon get them and their money."[18]

Jemison, working with the Iroquois Confederacy as well as tribal leaders from Allegany, Cattaraugus, Tonawanda, and Tuscarora, began the push for Latimer's candidacy. They, with the tacit approval of Indians from Onondaga and St. Regis, drafted petitions, wrote news articles and helped found a pan-Indian organization, the Intertribal Committee for the Fundamental Advancement of the American Indian. Reminiscent of Minnie Kellogg's early writings, the committee affirmed that the time was ripe for the abolition of the bureau to end what it claimed was "bureau dictatorship over the Indians," a position supported by Latimer. To these Indians, a "new deal" meant a complete change, not merely reform.[19] In February 1933, just prior to Collier's appointment, they clearly set forth this position by insisting that they were objecting to the "policies of the Indian bureau and certain so-called benevolent societies who apparently work hand in hand with it and are to a certain extent supported by it."[20] Knowing that Collier had the inside track on being appointed commissioner, they affirmed that they did not want another reform-minded Indian commissioner. Jemison later explained: "We are weary unto death of the propaganda for a continuance of the bureau to further 'protect' the Indian which is spread by the so-called Indian Defense Association and other societies which are sponsored by wealthy people in the name of charity, many of whom have never seen an Indian, would not know one unless he had on full tribal regalia, have absolutely no knowledge of reservations or the actual conditions thereon, but who think they know exactly what is best for the Indians."[21]

In a series of four articles that appeared in the *Buffalo Evening News* and other newspapers of the North American Newspaper Alliance in April 1933, Jemison frequently quoted from Montezuma, exposed the bureaucratic inefficiency and insensitivity of the BIA, and pushed Latimer for the next commissioner. She asserted:

> We consider that we are in a better position than anyone else to know what we need and that we have an equal right with all other people in this, our America, to voice our desire. We want, as commissioner, a man in whom we can trust. There are but few. We have been so victimized in the past. A man who will give an understanding ear to our expressions, and who, having heard, can and will sponsor legislation to promote our welfare, not as wards but as free men and women. Not a politician. But a bold and fearless man who will smash through the maze of red tape and restrictions in the bureau, remove them and give the Indian at last an opportunity to learn how to manage his own affairs by actually doing it.[22]

To Jemison, a reformer like Collier with new experiments in reorganization meant prolonging the suffering of the shackled Indian masses by focusing attention away from Montezuma's goal of abolition. She pointed out that President Hoover's appointments were also originally hailed as reformers committed to helping the Indians, but that they had done too little to alleviate problems and only contributed to more restrictions on Indians as well as a more bureaucratic, powerful, and repressive bureau.[23] She insisted that the Iroquois were now firmly behind Montezuma's goal of abolition and were pushing for Latimer's appointment as commissioner. Employing Montezuma-Latimer styled rhetoric, Jemison continued: "Yes! Abolish the Indian Bureau! The greatest example in the United States today of over-developed bureaucracy. Abolish this bureau with its un-American principles of slavery, greed and oppression and let a whole race of people, the first Americans, take their place beside all other people in this land of opportunity as free men and women."[24] Consequently, Collier's appointment to the commissionership was a major loss to Jemison as well as a vocal and influential group of Iroquois leaders.

Jemison's activism was also prompted by the terrible conditions found on her reservation. Since most Senecas worked off the Cattaraugus Reservation in factories in or near Buffalo or were employed as structural iron workers, they were not insulated from the devastating effects of the Great Depression. Unemployment was high, and many Indians depended on work relief to survive. Throughout the period after 1929, these Indians frequently complained that state and later federal programs designed for their needs — including road work and school construction projects — discriminated against the Indians by hiring only non-Indians or required American citizenship, voter's registration cards, and loyalty oaths that ran counter to Iroquois beliefs in sovereignty.[25]

The worst conditions at Cattaraugus were in the area of public health. In 1934, the death rate caused by tuberculosis on the reservation was six times higher than in the non-Indian world.[26] The continued pollution of Cattaraugus Creek, which traverses the reservation, was a major source of the spread of disease. Jemison described the causes of the pollution and its impact on public health in a letter to President Roosevelt on June 20, 1935:

> This sewage disposal (from the State Hospital for the Insane at Gowanda and the Thomas Indian Orphanage at Iroquois) together with that from the Village of Gowanda, the tannery and glue factory located therein, renders the Cattaraugus Creek unfit for any 'free use and enjoyment' by the Indians and makes it a constant menace to the health of whites and Indians alike throughout its entire course of twelve to fifteen miles. My own son will carry scars to his grave from an infection he contracted from swimming in that creek and there have been cases of typhoid fever, infantile paralysis and spinal meningitis resulting in both death and helpless cripples among our Indian children and thought to be traceable to the same source. As far as conserving the fish goes, the clearing up of this pollution situation would save more fish than the Indians could take there from if they engaged actively in the fishing industry. One has only to walk along the banks of Cattaraugus Creek early in the spring when many fish go up the creek during the spawning season to see the results of this poisoning in great numbers of dead fish floating down stream. So I repeat, the State of New York should be engaged in the business of conserving the lives of human beings rather than persecuting them for the few fish they take to sustain their lives.[27]

As a result of these and other Indian complaints against the New York State Department of Conservation, the Council of the Seneca Nation appointed her as their lobbyist in Washington against the Seneca Conservation Act of 1927. From January 1933 to June 1935, she actively campaigned to overturn the act. Working with Seneca President Ray Jimerson and Robert Galloway, the attorney for the Seneca Nation, she convinced New York Congressman Alfred Beiter to introduce legislation to overturn New York State Department of Conservation jurisdiction. She used the two arguments that the law violated Iroquois rights as guaranteed under the

Treaty of Canandaigua and that state officials were harrassing the Indians.[28] After calling it a direct violation of the treaty, President Jimerson, in a letter to Commissioner Collier, explained the Senecas' position:

> This Act has been a source of great aggrivation [sic] and unnecessary suffering to the Seneca Indians generally. The officers of the State [N.Y.] Conservation Department have been unduly diligent in their efforts to arrest Indians upon the reservations, even employing an air-plane [sic] for the purpose of detecting violators in some instances. On the other hand, the Seneca Nation has been unable to force the white fisherman to purchase a license from the Indians to haul seine in the Cattaraugus Creek and have received no cooperation from the State Department in preventing them from so doing. Many of the Indians have been fined excessively and several have spent considerable time in jail. And the expense of the litigation caused by this said Act have been great to the Nation.[29]

In June 1935, just after Iroquois rejection of the Indian Reorganization Act, President Roosevelt vetoed the Beiter Bill, much to the anger of the Senecas. In reaction, Jemison wrote a four-page letter of protest in which she criticized Roosevelt's action, claiming his veto was motivated by Iroquois opposition to John Collier and their voting down the IRA, and insisting that the president reread the treaty of 1794 and fire the commissioner of Indian affairs.[30] The failure of this campaign to overturn the Seneca Conservation Act contributed to her increasing activism in the mid and late 1930s and to her overwhelmingly negative reaction to Commissioner Collier, the IRA, and the Roosevelt administration as a whole.

Jemison's program was clearly spelled out throughout the 1930s: (1) remove Commissioner Collier, (2) repeal the IRA, and (3) abolish the BIA. In Washington, she actively became involved in the work of the American Indian Federation, a widely diverse group of Native Americans influenced by the writings of Montezuma. The organization has been generally interpreted as being composed of a group of super patriotic bigots, anti-Semitic inquisitors, assimilated Indian mixed bloods, fundamentalist Christian religious fanatics and even pro-Nazi, pro-Bundist zealots.[31] Although there is some truth to these generalizations, the goal of the American Indian Federation was much more mundane and Indian-oriented. Much of its right-wing rhetoric of protest has obscured its distinct objectives, the previously stated threefold program espoused by Jemison. When the American Indian Federation failed to secure the achievement of these goals by

Alice Lee Jemison, Cornelius Seneca, and Elnora Seneca (left to right), late 1930s, Washington, D.C. Photograph courtesy of Jeanne Marie Jemison.

1938, it splintered into several distinct factions and became ineffective until its demise after the onset of World War II.

Besides Jemison, the organization's leadership was largely dominated byIndians from Oklahoma and reflected much of that state's allotted Indian populations' uneasiness about Commissioner Collier's emphasis on tribal communal models. These Indians, led by American Indian Federation President Joseph Bruner, a wealthy full-blood Creek and peyotist from Sapulpa, advocated complete Indian participation in the American body

Joseph Bruner, president of the American Indian Federation and Creek chief. Photograph courtesy of the National Archives.

politic and argued against the continuance of the BIA. This Oklahoma-
based group included O. K. Chandler, one-eighth Cherokee, an attorney, and
former controversial Indian agent from Miami, and W. W. LeFlore, one-
eighth Choctaw and a teacher from Bennington.[32] The American Indian
Federation also included prominent Indians from Arizona, California,
Michigan, New York, North Carolina, Oregon, and South Dakota, many of
whom had little in common with their Oklahoma brethren. These members,
like Jemison, were drawn to the organization by local reservation grievances
against the Indian Service. Consequently, these members varied widely in
their objectives, except in their support of the previously stated threefold
goal. Besides Jemison, the non-Oklahoma members included Thomas
Sloan, an Omaha Indian attorney and former president of the Society of
American Indians; J. C. Morgan, later the president of the Navajo Nation;
Fred Bauer, vice-chief of the Eastern Band of Cherokee Indians; Adam
Castillo, a leader of the California Mission Indians; Rupert Costo, the
distinguished Cahuilla Indian journalist and later editor of his newspaper
(*Wassaja*) modeled after Montezuma's earlier paper; members of the so-
called Black Hills Treaty Council; and, quite significantly, two Iroquois
traditionalist chiefs.[33]

Although her own criticism of the Indian New Deal was largely based
upon her Seneca background and what she perceived to be a threat to
Iroquois sovereignty guaranteed by treaties, Jemison, as the Capitol Hill
lobbyist, and the "brains" of the American Indian Federation, went beyond
her own tribal affiliation to defend and espouse the causes of other Indian
nations. Commissioner Collier and Secretary Ickes felt the wrath of Jemison's jibes throughout the New Deal. Her accusations against Collier were
manifold: his heavy-handed and insensitive conservation measures in the
herd reduction program among the Navajo; his failing to appropriate funds
to allow Indians objecting to the commissioner's program to come to
Washington to testify; his threatening Indians who signed petitions against
Collier or the IRA with a loss of jobs and rations; his wasteful spending of
congressional appropriations for Indian affairs; and his overall administrative incompetence.[34]

She was an active defender of the rights of the Eastern Band of
Cherokee Indians and worked with her lifelong friend, Cherokee Vice-Chief
Fred Bauer, to prevent the Interior Department from splitting their Qualla
boundary reservation in two. Secretary Ickes had acceded to the Park
Service's and other political pressures to build the Blue Ridge Parkway — a
1,000 foot right-of-way 13 miles in length — through the reservation to
promote tourism in the nearby newly opened Great Smoky National Park.

Without Bauer's and Jemison's work in organizing Indian and non-Indian resistance, much more Indian land would have been taken. Instead of dividing the reservation, a "compromise" was eventually worked out, whereby the parkway, although taking some Cherokee land, today skirts the northern boundary of the reservation.[35]

Jemison also devoted much of her time in this period to the problems of California and Sioux Indians. In both instances, she and large numbers of these Native Americans from both areas questioned the legality of the IRA referendum and suggested government voter manipulation and fraud. Jemison's defense of California Indian communities also centered around attempts to win recognition of eighteen treaties made by these Indians with the federal government but never formally ratified by Congress and to gain reparations benefits for the survivors of the heinous treatment accorded to these Indians during and after the Gold Rush years.[36]

Although there were many assimilationist-minded people in the American Indian Federation, it was one of the earlier national lobbying efforts that tried to influence policy. Jemison and other members of the organization saw that blanket uniform policies carried out from Washington often did more harm than good. In a *Washington Times* letter to the editor in 1935, Jemison maintained: "There never has been and never will be but one method to deal with the Indian problem which has been created by the Indian Bureau."[37] Jemison put it best in a speech to the Black Hills Indian Treaty Council at Kyle, South Dakota, on July 27, 1938: "The Wheeler-Howard Act provides only one form of government for the Indian and that is communal or cooperative form of living. John Collier said he was going to give the Indian self-government. If he was going to give us self-government he would let us set up a form of government we wanted to live under. He would give us the right to continue to live under our old tribal customs if we wanted to."[38]

In all cases, she attempted to win a hearing for varied Indian interests before Congress, and it is clear from a reading of the major legislative hearings of the 1930s that she had an influence on leading congressional critics of the BIA in the period, most notably Congressman Alfred Beiter of New York, Virginia Jenckes of Virginia, Usher L. Burdick of North Dakota John S. McGroarty of California, Senator Burton K. Wheeler of Montana, and Special Counsel to the Senate Indian Affairs Subcommittee Albert A. Grorud. They sponsored legislation to limit or repeal the IRA and/or to incorporate the American Indian Federation, made speeches opposing Collier's programs, or badgered the commissioner with their insistent questioning before congressional committees.[39]

In fairness to Collier, not all of Jemison's attacks against him or the BIA were made responsibly. Her strong conservative political leanings combined with her lifelong emotional, nearly fanatical, commitment to Indian civil and treaty rights, led her to make accusations that were often overblown and exaggerated. She frequently red-baited, charging that the Interior Department had been seized by communists intent on undermining American as well as Indian freedoms. Although she was accurate in charging Collier with experimenting and tampering with existing Indian political systems, in her zeal to win support for the abolition of the BIA from Capitol Hill and the American public, she accused Collier of being a dangerous subversive and a tool of the American Civil Liberties Union. To Jemison, the mere facts that many of the Interior Department's officials were outspoken activists and were associated with the ACLU — Allen Harper, Collier's trusted field representative and coordinator for the Technical Cooperation-BIA program; Robert Marshall, chief forester; Nathan Margold, solicitor; Mary Heaton Vorse, editor of the bureau biweekly magazine *Indians at Work,* as well as John Collier and Harold Ickes themselves — were proof positive of their treason. Willard Beatty, director of Indian education, was also labeled by Jemison as a subversive for his past affiliation with the Progressive Education Association and for his radical departures and experiments in the curriculum of Indian schools.[40]

Throughout the New Deal era, Jemison surrounded herself and was surrounded by right-wing critics of the Roosevelt administration. As a conservative adversary of the Indian New Deal, she accepted and was accepted by nearly every Roosevelt-hater in the country, from the Daughters of the American Revolution to William Dudley Pelley, head of the Silver Shirts of America. Because of her fervent anti–New Deal thrust that exposed the poor conditions of Indian life in the 1930s, her articles were reprinted by widely circulated fascist publications to justify attacks on Roosevelt from the right. Since her commitment entailed a relentless, Montezumalike holy war against the BIA, she was not averse to appearing throughout the period on the same platform or at the same congressional hearing with leaders of the "radical right" in America, including Pelley himself. In most difficult times when her finances ran out completely, she accepted financial help from right-wing extremist James True, editor of the fascist and anti-Semitic newsletter *Industrial Control Report,* in order to support herself and her family and continue her opposition to Collier, the IRA, and the BIA.[41] Confronted by this revelation before the House Committee on Indian Affairs in 1940, she described her predicament:

Now in 1937, things were particularly hard. There were many times that we did not have enough to eat. Sometimes the children could not go to school because they were too hungry, and I have appeared before committees when I was faint from the lack of food. In fact, in April of that year, while appearing on the Wheeler-Howard matter before the Senate committee, I did faint and the hearing had to be adjourned until I recovered. The children and I lived in one room at that time, and the rent was $6 a week. But we were unable to pay that for 6 months or more. The landlord was very patient, but finally could not wait any longer, so one day when we were all out of the room he put a padlock upon the door, and we were literally put out into the street without anything. It was in September, just before Labor Day. I had not seen my mother for almost 4 years, and she arrived on a visit on Labor Day to find us without even a room to live in. She can verify what I am telling you now. She and my uncle [Cornelius Seneca, president of the Seneca Nation] wished to take us home with them, but I refused to go. So, in October, Mr. True circulated the appeal which Mr. Collier put into the record, and through it my room rent was paid in full, and we got back our clothing and federation files and records. And, let the record show that Jim True is a fine, sincere, Christian gentleman, and he is my friend.[42]

Consequently, it is easy to see how the federal government was able to portray her as an Indian Nazi. This allegation was further confirmed in the American public's eyes when she led Seneca resistance to the Selective Service Act of 1940.[43]

Although Jemison herself was guilty of irresponsible red-baiting, government officials themselves used flimsy hearsay testimony to slander her. Since there were members of the American Indian Federation, such as E. A. Towner, that flirted with Nazism by wearing German-styled swastika armbands or distributing Nazi literature at their annual conventions, historians have treated the organization as a whole as ideologically fascist or Nazi. Yet, Jemison's Indian newsletter, The First American, published in this period, reveals that her interests were almost entirely concerned with congressional Indian legislation, violations of Indian civil liberties, improving the overall image of the American Indian, the repeal of the IRA, the removal of Commissioner Collier, and the abolition of the BIA. With few exceptions, she was basically a one-issue political activist, and her cause was furthering Montezuma's abolitionist movement. Most significantly, despite the accusations, Jemison passed every loyalty check made by the FBI and was able to secure federal employment by 1941.[44]

It should also be noted that by 1937 the Indian New Deal as well as the New Deal as a whole was in serious political trouble. The conservative coalition in Congress began to assert the power that it had relinquished during the economic emergency of President Roosevelt's first term. The "court-packing" fight of 1937 also undermined the administration's influence on Capitol Hill. Commissioner Collier and Secretary Ickes, never liked by many congressional leaders, had also begun to face the wrath of a newly assertive Congress. Most of the major pieces of legislation of the Indian New Deal had all been introduced and passed during Roosevelt's first administration. Equally significant, Senator Wheeler, by 1937 the leader against Roosevelt's attempt to pack the Supreme Court, introduced a bill to repeal the IRA, the very piece of legislation he had sponsored into law.[45] Just as the president had purged his foes in the congressional primaries of 1938 and 1940, Collier and Ickes, now under attack by Congressman Dies' House on Un-American Activities Committee, began to retaliate against their enemies. It appears as no coincidence, then, that the day after Jemison testified about communism in the Interior Department before Dies' committee, Ickes first alleged that Jemison, code-named "Pocahontas," was a Nazi go-between. The FBI file on Jemison also reveals that her two major accusers of alleged Nazi activity were the secretary of the interior and the commissioner of Indian affairs, precisely the same two administrators subjected most to Jemison's attacks.[46]

By the late 1930s, the American Indian Federation began to schism. Jemison broke with the leadership over their abandonment of the movement to concentrate on overturning the IRA, removing Collier, and abolishing the BIA. The leadership had turned its efforts, among other things, to the so-called "Settlement Bill," an attempt to win a sum of $3,000 for every Native American in the country. To Jemison, this was a detour from the initial aims of the organization.[47] Despite this break, she continued to testify before congressional committees from 1938 to 1940, including Senator Elmer Thomas' Senate Indian Affairs Subcommittee and the Dies' Committee, against "Collierism," "bureauism," and communists in government.[48]

Because of family economic necessity, federal limitations on government employees' political lobbying, and the climate of the country after Pearl Harbor, Jemison muted her outspoken stance against Washington throughout the 1940s when she held a job at the Bureau of the Census. Instead, she increasingly directed her attacks against the State of New York in its successful campaign to secure civil and criminal jurisdiction over the Iroquois.[49] Nevertheless, by the early 1950s, as editor of the

The First American, a newsletter which she once more published in the Washington area, she again became vocal about Bureau of Indian Affairs mismanagement.

The ultimate irony of Jemison's important career as a political activist was that her work over three decades for self-determination of Indian nations was distorted by the congressional establishment of the 1950s through the policy of termination and had effects on Native Americans opposite from those she had intended. Though she wanted to help American Indians by abolishing the BIA, her arguments for its abolition added fuel to a policy that proved more of a detriment than a cure.[50]

In sum, Jemison was an Iroquois woman, a political disciple of Montezuma as well as an evangelical abolitionist. As a political conservative, her fear of an all-dominant, omnipotent government complemented her basically conservative Native American heritage that was suspicious of all non-Indian governmental authority. The end result was a critic who insisted upon the sanctity of Indian treaty rights while labeling the Indian New Deal's experiments a financial boondoggle, communist-inspired and anti-Christian. Although her remarks before senate and house committee hearings echoed much of her organization's right-wing rhetoric of protest and represented much of the sentiments of the Oklahoma faction within the American Indian Federation, Jemison's protests also reflected much of the Iroquois thinking of the period. Her belief in Iroquois treaty rights, coupled with an Iroquois vision of sovereignty that never wavered, came into conflict with Commissioner Collier and his views throughout the New Deal years.

At a congressional hearing on February 11, 1935, Jemison affirmed her belief in the sanctity of the Treaty of Canandaigua, insisted that the "situation in New York State is entirely different from any other Indians in the United States," and concluded that, under the terms of this and other treaties with the federal government, "we have always had self-government among the New York Indians."[51] At the same hearing Collier totally dismissed this interpretation that the Iroquois were independent sovereignties who "never came under the jurisdiction of the United States and only by courtesy and consent under the jurisdiction of the State of New York [and] that they are independent sovereignties, dependent, but subject to nothing but a ghostly guardianship." After all, Collier argued, the Supreme Court has repeatedly held that the "sovereignty in an Indian group is dependent on the will of Congress, and that Congress may invade, modify, regulate, or abolish it."[52] Hence, two divergent belief systems, one ascribed to by Jemison and a significant number of Iroquois and the other held to by the non-Indian world and its legal institutions, clashed throughout the New Deal.

4

RAW DEAL

The Iroquois of New York and the Indian Reorganization Act of 1934

Leave us as we were.

Chief Jesse Lyons (Onondaga)
Syracuse Herald, July 27, 1933

... and when have we believed in the Government and not been fooled.

Unknown Tonawanda Seneca
Listen for a Lonesome Drum

If the Federal Government will not stand back of the agreements of your Treaty of 1784/89, then of what avail is further legislation.

Lulu G. Stillman
Advisor to Six Nations
Letter to the Six Nations,
March 29, 1934

THE ENTIRE IROQUOIS NEW DEAL in New York was colored by the bitter struggle over the IRA of 1934. Unlike their brethren in Wisconsin, New York tribesmen overwhelmingly rejected the act in 1935 and sought its repeal right through 1940. Many agreed with Melvin Patterson, a journalist of Tuscarora ancestry, in his evaluation of the act as "the rawest deal ever perpetrated by an administration."[1] Nearly 50 percent of all eligible voters—an unusually high turnout by the Iroquois who traditionally avoid political participation in the non-Indian world—went to the polls, reflecting the intense campaign surrounding the act. More than 80 percent of all the Iroquois who participated in the referendum voted against the act:[2]

Reservation	Eligible Voters	For	Against	Not Voting	Election Date
Allegany	548	37	298	213	June 10, 1935
Cattaraugus	864	101	475	288	June 14
Onondaga	350	17	206	127	June 15
St. Regis	800	46	237	517	June 8
Tonawanda	338	42	175	121	June 11
Tuscarora	225	6	132	87	June 12
Totals:	3,125	249	1,523	1,353	

The original bill introduced in Congress in 1935 was forty-eight pages long, containing four separate parts. Title I granted all Indians the freedom to organize for purposes of local self-government and economic independence. It provided for the establishment of tribal elections, tribal constitutions, and tribal corporations; a revolving loan fund to assist organized tribes in community economic development; and the encouragement of Indian employment in the Indian service by giving preference in hiring by waiving civil service requirements. Title II, which dealt with Indian education, affirmed that the purpose and policy was "to promote the study of Indian civilization, including Indian crafts, skills and traditions." Under this part of the act, vocational and college scholarships and educational loans were also included. Title III was directly related to Indian lands, ending the land allotment policies of the Dawes Act and providing for the purchase of new land for the Indians. Unallotted lands were to be returned to the tribal councils. Conservation efforts were to be encouraged on existing Indian lands by the establishment of Indian forestry units and by herd reduction on arid land to protect range deterioration. Title IV, which was later deleted from the bill, proposed the creation of a Court of Indian Offenses which would have original jurisdiction in all cases involving federally recognized tribes. The bill defined "Indian" as members of any recognized tribe under federal jurisdiction, those descendants of tribal members who resided within the boundaries of any reservation on or before June 1, 1934, and all other persons of one-half (later amended to one-quarter) or more Indian blood.

As passed by Congress and signed by the president on June 18, 1934, the IRA required a tribal plebiscite before its acceptance. According to Section 18: "This Act shall not apply to any reservation wherein a majority of the adult Indians, voting at a special election called by the Secretary of the Interior, shall vote against its application."[3]

The major supporters of the IRA in New York, few in number, included John L. Snyder, a Seneca, an attorney from Cattaraugus Reservation; Frank D. Williams, a farmer and chairman of the Tuscarora Agricultural Association; and Edgar Rickard, a chief of the Tuscaroras. Snyder saw the IRA as "designed to correct and repair the wrongs done Indians" and to provide them with "equal protection of the law."[4] He proved unsuccessful at silencing his Seneca opponent in the IRA controversy, Alice Lee Jemison, or convincing her that John Collier was "sincerely interested in the welfare of Indians generally."[5] Williams, in contrast, was more interested in the revolving credit fund program provided in the act. His support of the IRA included making a speech on behalf of the act and his offer to Commissioner Collier of service in connection with explaining it to other Iroquois. Although his motivation is unclear, Edgar Rickard had supported Collier for commissioner in 1933 and had helped bring him as a speaker to the Niagara Falls area in September 1934.[6] According to his brother Clinton, Edgar's political rival on the reservation, his positive "attitude toward this legislation [IRA] brought about a decline in his influence in the community and on the chief's council — for our people were strongly opposed to Washington's attempts to reorganize our traditional government and customs."[7]

The IRA was largely rejected in New York because of reasons unrelated to the act itself. Although the government's selling of the Indian New Deal left much to be desired, age-old Iroquois concerns and perceptions, both real and imaginary, were central to the IRA's rejection. The unique Iroquois view of sovereignty blended with memories of past injustice suffered by these Indians and created a formidable opposition movement to the IRA. Unlike their near-landless cousins in Oklahoma and Wisconsin, the Iroquois in New York retained approximately seventy-seven thousand acres of land, most of which was held in communal fashion.[8] These Indians had fought successfully to maintain their land base, however reduced from their ancient grandeur, despite the allotment of some of their lands and serious attempts to subdivide Allegany, Cattaraugus, and Onondaga reservations in the nineteenth and early twentieth centuries.[9] One Seneca expressed the feeling about sovereignty and previous land losses to a visitor to Tonawanda Reservation in 1935:

I shall vote against accepting the bill.... We are a nation, living on land of our own. We are not citizens of the United States and I hope we never will be. We must insist on our rights as a separate territory not responsible to any other government. We must rule ourselves. We must not pay taxes to the United States or we will lose our status as a separate nation. Over near Oneida a little while ago some white farmers tricked an Indian into paying taxes on his tax-free land. Now the whites own the land and the Indian is penniless. We must not let that happen to us.[10]

Lingering fears and one hundred fifty years of distrust of the dominant non-Indian world could not be removed overnight by one piece of comprehensive legislation designed to help all tribes in the United States however different from each other they may have been. Another Seneca, despite his faltering English, put it most accurately: "we have been fooled time after time that most of the Indians have lost faith in the Saxon Race we certainly have had some raw deal in back history we have never had a square deal."[11]

Despite the revolutionary features of the act — its cultural pluralistic educational philosophy; Indian preference in hiring; revolving credit loan program for economic development; and the encouragement of Indian higher education by the establishment of scholarship assistance — the majority of Iroquois viewed the act with suspicion. Why should the United States government help the Indians when so often in the past it had turned its back and allowed New York State to take advantage of the Six Nations? Why should Washington *now* fulfill trust responsibilities toward its red brothers? Reminiscent of Deskaheh and the Grand River traditionals' warnings about Canadian intent under the Soldier's Settlement Act after World War I, one Seneca maintained: "You can't make me believe that the [U.S.] Government offers loans to us without asking security. Suppose we don't make money without plows. Suppose our horses die before we can pay back. What then?" He added that the government, undoubtedly upon default, would appropriate Indian homes.[12]

The Iroquois' questioning of motives of policy-makers could also be traced to concerns pertinent to the atmosphere in the 1930s as well as to important events in the decade prior to the Indian New Deal. The Great Depression had made a previously poor situation even more intolerable, leading to further suspicions of the non-Indian world. According to Chief Clinton Rickard:

Chief George Rickard, W. K. Harrison (Indian agent in New York) and Chief Clinton Rickard (left to right), 1932. Photograph courtesy of Beulah Rickard Lillvick.

The Great Depression that was sweeping the United States in the 1930's hit our Indian people everywhere particularly hard....During the distressing time of the depression, we had the utmost difficulty in securing enough money to buy seeds, horses, mules or other necessities required for agriculture. When we were unable to farm, we were unable to be self-reliant. Our hunting was no longer sufficient to support all of us during the year, but could be used only as a supplement. We looked for wage work off the reservation but were discriminated against because of our race. The white people were taken care of first, and those of our men who were fortunate enough to find work were usually soon discharged to give the job to a white man. Even a recent European immigrant was always given preference over an original American. When we sought relief, we were turned away with the comment that our reservation was not in any relief district. White men less destitute than we were readily given work.[13]

Between 40 and 50 percent of the Indians in New York State were receiving some welfare assistance by the mid-1930s.[14] The magnitude of the crisis was expressed by two Onondaga chiefs in a letter to Governor Herbert Lehman in February 1934: "There are a number of Indians [Onondaga] who are in destitute circumstances, most of them heads of families, about thirty-four in number. They are willing to work, in fact, are anxious to get any kind of work that they can do but the larger part of the thirty-four are going to be absolutely destitute in a very short time. We are writing you in the hope that something may be done through the cooperation of the Federal or County Government that those men can be put to work."[15] As late as 1939, a government survey still showed 24 percent of the Iroquois as unemployed, while C. H. Berry, superintendent of the New York Agency, reported "that practically the entire population of this [Onondaga] reservation ... is on relief at some time during the year."[16]

The period from the early 1920s to the appointment of John Collier as commissioner in 1933 also undermined any attempts at acceptance of any governmental legislation affecting the Iroquois in the New Deal era. The complete nonrecognition of the Everett Report is a case in point. To the Six Nations, governmental insensitivity to Indian interests had once again been revealed by the burying of Everett's findings.[17] It is significant to note that the commissioner's stenographer, Lulu G. Stillman of Troy, a non-Indian, was later an important critic of Collier and the IRA and was especially influential in Tuscarora, Mohawk, and Oneida circles. Her distrust of New York State's intentions, based on her work for Everett, made her suspicious of all governmental intentions be it Albany or Washington. Her advocacy of the carrying out of treaty rights instead of new legislation won many admirers. Talking down the IRA, Stillman argued that it was meant for western tribes not the Iroquois, that it would result in increased governmental regulations and intervention in the Iroquois world and that it was a first step in securing New York jurisdiction over Iroquois affairs in the manner of the Snell Bill of 1930. These arguments, almost in toto, were adopted by the Iroquois in their resistance to the IRA. Moreover, Stillman drafted the Mohawk Council's petition objecting to the IRA and circulated her own protest against the act to all the Iroquois councils.[18]

On April 16, 1934, in an open letter to the leaders of the Six Nations in New York, Stillman specified her complaints about the Wheeler-Howard Bill, and insisted that it was her "personal opinion that a Government which has not or does not recognize and enforce its obligations under treaty stipulations (1784–1789) in all probability will find some way of evading further obligations under any legislation passed today over Indians." Despite the lack of hard evidence, she warned that there appeared to be a movement "afoot to allot your lands and that means taxes in the future, citizenship and loss of the little lands that remain your inheritance." She suggested that the Iroquois reform their existing councils by ridding them of corrupt leaders instead of following the Collier path to the same fate as their landless brethren in the west.[19] As the most respected outsider in Iroquois political circles who had supported the long crusade to win their lands back, Stillman clearly had torpedoed the Collier program in New York.[20]

Despite its unreality, the fear perpetuated by Stillman that the IRA would somehow hand over federal governmental jurisdiction to New York State was especially great in Iroquois country. Memories of recent attempts to accomplish this goal, most notably the Snell Bill introduced in Congress in 1930, made the Six Nations question any piece of legislation coming from Capitol Hill.[21] Collier, himself, had expressed the need to redesign the responsibilities of the federal and state governments to the Iroquois as early as September 1933. In an exclusive interview, Collier had questioned the "general indefinite policy of the federal government" and insisted "we should get in squarely or get out entirely" in order to remove the "twilight zone" status of New York's Indians.[22]

The Iroquois also took issue with specific features of the legislation. On every reservation the IRA's voting precedures were called into question. Since a majority of eligible voters in the referendum, according to Section 18, had to vote *against* the act to nullify its enforcement, many of the Six Nations suspected that it was another white man's trick to dupe the Indians. The traditional boycott of white elections for Iroquois ethnic boundary maintenance purposes was partially overcome in the IRA elections because of fear that the federal government was sneaking something past the Indians through a highly irregular voting set-up.[23]

The Iroquois in New York objected to the IRA's definition of "Indian," which ran counter to Six Nations' custom.[24] The matrilineal Iroquois were strongly opposed to any legislation employing blood quantum as a criteria or allowing the large number of nonenrolled Indians living among them tribal privileges. Alice Lee Jemison voiced her strong objection to this feature of the act:

> We [Seneca Nation of Indians] have taken to our reservation Indians from other tribes dispossessed of their lands. We have many Indians there who are not Senecas. We have practically all of the Cayugas, some of the Onondagas, some Mohawks, some of the Oneidas. We have Indians on our reservation from the Western states. We have half-breeds living on

our reservation. These are people whose fathers were Senecas, perhaps, but their mothers were white or belonged to other tribes. The citizenship status of Indians on my reservation follows the mother. That gives one the right, if he is Seneca, to hold lands and vote at tribal elections. All of these other people who live on our reservations do not have that right.... All of them are, however, most anxious to see the Wheeler-Howard bill put into effect in order that they may hold lands legally on our reservation and have a share in our tribal affairs. If that is done, our Seneca Nation will be entirely destroyed, because the new chartered community that will be set up will not be the Seneca Nation of Indians but will consist of other persons who on June 1, 1934, were living on our reservation.[25]

Furthermore, the IRA permitted women to participate in the referendum. Although women played a prominent, if not predominant, political role in Iroquois society, this allowance of suffrage ran counter to tradition where they exerted influence from behind the scenes.[26]

In other areas, the IRA was also seen as a new threat to the existing way of life. Fearful of any loss of what they perceived as their autonomy, many Iroquois reacted negatively to the act. Jemison, during a later effort to repeal the IRA nationwide in 1940, maintained that there "is no self-government in the act, all final power and authority remains in the Secretary of the Interior, which is exactly where it always has rested heretofore." She added that in certain areas, such as in the control of grazing and timber operations, the secretary of the interior's power expanded under the act.[27] Other Iroquois expressed concerns that the act gave the secretary of the interior a "stranglehold" on the assets of the tribes.[28] Many agreed with Ray Jimerson that the act was "too long and complicated, is full of new rules and regulations, and is subject to Bureau interpretation."[29] To conservative reservation communities suspicious of new reformers and their experiments, the IRA meant tampering with stability and order. Jesse Cornplanter, the noted Seneca artist, author, and raconteur claimed that the existing relationship was perfectly satisfactory since "the only time we sees [sic] our Agent is when he dishes out the Gov't Goods, etc."[30] He and many other Iroquois believed that the desire to be left alone was more important than change that might or might not bring benefits. Reflecting back on the IRA defeat, Cornplanter wrote Collier in 1940: "We have lived all those years without the intervention of the Indian Bureau, so we did not accept the Wheeler-Howard Act and what it represents."[31]

It is clear that many Iroquois remembered Deskaheh's message and his warnings about outside interference. If Canada could impose elected systems upon traditional peoples, any United States attempt to follow that course, however dissimilar, had to be rejected outright. Despite his Canadian birth, Deskaheh remains to this day the major Iroquois patriot of the twentieth century to New York's Indian populations.[32]

Diverse factors on each reservation contributed to the IRA's defeat. At Onondaga the act was voted down because of time-old Iroquois concerns. At that reservation, the Indians insisted that the United States government had no right to unilaterally pass laws that affected the sovereignty of the Iroquois Confederacy guaranteed by treaty or had the right to bypass the League's Council by negotiating with individual Iroquois tribes.[33] At Tonawanda, the IRA issue became involved in an approaching tribal election. Aaron Poodry, Norman Parker, and their party attacked it and used it as a springboard to put them back into political control.[34] At St. Regis, the IRA debate became confused with the existing bitter rivalry of the elected tribal and hereditary life chiefs, leading Mohawk women to interfere with the carrying out of the plebiscite.[35] The Tuscarora referendum was affected by the rivalries of the two brothers, Edgar and Clinton Rickard, despite the IRA's near unanimous rejection on the reservation.[36] At Allegany, the fears, based on past history, that the IRA was somehow connected with earlier attempts by white lessees in Salamanca to obtain title, contributed to the act's rejection.[37] At Cattaraugus, where the center of IRA opposition existed, Alice Lee Jemison's influence and the IRA voting procedures were predominant in the Senecas' killing the IRA.[38] Moreover, the Iroquois on each reservation, especially the Seneca Nation which already had an elected system dating back to 1848, saw the act as superfluous mass legislation that offered more for western tribes.[39] Furthermore, to the Onondagas as well as the Allegany and Cattaraugus Senecas, the IRA's deemphasis on allotment had little direct meaning because of historic communal land patterns.[40]

Time has finally revealed an obscure factor that also worked against Iroquois acceptance. Unlike other nations who accepted the IRA and later regretted coming under its provisions, the Iroquois in New York, studying the act quite carefully and reading between the lines, saw an inherent danger in the act that few tribes perceived. With the historic problem of factionalism in Iroquois society, some saw the act as a potential contributant to renewed intratribal strife. One Onondaga wrote to Collier: "If this Bill is passed, agitators and those of not too well balanced minds may repeatedly call for and cause an election."[41] Others feared the impact of federal moneys which they claimed would lead to further tribal council corruption and which would not filter down, in any case, to the people.

Confusion was everywhere evident about the IRA and its aims. Many Iroquois agreed with Clinton Rickard's view that there "were many in the community who did not understand just what it was John Collier wanted us to do."[42] Part of the problem was Collier's own ambiguity about why he was advocating that the New York Indians come under the act. Even Collier himself in June 1934 confessed to Senator Royal S. Copeland of New York "that the legislation was less designed for his state's Indian populations but for those in the west who have been rendered landless by the allotment system."[43]

The campaign to convince the Iroquois in New York to accept the IRA was further impeded by Collier's own tactical mistakes. Aware that he was opposed for the commissionership by the Iroquois leadership, Collier failed to make personal visits to Iroquoia after September 1933 to win support for himself and his ideas. Although he'd meet with some Iroquois leaders in Washington who were protesting passage of the Wheeler-Howard Bill, he never bothered, unlike his approach in Oklahoma and Wisconsin, to send any of his special assistants in the Indian Service to answer the queries of the Iroquois until the weeks before the referenda were scheduled to be held. Instead, he instructed W. K. Harrison, the Indian agent in New York, and William N. Fenton, the Indian Service community worker based at Tonawanda, to hold public meetings on the act and distribute copies and information door-to-door on the reservations.[44] Despite warnings from Fenton about the extent of the opposition, especially among the Senecas, Collier held back sending other Indian Bureau personnel to push the act. Fenton informed Collier: "They (Senecas) certainly will not vote for a measure which the Office of Indian Affairs does not deem of sufficient importance to send a speaker *to the reservation* to explain."[45] In late May, ten days before the scheduled referenda, Collier sent Henry Roe Cloud, the superintendent of Haskell Institute and noted Indian educator, to explain the act and conduct the vote on the IRA.[46]

Fenton, Harrison and, Roe Cloud held discussions throughout Iroquoia about the act, attempting to calm the universal fears that the legislation would somehow abrogate Iroquois treaties made with the federal government. Meetings were held at the gymnasium at Tuscarora, the court house and Presbyterian church at Tonawanda, at the Onondaga Longhouse, the Rochester Municipal Museum, the Forresters' Hall at St. Regis, and even at

Henry Roe Cloud, Akron, New York, June 10, 1935. Photograph by William N. Fenton, courtesy of the William N. Fenton Collection, U.S. Indian Service Photographs, 1935–37.

Moses White and Chief Joseph Tarbell at the time of the Indian Reorganization Act referendum at a lumber camp, Sevey, New York, June 5, 1935. Photograph by William N. Fenton, courtesy of the William N. Fenton Collection, U.S. Indian Service Photographs, 1935–37.

several lumber camps in the heart of the Adirondack Mountains. Working with interpreters, they ran into serious problems from the beginning. It is clear that each, despite his outward official support for the act, had misgivings about it or about Collier himself. Fenton, an anthropologist hoping to keep trust with the Iroquois and aware of their vocal opposition, had earlier opposed any changes in their political systems. He later supported the act because he feared that the educational and economic pro-grams provided would be lost if the IRA was rejected. Harrison, an old-guard bureau employee, was no friend of Collier since the commissioner had suggested as early as 1933 that he be replaced. Roe Cloud, a Yale-educated Winnebago Indian, saw the act as intended for landless western Indians rather than the Iroquois. His talks, intentionally or otherwise, further confused these Indians with his extensive references to and maps of western reservations.[47]

What the three men were totally unprepared for was the highly coordinated campaign against passage of the referendum being undertaken by the Iroquois. Emergency meetings had been taking place since February, coordinated by Alice Lee Jemison from her home on Cottage Street in Buffalo. At one of these strategy sessions, sixty-five Iroquois — including two members from the councils of the Cayugas, Seneca Nation, Tonawanda Senecas, and Tuscaroras — plotted a single course of action. At these types of gatherings, the Iroquois, especially in western New York, made special arrangements to bring their old people, the infirmed and those without transportation to the polls to vote down the IRA.[48]

The fervor against the act can be explained in part because the New York Iroquois saw the struggle in larger terms. They perceived themselves as leaders of the Indian world and as members of independent sovereign nations free of bureau interference, and quite distinct from other Indians. Accordingly, Jemison, before a congressional hearing in February 1935, claimed that the Senecas "thus far escaped the ravages of Bureau control. The Indians that are suffering under that Bureau are our brothers, and we are here to assist them."[49]

The furor over the IRA culminated with the holding of the first referendum on June 8 at St. Regis. On that day, the plebiscite was temporar-ily halted when Mohawk clan mothers prevented the opening of the election site by threatening to remove the clothing from the janitor who had the keys if he foolishly decided to cross their path. The elected chiefs called in New York State troopers and two members of the border patrol. The referendum was shifted from Forresters' Hall to the Mohawk school. The women, however, refused to abandon their plans. State and federal police kept the mob from seizing the ballot box. The women were eventually placated when ballots were taken to a number of handicapped Indians unable to reach the polls and when Roe Cloud diplomatically recommended to the women that they wire the commissioner about their objections.[50]

Despite the eventual resumption of voting, few eligible Mohawks participated since, as Fenton described, they identified "casting a ballot with citizenship, taxes and ultimate loss of their lands."[51] Once again, suspicions of the non-Indian world based upon historic factors of land loss produced a situation unfavorable to acceptance. This Mohawk boycott was also conditioned by local factors that went well beyond the IRA itself. Fenton attempted to explain one of these reasons to his superiors in Washington: "At present, about twenty-five percent of the people elect the chiefs. The others do not recognize the legal government, insist on the old life chiefs, and refuse to come to the polls. Hence they object strenuously to coming to the polls and voting for or against the IRA. Many will stay home and still violently oppose the act."[52] Since 517 out of 800 eligible voters did not participate, the Mohawks, because of Section 18 of the act, technically accepted the legislation. Nevertheless, Collier, realizing that only forty-six Mohawks voted for the act and now fully aware of the predominant New York Iroquois attitude against it, wisely never pushed for Mohawk tribal reorganization.

In sum, a combination of factors helped to kill the movement for tribal reorganization in New York. It is clear that the IRA was largely dead in New York before it was even conceived in the minds of John Collier and his assistants in the BIA. Historic concerns that were unique to the Six Nation —the belief in continued sovereignty under treaties with the United States, fears of changes in jurisdiction, and the ethnocentric world-view of these Indians that set them apart in their mind from western tribes — played a significant role in the rejection of the IRA.

Distrust of the non-Indian world was not alleviated by Collier's tactical errors and by the act itself, with its strange voting procedures, its new rules and regulations, its lack of application to some of the realities of Indian life in New York. Past suspicions were fueled both by a commissioner, associated with western tribes who was not the first choice of the Iroquois leadership and by the activities of two women—Alice Lee Jemison and Lulu Stillman. The historic fears that citizenship, allotment, taxation, and loss of lands were behind everything emanating from Washington as well as Albany worked against acceptance. In addition, a decade of distrust from the era of the Everett Report to the harsher realities of the Great Depression contributed to the IRA's demise in New York.

5

A REVOLUTION AT ONEIDA

Tribal Reorganization and the Indian New Deal in Wisconsin

The Reorganization Act is recreating a reservation and houses are being built with government assistance. The government loans the Indian from $600–1,000 and it is paid back on the installment plan. An Indian may sell this land to another Indian but never to a white man.

Oscar Archiquette (Oneida), 1939

UNLIKE THE IROQUOIS IN NEW YORK, most Oneida tribal elders in Wisconsin consider the New Deal era as the positive turning point in their modern history. For the majority of these Indians, the 1930s marked the establishment of an elected tribal system of government out of the political disorder of the past; the repurchase and reclamation of tribal lands; the building of so-called "New Deal homes" to replace dilapidated log cabins; the drilling of wells for each new home to end the need to haul water from springs; relief employment sponsored by the Civilian Conservation Corps (CCC) and the Works Progress Administration (WPA); and finally, the WPA Oneida Language and Folklore Project, one of the earliest language and oral history programs among the Indians of the United States. In reality, the New Deal witnessed a revolution at Oneida whose impact is still being felt by these Indians today.[1]

The Oneidas first began emigrating to the Wisconsin wilderness in 1823 after years of increased pressures by whites to get at their New York lands and at the urging of Eleazar Williams, an Episcopal lay reader, catechist, and self-appointed leader of these Indians. By 1838, 654 Indians had relocated on 65,426 acres, about 100 square miles, along Duck Creek near Green Bay on lands purchased from the Menominees. Politically divided into three separate factions from their days in New York — the First and Second Christian and Orchard parties—the Oneidas replicated their divisive history in Wisconsin. They settled in two areas, with Methodist Oneidas occupying the southern portion of the reservation and Episcopals occupying the northern part. Within these divisions, eight separate neighborhoods developed that still have significant political influence. As members of the three Oneida factions arrived from the East, their leaders attempted to assert their hereditary rights, chief's prerogatives and other claims to power that they had had in New York, resulting in the carry-over of previous factional behavior. To further complicate these serious divisions, a sizeable number of Oneidas, the so-called "Homeless Indians," moved westward from New York and Canada after the sale of their lands in New York. Following fifty years of bitter debate about their status, these latecomers were adopted into the tribe.[2]

The uprooting of these Indians also contributed to structural changes in Oneida politics and society. Over a one hundred-year period, clan affiliation virtually disappeared as a factor of importance in Oneida politics. In the same period, encouraged by outside white influences, especially missionaries, the Oneida social structure became patrilineal, evolving from the traditional Iroquois matrilineal model.[3]

The Oneida economy was also faced with dramatic changes. Agriculture, largely of a subsistence nature, was the basis of the economy before the Civil War, and Oneidas supplemented their farming with hunting game in the heavily forested land, fishing in Duck Creek, and gathering wild berries, which they consumed or sold to traders in Green Bay. By the 1870s, the Oneidas were slowly drawn into the lumber industry as employees in the exploitation of their rich pine forests. Just as they had abandoned much of their agriculture for the market economy of the European fur trade during the colonial era, they once again became increasingly dependent on white commercial interests. The results were uncontrolled timber stripping of their lands, serious soil erosion, low leasing arrangements, and increased consumption of alcohol. The Indian agent for the Oneidas observed in 1875 that unprincipled white men were making fortunes by creating "sawmills as near to the reservation as possible, buying off the Indian timber at much less than its value, selling the same to suit themselves, and often times paying for it in goods at exorbitant prices, which in many cases are exchanged for whiskey."[4]

In 1887, the Dawes General Allotment Act was signed into law, which gave the president the discretion to allot reservation tribal lands to individual Indians, the title to be held in trust by the federal government for twenty-five years. Heads of families were to receive 160 acres; individuals over eighteen years of age were to receive 40 acres while those under that age were to be allotted 26 acres each. All surplus lands after the allotment were to be sold and thrown open to settlement.[5] Despite strong Oneida resistance to the act, President Benjamin Harrison approved an order for the making of allotments in severalty to these Indians.[6] On June 13, 1892, allotment began with the issuance of a total of 1,524 allotments and 20 trust patents to the Indians. The trust period was extended for another year in 1917. Even before the trust period was allowed to finally expire on nearly all the Oneida allotments in 1918, a federal "competency" commission began issuing fee patents to Oneidas of less than one-half Indian blood in order to quicken the pace of assimilation. By the time of the New Deal, only twenty-one allotments were still being held in trust for the benefit of the allottee or his heirs.[7]

Despite the overly optimistic forecasts of Indian agents,[8] the allotment policy proved a total disaster to the Oneidas. In August of 1937, Commissioner Collier described the tragedy that befell the Oneidas: "They lost more than 95 percent of all their land under the fee-patenting operation. They are one of the extreme examples of the disastrous operation of the old type of allotment such as we had under the 1887 act."[9] In reality, the Oneidas and their Wisconsin neighbors the Winnebagos were the two tribes most devastated by the Dawes Act.[10] After the issuance of fee patents by the federal "competency" commission or at the end of the trust period, Oneida lands became subject to taxation, resulting in new and impossible tax burdens, foreclosures, and subsequent tax sales of property. Moreover, land speculators, in collusion with the corrupt Indian agents, and, on occasion, Oneida leaders themselves, immediately set out separating the Indian allottee from his allotment. The Oneidas, largely uneducated rural people, were encouraged to fall into debt by borrowing money or mortgaging their homesteads to buy musical instruments, carriages, and livestock, all of which they generally did not need. Some of their homes were subsequently lost because of their inability to pay back loans. Whiskey was employed in outright swindles to dispossess them.[11]

Thus, by the time of the New Deal, the Oneidas had less than 90 acres of tribal lands and approximately 700 acres of land held in individual allotments.[12] To survive, these Indians worked as laborers in the mills at Green Bay or as hired hands on farms in the surrounding white communities. Quite significantly, many Indians left Oneida for Chicago, Detroit, Milwaukee, and Minneapolis during the first four decades of the twentieth century. Although these migrations separated kinship ties and created new divisions, these Indians never fully severed their ties to the shrinking community. This out-migration was also accelerated by World War I. One hundred-fifty Oneidas enlisted and many of the survivors were reluctant to return to the economically depressed and largely landless community.[13] By 1932, only 1,415 of 3,131 Oneidas lived at or in the immediate environs of Oneida.[14]

Conditions at Oneida were abysmal even before the Great Depression. One prominent Oneida insisted, before the senate Indian affairs subcommittee in July 1929, that the "people are all poor and have no money with which to live." He added that the Indians "are losing their homes and many are destitute on account of taxation and the high cost of living."[15] The senate subcommittee later heard testimony from the superintendent at the Keshena Agency who indicated that the Oneidas had only a few small parcels of land left.[16] Racial discrimination also impeded Oneida economic and educational progress. The narrow-minded superintendent of the Tomah Indian School, one with a large Oneida student body, outlined his analysis of the problems of educating Indians in 1929: "Of course some are poverty stricken due to their own improvidence. I don't blame them any, they're Indians, and that's their way."[17]

With the onset of the Great Depression, the Oneidas' problems went from bad to worse. One anthropologist, who was at Oneida in the 1930s, described the changes:

> In the ensuing years many of the people lost the jobs they had held in nearby towns. Many of the Oneidas scattered over state and country also lost their jobs and had no chance but to return to the only home they knew, Oneida. The influx of the jobless tended to make the home problem more acute; meager resources were rapidly dissipated to a depression subsistence. The drop in prices of farm produce also had its effect as this was the only source of income for some. By this time the landholdings had dwindled to an average of ten acres per family, which made increased production impossible. A state survey showed that at least eighty acres of land in that area was necessary for economically sustaining a farm.[18]

By 1930, 77 percent of these Indians were receiving public assistance. The Indian Bureau in the early 1930s, in order to alleviate starvation, sent fifteen hundred Navajo sheep to Oneida. Unfortunately, the sheep were too scrawny, having little meat on them after butchering. Other relief efforts included the sending of Red Cross flour as well as surplus army clothing. Despite these efforts, Oneidas frequently complained of prejudice and discrimination by relief officials.[19] By the mid-1930s, the superintendent of the Keshena Indian Agency, whose purview included the Oneidas, appealed to Washington on their behalf claiming he knew "of no condition within this area that is in such dire need of assistance." He reported that the conditions "among the Oneida people are extremely bad, with practically every Indian on relief, and very little land held in Indian ownership. In the village of Oneida ... as many as four and five houses can be found grouped on one small lot of land with no garden room and several families occupying each house."[20]

The failure of the United States government to deal effectively with any and all of these massive problems worked to reinforce Oneida suspicion of Washington Indian policy-makers. The Oneidas could point to a long line of government ineptness and corruption in their dealings with the non-Indian world: the emigration westward, the Dawes General Allotment Act of 1887, corrupt Indian agents who failed to protect them from land swindlers and timber strippers, the nonrecognition of Oneida land claims, and many other examples of overall incompetence. This historic failure in carrying out the trust relationship with these Indians provoked Oneida ire and allowed for Indian politicians, some honest, others dishonest, to arise and advocate their own solutions to thorny problems. By the late 1920s and early 1930s, three separate political groups, each with large followings, vied for power at Oneida. The bitterness and resulting recriminations caused by the allotment policy coupled with the historic divisions within the tribe to produce increased fractionalized political behavior. Consequently, measures needed for tribal relief, reform, and economic development were postponed and became subordinate to the ambitions of self-proclaimed head chiefs.

One of the most influential of these factions was the so-called "Kellogg Party." Headed by the previously mentioned Minnie Kellogg, the party's central focus was the pursuit of Iroquois claims to land in New York. Through her perfect command of both English and the Oneida languages, she held meetings at Oneida from the early 1920s onward, collecting moneys for the cost of pursuing the claim. Kellogg and her followers had several methods of collection. By eloquently espousing an issue of utmost importance to these Indians, they were able to register Oneidas and other Iroquois who paid into the claims movement and were given tax receipts in return. These due bills indicated the contributor was entitled to 10 percent interest

TAX CERTIFICATE SIX NATIONS CONFEDERACY

This certifies that Mr *Ephriam Schuyler*

has paid $ *10⁰⁰* enrollment fee and $ *5⁰⁰* taxes to The Six Nations Confederacy, and this money draws 10 per cent interest and 40 per cent bonus from this date and is to be repaid from the first money recovered in our claim against the State of New York.

This tax certificate is transferable and will be paid as stated above to the person presenting same, properly endorsed.

GEORGE E. THOMAS,
Head Chief.

W. K. CORNELIUS,
Treasurer.

This is the kind of receipt used in collecting money under false pretense started in 1921

Kellogg tax certificate, Six Nations Confederacy claim, 1920s. The handwriting at the bottom of the certificate was done by Oscar Archiquette who explained the certificate's meaning in an interview conducted by Dr. Robert W. Venables, 1970. Photograph courtesy of Dr. Robert W. Venables.

and a 40 percent bonus when the first money was "recovered in our claim against the State of New York." In addition, they formed claims clubs on nearly every Iroquois reservation in the United States and Canada, charging dues for membership or levying a tax of approximately $1.25 per month on each individual. Long after the Kelloggs' final legal appeal in pursuit of the claim ended in 1928, she and her followers were still collecting money. Although the exact extent of their fund-raising cannot be ascertained, numerous Indian protests to the Interior as well as the Justice departments about the Kelloggs' activities and the bitter memories of the incident by Iroquois elders today confirm that many lost their savings and property. Moreover, since the Kelloggs also told the Oneidas not to pay taxes on their allotments because they claimed the Dawes Act's application to them violated existing Iroquois treaties, some Oneidas lost their land for nonpayment of taxes.[21]

To poverty-stricken Indians, the Kellogg Party seemed the only way out

Laura Cornelius "Minnie" Kellogg, from *Our Democracy and the American Indian* (Kansas City, Mo.: Burton Publishing Co., 1920).

of a desperate situation. Their willingness to contribute was further encouraged by the Kellogg Party's insistence that only those who contributed to the continuing costs of the venture would collect if the Iroquois won the case. The Kelloggs were also able to win support at Oneida and other Iroquois communities because their activities emphasized solidarity with traditionalist Iroquois politics, culture and values. Traditional approaches to Iroquois medicine and attempts at resurrecting the clan system were also encouraged. They even attempted to reinstitute the old league political offices suggestive of nativistic orientation. Mrs. Kellogg went so far as to revive Oneida chiefly titles associated with matrilineal lineages, brought longhouse leaders from Onondaga to Wisconsin to condole a council, and "arranged" for the raising of nine sachems by Iroquois traditionalists on a visit to New York.[22]

Despite the largely negative aspect of the movement, the Kelloggs also had more positive influences on Oneida and Iroquois existence as well. Their assertions of Iroquois claims in the 1920s, especially in the courts, served to keep the issue alive not only in Albany, Washington but at Oneida, Onondaga, and other Iroquois reservations in the United States and Canada as well. In the process, communications and awareness between eastern, western, and Canadian Iroquois increased. The long geographic, cultural, and religious separation that had begun with Oneida migrations westward in the early 1820s had been somewhat lessened by the Kellogg movement.[23]

A second faction, and the largest and most influential one by the early 1930s, was headed by William "Willie Fat" Skenandore. Usually armed to the teeth with law books, legal memoranda, and treaties, this short, chubby, self-educated man waged an energetic campaign to win recognition for the Oneidas and their land claims in his role as a self-styled head chief of his faction. As a frequent correspondent, he brought the claims issue and other Oneida concerns to the attention of influential congressmen and bureau personnel.[24] Skenandore's group "directly contested white power to levy taxes and sought through legal action to have the provisions of early treaties between the Oneidas and the United States confirmed and enforced."[25] It was this group that engaged most intensely with the Oneida faction favoring the Indian New Deal.

Skenandore was a controversial figure. As in the Kellogg case, Skenandore was frequently accused of fraud and collusion with non-Indian schemers. Like the Kelloggs, Skenandore attempted and used the fading clan structure to raise himself and his party to power. Like the Kelloggs, his actions were not altogether without benefit, especially in keeping the claims issue alive.[26] He constantly monitored any and all Oneida complaints about federal operations including payment of treaty annuities away from the Oneida community since the Indians had no means to drive to the government office because of poverty, the high unemployment rate among the Oneidas, and the high-handed attitude of federal relief administrators who made it nearly impossible to obtain assistance.[27] Unlike the Kelloggs, Skenandore's influence was primarily in Wisconsin, having little influence in New York and Canada among Oneidas and other Iroquois.

A third group was headed by Oscar Smith from DePere, Wisconsin. As head chief of his faction, Smith also appealed to the Oneidas' overriding

"Willie Fat" Skenandore, Oneida, Wisconsin, 1939. Photograph by Robert Ritzenthaler, courtesy of the Robert Ritzenthaler Collection, Milwaukee Public Museum.

concern with their claim. In a letter to Senator LaFollette in 1933, Smith
maintained that treaty rights precluded the Oneidas from coming under the
State of Wisconsin's jurisdiction even though they were nearly destitute and
starving. After claiming that the Oneidas "do not vote and therefore do not
pay taxes," Smith insisted that some "of us Oneida Indians do not wish to
relinquish our interest in the United States Government as stipulated in the
various treaties, and vigorously protest the interfering of the township

government." He urged LaFollette to make another on-site inspection of Oneida, to meet with his council, and to help the Indians submit the Oneida claim to the United States Court of Claims.[28]

By 1933, a fourth political force was beginning to take shape at Oneida. This group, headed by Morris Wheelock, a Carlisle-educated Indian from Milwaukee, was largely composed of Oneidas who had returned to the community from urban areas. These Indians were joined by other Oneidas who were fed up with the political conditions, corruption and unfulfilled promises of tribal leaders. Less concerned with land claims assertions, these Indians stressed the need for political order and economic development at Oneida. As early as October 1933, Wheelock, in a letter to Commissioner Collier, was explicit about his sharp differences with Kellogg, Skenandore, and Smith. He insisted that he was proud of being a United States citizen, that only "just a few of the land sales between the Indians and whites were illegal," and that major problems could be resolved by investigating the operations of the bureau, not by pushing land claims. He questioned the motives and actions of the various sets of head chiefs in raising money from indigent Indians and in thinking they knew "more about laws than the lawyers and judges themselves." Wheelock urged Collier to intervene at Oneida to put a stop to the divisive political behavior, to help rid the Oneidas of the "present fraudulent and faking self-styled chiefs of the non-existing Oneida government," and to provide direct aid in the form of "food, clothing, medical and hospitalization."[29] One month later, Wheelock wrote Collier insisting that he and his supporters were "very much interested in my people in getting a fair deal and not to have the so-called head chiefs of the Kelloggs, Skenandore, or Smith collecting funds to prosecute certain claims, and telling the Oneidas not to pay taxes."[30]

The factional behavior at Oneida spilled over into debates over the IRA. On April 23 and 24, 1934, two months before passage of the act, the Oneida faction headed by Skenandore attended a two-day meeting at Hayward, Wisconsin, with bureau officials about the impending legislation. Collier, unable to attend the conference because of congressional hearings in Washington, sent William Zimmerman, Jr., assistant commissioner of Indian affairs, to explain the Wheeler-Howard Bill. At that meeting, Skenandore announced that, on March 14, 1934, his council had approved a resolution, endorsed by 500 Indians, calling for "passage of the bill of Indian rights." The resolution praised Collier for his past efforts as a reformer, hailed him for including the Oneidas and other Indians in emergency relief and civil works programs "which relief has never before been accorded to us," and lauded him as the "Abraham Lincoln to the Indians."[31] Ironically, it was this very piece of legislation which Skenandore praised at Haywood that was to be his political undoing. Too busy doing legal research in Milwaukee during the spring and summer of 1934 and underestimating the strength of the Wheelock faction, Skenandore failed to see that the IRA provided a mechanism for a tribal political revolution at Oneida.

Wheelock's faction gained strength throughout 1934. Urban Oneidas, in desperate condition after returning to the community and without land, saw the IRA as legislation facilitating their reobtaining land. Wheelock also was aided by an alliance with Oscar Archiquette, a recent emigrant from Milwaukee, who had been born at Oneida to a prominent politically active family. With his strong command of the Oneida language and skills as an orator, Archiquette represented a formidable force in the tribe's political affairs until his death in 1971. By June 1934, Archiquette had become a strong advocate of the IRA and was pledging to Commissioner Collier his "utmost to explain the bill" to his people. He sought information and official assurances to counter Skenandore's claims that the IRA would abrogate Indian treaty rights and that land purchased for the Oneidas would be worthless and away from their landbase. By October, the Archiquette-Wheelock group had formed a board of directors, wrote a charter, organized themselves under the state laws of Wisconsin and held meetings with federal officials. Archiquette became the organization's president while Wheelock served as secretary. Through Archiquette's oratory and Wheelock's superior writing skills, this faction increasingly projected itself as a responsible group of Indians capable of carrying out the tribal rehabilitative features of the IRA.[32]

Skenandore, while in Milwaukee for much of 1934, had helped prepare a case asking the federal district court to set aside and declare illegal and void the allotment of the Oneida reservation. By suing the United States, the self-styled attorney hoped that the United States government could be held liable for the action that had nearly ruined the Oneidas. In December 1934, the precise time of the IRA referendum, the federal district court dismissed the case.[33] Because of this prolonged absence and the skill of his opponents, Skenandore's political fortunes had fallen to the point of no recovery by the end of 1934.

On October 17, after accusing his opponents of being a bunch of swindlers and "moonshiners," Skenandore asserted: "Last Spring this same group took advantage of my absence from Oneida for months, carrying on my studies at the libraries at Milwaukee for the benefit of the Oneida Indians

Oscar Archiquette, Oneida, Wisconsin, 1939. Photograph by Robert Ritzenthaler, courtesy of the Robert Ritzenthaler Collection, Milwuakee Public Museum.

as a whole, by spreading all sorts of ill propaganda against me, to get control of the affairs of the Oneida Indians, when it developed that the Indians were about to have a break and all they are after is to get what they can out of it."[34] Annoyed that he was allegedly denied the podium at a public meeting packed with his political rivals, Skenandore accused his opponents of being mostly white people and Stockbridge Indians.[35] Increasingly desperate because of his failure throughout 1934 to cultivate his political base, he chided his opponents for claiming that the federal government was going to buy lands at Oneida and build homes for the Indians without regard to questions of uncleared title, land claims concerns, and costs. Moreover, he criticized the bureau for the government's supplying information "to this new faction" and overall dealings with his political enemies.[36] Assistant Commissioner Zimmerman responded by strongly maintaining that the "government in dealing with the Indians does not consider the factional groups," and that the IRA was intended for the benefit of "Indians generally and not for one faction or the other."[37]

By December, Skenandore found himself in an impossible situation. On record as an original supporter of Commissioner Collier and the IRA, he could not easily backtrack from this position. Because he ignored his political backyard in his frequent legal adventurism, Skenandore's Oneida political opponents had seized upon the IRA issue as *their* program for tribal renaissance. Skenandore's dilemma was further complicated by the activities of Oneidas committed to the Kellogg and Smith factions. In the manner of Iroquois traditionalists, these groups urged their supporters to boycott the bureau-sponsored referendum on the IRA in order to reaffirm Iroquois sovereignty and the sanctity of treaties between the Six Nations and Washington.[38] This tactic only served to guarantee passage since those who stayed away from the polls were counted under Section 18 of the IRA as if they had favored the legislation.

Despite Skenandore's change of heart on the IRA and his frantic effort to tarnish the reputations of his rivals, the Oneidas voted to accept the IRA in a referendum on December 15, 1934. Six hundred eighty-eight Oneidas voted to approve the legislation; only 126 voted against the act. Significantly, 56 percent of the eligible voters — 1,030 out of 1,844 — did not vote.[39] Although the act passed by a substantial margin, it is clear that to many Oneidas, land claims assertions and treaty rights guarantees were still more important than another piece of legislation emanating from Washington promising a new day for Indians.

In early 1935, Morris Wheelock was elected the first Oneida tribal chairman under the IRA. The economic crisis that his people faced was one of the worst affecting any Native American tribe. The debate over the IRA referendum had raised expectations about a restored land base, but Oneida factionalism nonetheless did not totally disappear with the acceptance of the IRA. Consequently, Wheelock had to contend with raised hopes, the harsh realities of Indian existence in the Great Depression, and, at the same time, the political losers of the IRA referendum.

Skenandore, Wheelock's major opponent, attempted to recoup his losses throughout the mid- and late 1930s. Skenandore became increasingly vocal in his criticism of the IRA. Almost immediately after his faction's defeat, he insisted, in a petition to the Indian Bureau, that no provision of the IRA "can meet our situation except the restoration of our original Reservation, under the Treaty of January 15th, 1838."[40] In newspaper articles and in testimony before the Senate subcommittee of the committee on Indian affairs, he accused Commissioner Collier and other Indian service personnel of making false promises about restoring the Oneida land base, of employing authoritarian measures to perpetuate the Indian Bureau, and of continuing to permit the unlawful confiscation of Oneida lands by mortgage foreclosures and tax deeds contrary to Indian treaty rights guarantees. Even after being stripped of his title as chief, Skenandore persisted in his legal and political crusade.[41] As late as 1939, after showing his numerous legal briefs and documents to one visiting anthropologist, Skenandore clearly set forth his position: "I don't believe in the Reorganization Act because it isn't necessary to the Oneidas. All the Oneidas need is the Government to recognize their rights and take the lands and give them back to the Oneidas. The Indian Bureau should be eliminated. It doesn't help the Indian. It only misrepresents them. The Indians are still wards of the Government. I believe that the Indians should be given back their lands and their treaty rights recognized."[42]

The Wheelock faction had used the Indian New Deal to seize power at Oneida and was to employ New Deal programs to hold onto power through the 1930s. By April 1935, the superintendent at the Keshena Agency reported to Collier that the Oneidas "are very well organized and had been holding meetings regularly, enthusiastically waiting for land relief of some character."[43] New Deal programs providing work relief under WPA and CCC began in earnest in 1935 and were the mainstay of the limited tribal economy of the 1930s. The tribal business committee certified Oneidas as eligible for work relief and other new government services, thus providing the party in power a strong measure of power and patronage during the Great Depression. A building repair project was started in August 1935. Although a total of 169 buildings were repaired at a cost of $12,501.98, efforts at long-range economic development, government land repurchase, and wider tribal reorganization were postponed in the aftershock of the IRA referendum.[44]

In 1936, the Oneidas, through the efforts of the Indian Service, drew up a constitution and bylaws under which these Indians would operate as a political entity, the "Oneida Tribe of Indians of Wisconsin." On November 14, 1936, the Oneidas overwhelmingly adopted the new constitution and bylaws by a vote of 790 to 16. It is evident that Skenandore's influence had largely been reduced in the two years since the IRA referendum. In December 1936, Secretary Ickes formally approved the constitution and bylaws. By May of the following year, the Oneidas also approved a tribal charter of incorporation after an extensive campaign organized jointly by Wheelock and bureau personnel.[45]

Commissioner Collier spelled out his plan to aid the Oneidas before a Senate hearing in August 1937. After insisting that he was working within the limits of available funding, he maintained that the Interior Department "optioned nearly $50,000 worth of land up there, to be used as home sites and garden tracts, to be occupied by those Indians who will do labor and engage in sundry secondary agricultural pursuits. That is all we can do in that region."[46] At the same hearing, a land acquisition report was entered into the record that further elaborated on Collier's aims for community betterment:

> The ultimate objective of the (IRA land) program is to provide each family with sufficient land to insure it a livelihood through berry growing and truck farming. If each family could grow 2 or 3 acres of berries, it is conceivable that a canning industry could be constructed and operated on a cooperative basis by an Indian organization. The nearby villages and canneries provide a ready market for such vegetables as string beans and peas. These industries coupled with subsistence farming, will undoubtedly place this group of Indians on a self-sustaining basis, and besides the great social and economic benefit derived, will relieve the Federal Government of a very appreciable relief burden.[47]

Although the Indian New Deal never resulted in total Indian self-sufficiency at Oneida, it did produce from 1937 onward major political, economic, and social changes. Newly incorporated with elected officers and regular elections, the tribe now had more unified group action than in the past. The Tribal Business Committee wielded great powers of governance as few past councils since the Dawes Act had done. Despite the opposition from some neighboring non-Indian farmers hoping to limit the growth of the Oneida land base,[48] the United States government, with the cooperation of the Tribal Business Committee, began taking options and repurchasing land.

Although much of the land was submarginal in nature, the Indian Service consciously attempted to overcome the checkerboard pattern of Oneida lands that had occurred under allotment by purchasing lands in adjacent tracts wherever possible. By 1939, approximately 1,200 acres had been repurchased for Oneida use, nearly 60 percent of the present tribal land base of 2,106 acres.[49] Consequently, throughout the late 1930s the Tribal Business Committee awarded house-lot assignments and farming privileges on these newly acquired lands. Virtually every meeting of this governing body in this period dealt with the immediate issue of land and land assignments. At one of the sessions held on December 7, 1937, the Oneida Executive Board assigned a total of 185 acres to nine different individuals in parcels of land mostly under twenty acres.[50]

The power of the Tribal Business Committee was also greatly increased with its ability to borrow money from the federal government under the provisions of the IRA. By December 1937, the Oneidas were awarded $5,000 of IRA revolving loan funds. Despite the ever-present problem of governmental red tape, Morris Wheelock looked optimistically to the future: "The Oneida Indians have good land, good markets and are versatile in many lines. They should borrow funds to advance their interests and by doing so can greatly increase their economic conditions. With a large quantity of IRA lands already purchased and assigned to individuals, there is no reason why the members of this Tribe should not advance economically through the use of Credit Revolving Funds."[51] One year later, the Oneidas, through their Tribal Business Committee, received an emergency grant of $38,000 in order to: "finance the rehabilitation of Indians in stricken, rural, agricultural areas by means of loans or grants, or both, to enable them to construct or repair houses, barns, outbuildings, and root cellars; to develop wells and springs for domestic water; to clear and improve lands for gardens or small farms, and to purchase land for such purposes when necessary; to make furniture and other handicraft products; and to establish, maintain, and operate other self-help projects.[52]

In the process, New Deal homes, a total of twelve by 1939, "began to replace the dilapidated log cabins that previously had been found at Oneida; wells were drilled for each new home. The tribe borrowed for its members up to $1,000 for the purpose of buying building materials; while labor was furnished by the WPA and employed Indian workers on relief."[53] By 1939, 200 Oneidas were employed on WPA projects, including the building of a dam at Kaukauna, the Oneida Language and Folklore Project as well as in house construction. Moreover, "approximately 1300 of the 1500 Oneidas

New Deal house constructed by Oneidas on work relief, Oneida, Wisconsin, 1939.
Photograph by Robert Ritzenthaler, courtesy of the Robert Ritzenthaler Collection,
Milwaukee Public Museum.

(Indians living at Oneida) were receiving government aid, either surplus
commodities, W.P.A., outdoor relief, old-age pensions, dependent-children
pensions, or C.C.C. aid."[54]

   Despite the significant changes for the better, the Oneida New Deal had
its limitations. Community self-sufficiency was never achieved, and more
Indians were receiving public assistance by 1939.[55] Moreover, even some of
the Indian New Deal's ardent supporters such as Archiquette later complained that the IRA revolving credit fund was too small for the Oneida's
pressing needs. Although lands were obtained, the old Oneida reservation as
it existed before 1887 could never be restored. Land claims assertions to the
Oneida homeland in New York were sidetracked in efforts to rebuild the
Wisconsin community. Their reemergence as a major issue had to wait until
the 1960s and 1970s.

The Indian New Deal at Oneida represented something quite different from the New York exerience. Despite the depressed economic conditions of the Iroquois in New York, the Oneidas in Wisconsin were definitely in worse shape. Consequently, these Indians had less to lose than their eastern brethren and were more willing to take the chance of accepting New Deal programs.

The motives behind acceptance of the Indian New Deal were not simply a renewed effort by Oneidas to rebuild a land base that had been lost under the Dawes Act. The IRA referendum and its consequences provided outsiders an opportunity to seize power from an older guard that had exclusively been associated with the pursuit of tribal land claims and treaty rights guarantees. Their new seat of power was further secured through the infusion of federal programs at Oneida, and with them, land, money, and work relief. Consequently, some of the newly returned Indian population, who made up an important part of the Wheelock-Archiquette faction, were to be aided by these programs and were integrated back into the Oneida community during the 1930s.

One surviving member of the original Oneida Tribal Business Committee revealed another reason for the success of the coup of 1934. After insisting that the New Deal was "the best thing that ever happened," he added that "no tribal governing mechanism to stop fraudulent land sales existed before the IRA." The state of disorder among the Oneidas following the Dawes Act became more confused as time went on and "some of our best educated people took advantage of us and lined their pockets to help dispossess us."[56] Hence, at least to some Oneidas, the Indian New Deal provided the means for tribal reorganization, and with it, tribal reform. "Chasing the rascals out" had a definite meaning at Oneida in 1934.

The Indian New Deal had produced significant results for the 3,351 Oneidas of Wisconsin including tribal relief, rehabilitation, and political reorganization through the creation of a Tribal Business Committee.[57] Most important, the 1930s gave a community that had been nearly destroyed hope for some future betterment.

6

SOMETHING OLD/SOMETHING NEW

The Seneca-Cayugas of Oklahoma in the Age of Tribal Reorganization

The New Deal council established by incorporation in the 1930s set up the entire tribal operation that exists today. That in itself was a major accomplishment.

Chief James Allen
Seneca-Cayuga Tribe of Oklahoma
August 17, 1979

THE OKLAHOMA SENECA-CAYUGA experience largely parallels Wisconsin Oneida history from the 1820s to the present day.[1] Both were affected by early pressures for removal. Each migrated to the west in several stages. The two were nearly destroyed by the Dawes General Allotment Act of 1887 and its consequences. Both developed their current tribal structures during the New Deal years, 1934 to 1941.

Finding themselves with only 104 acres of tribal lands in 1936,[2] the Iroquois in Oklahoma consolidated and reorganized as a new tribal entity known as the Seneca-Cayuga Tribe of Oklahoma the following year. To these Indians, the constitution, bylaws, and charter accepted by the tribe are the most important documents of their recent history and are the "last word on most matters."[3] Consequently, the twenty-two-hundred-member tribe today has a total of 1081.08 acres as a result of government-encouraged land repurchasing efforts under the Oklahoma Indian Welfare Act. Despite these significant changes, much remained the same. The Grand River Dam project of the late 1930s flooded significant acreage of their recently repurchased lands and limited future attempts to rebuild their land base out of their original Oklahoma treaty lands. Importantly, individually owned Iroquois allotments have declined significantly since 1936, from 7,725 to 2,257.74 acres.[4]

The trek by two bands of Iroquois Indians residing in Ohio to the trans-Mississippi West began in the early 1830s. These Iroquois tribesmen, who, besides Senecas and Cayugas, included Mohawks, Oneidas, Onondagas, and remnant populations of eastern Algonkian tribesman, had settlements in the Ohio country at least dating from the mid-eighteenth century. To some extent, these Indians were largely independent of Iroquois League control. From 1807 onward, Cayugas from the Buffalo Creek Reservation in New York joined these Ohio Iroquois. By 1819, two separate reservations had been established by treaty in Ohio, one composed of Indians referred to in the literature as the "Senecas of Sandusky" and the other a mixed band of Senecas and Shawnees around Lewiston, Ohio. The Senecas of Sandusky concluded a treaty with the United States government on February 28, 1831, whereby they ceded all claims to their Ohio lands totaling forty thousand acres. In return, they were to receive approximately sixty-seven thousand fertile acres in Indian Territory north of the Cherokee Nation adjoining the Missouri border. In late 1831, 400 Sandusky Senecas began their eight-month journey from Dayton, Ohio, to their new lands along the Cowskin River in northeastern Indian Territory. Delayed by floods, winter storms, and deaths of their kinsmen en route, they arrived at their new home on July 4, 1832, only to find that part of their land west of the Neosho River had already been assigned to the Cherokees. A second mixed band composed of 300 Senecas and Shawnees also set out for Indian Territory. Only 258 of these Indians arrived along the Cowskin River on December 13, 1832, the remainder succumbing to cholera and other illnesses during the journey. Upon their arrival, they also discovered that their lands had been assigned to the Cherokees. Eventually on December 29, 1832, thirteen Sandusky Seneca and eleven Seneca-Shawnee leaders signed another treaty with federal officials along the Cowskin River in Indian Territory, after adjudication by a presidential commission. The tribes ceded all their lands west of the Neosho or Grand River in exchange for an equal amount east of the Neosho, north of the Cherokee border and east of Missouri in present day Ottawa County, Oklahoma.[5]

These Iroquois people never lost contact with their mother culture at Onondaga and at Brantford, Ontario. They carried their Iroquois religious traditions westward. Periodic interaction between eastern and western Iroquois did exist. These Indians were joined in the period, 1846–52, by new

York Iroquois, mostly Cayugas, who had agreed to exchange their claims in the east for Kansas lands in the nefarious Treaty of Buffalo Creek of 1838. Although most of these Indians died during the removal process or returned to New York, a small number remained in Indian Territory.[6] After the Civil War, new emigrants, mostly Cayugas, from both the Six Nations Reserve and Cattaraugus arrived in Indian Territory. As late as December 1881, thirty-two more Iroquois, twenty-six from Brantford and six from Cattaraugus arrived. Eleven of these Indians were to return to the East only after much administrative confusion about jurisdiction on the part of Indian agents and their supervisors in Canada and the United States.[7]

Throughout the nineteenth and twentieth centuries, family connections with the eastern Iroquois were maintained, Iroquois languages, especially Cayuga, were retained, and Iroquois ceremonialism remained vibrant. In the 1880s, the Oklahoma Iroquois' traditionalist religion was infused with vitality by the appearance of at least one Iroquois Longhouse preacher of the Code of Handsome Lake from Six Nations Reserve.[8] Moreover, the Cayugas in the West, who maintained a separate tribal existence until the 1920s, negotiated treaties with the federal government in council with their brethren in New York until 1871 and receive their annuities under treaty from New York State up to the present day. Hence, despite a fifteen-hundred-mile separation from their mother tradition and the differences of environment, these western Indians remain distinctly Iroquois. To this day, some of these tribesmen speak a dialect of the Cayuga language. The Seneca-Cayugas celebrate the annual Iroquois Green Corn Festival each August. A version of the peach stone game, typically found among Iroquois Indians in New York, is also played by these Oklahoma tribesmen.[9]

The transplanting of Iroquois existence to the West hardly went smoothly. During the 1850s and 1860s, they found themselves engulfed by sectional lawless activity referred to as "Bleeding Kansas" and eventually by the Civil War, sustaining heavy property damages and losses.[10] In a new treaty with the federal government in 1867, the Sandusky Seneca and Seneca-Shawnee bands were consolidated into one tribe after the dissolution of all tribal ties between Seneca and Shawnee. The treaty reaffirmed Seneca possession to approximately sixty-five thousand acres of land in what is now northeastern Oklahoma, after securing agreement to allow Ottawas and Wyandots to resettle in lands previously allocated to the Senecas. Despite this forceable attempt to unify tribal affairs, Iroquois society remained split in the West. The presence of diverse Iroquois peoples emigrating at different times could only produce at best a state of tribal confusion. As early as 1873, one Seneca leader appealed to Washington to intercede in order to reconcile tribal division. Despite the Seneca names applied to these peoples —Senecas of Sandusky, Neosho Senecas, Cowskin Senecas, Seneca Nation, or Senecas — a large segment of the population was clearly Cayuga. A separate Cayuga tribal structure existed until the mid-1920s and in weakened and modified form until 1937, while Senecas, by the 1870s, elected a tribal council of three councilmen and three chiefs until 1937. These different councils existed side by side and often vied for power until just prior to the New Deal era.[11]

Even before the Dawes Act of 1887, these Indians complained about Cherokees, Quapaws, and whites who trespassed and stripped timber off their lands, about the improprieties of their Indian agents, illegal grazing on their lands, not receiving annuities, whiskey traders, attempts to establish a territorial government and about white efforts to consolidate the Iroquois with the Cherokees.[12] Despite tribal protests about the increasing assault on their treaty lands, the Dawes Act went into effect in a similar manner as it had in Wisconsin.[13] By 1888, the federal government allotted half the existing Seneca reservation as guaranteed by the Treaty of 1867 in 40- to 160-acre tracts. As in the Oneida case, full United States citizenship immediately accompanied allotment and fee patents were awarded the Indians after a twenty-five year trust period. Eighty acres were set aside as tribal ceremonial grounds while forty acres were reserved for the Quaker meetinghouse. In 1902 and 1903, the government allotted most of the remaining lands with 120 acres assigned to Indians born since the first allotment. In the same years, the government declared ten thousand of the approximately thirty thousand remaining acres as surplus lands and threw the land open for white purchase and settlement under the provisions of the Dawes Act with the moneys raised earmarked for Indian education.[14]

The Oklahoma Iroquois faced pressures not unlike their Wisconsin brethren under the allotment policy. These Indians were handicapped from the start by their location which was adjacent to the country's leading lead and zinc mining area. This tri-state district of southeastern Kansas, northwestern Missouri, and northeastern Oklahoma included the boom towns of Baxter Springs, Kansas, Joplin, Missouri, and Picher and Miami, Oklahoma.[15] Unlike their Quapaw Indian neighbors whose lands contained precious metals, the Oklahoma Iroquois had rich agricultural and timber lands that supplied the neighboring communities. In the 1890s, an increasing number of these Indians found it easier or profitable to lease their lands to whites who were flooding into the area. One Indian agent complained to

Washington that "shrewd mixed bloods and mercenary white man" were taking advantage of the Indians' ignorance in these matters to obtain outragiously low leasing arrangements.[16] Land speculators by the mid-1890s began to advertise the area as a veritable paradise containing rich lands, minerals, and timber as well as possessing the "most beautiful and picturesque streams in all the south and west." The same prospectus described the Quapaw Agency, that included the Iroquois, as having two-thirds of its population as "well-to-do white men cultivating fields."[17]

On occasion these land-hungry whites worked with agents to divest Indians of their land and its resources. Unsupervised leasing arrangements under loopholes of the Dawes Act allowed for illegal grazing, squatting, and timber stripping on Iroquois lands.[18] Some agents either encouraged this process for personal profit or ignored it to win favor in the local white communities.[19] In 1898, the Indian agent wrote that leasing had been so successful that he recommended the right of the more "progressive" Indians of the Quapaw Agency to circumvent the Dawes Act by selling a portion of their lands before the end of the trust period.[20] Despite the warning of the Justice Department, control of Indian property, especially timber, was also obtained by whites by securing legal guardianship over the largely uneducated Indians who were not of legal age or not yet declared competent.[21] Not all agents condoned these actions, and some filed complaints about the activities of squatters and lessees. In one of these instances, local whites, who had been removed from the agency, sued the agent for damages and threatened the poor man's life.[22]

The assault on tribalism also took other forms. After the founding of the Seneca Indian School in 1872, schisms within the tribe along religious lines became more and more evident. Quaker proselytizing, despite strong tribal resistance, gained impetus a decade later with the work of missionary Jeremiah Hubbard and his Cayuga convert John Winney. In the 1890s, the nondenominational missionizing activities of Matthias Splitlog, a wealthy Cayuga, also encouraged Iroquois conversion. As early as 1882, 42 out of 222 Iroquois had been converted.[23] One year later, these Indians appealed for tribal lands to build a church and burial grounds, a move resisted by tribal authorities. The commissioner of Indian affairs responded by allowing these Quaker converts three acres to build, since to him the "most ignorant and superstitious" Indians had to be ignored — allegedly for the progress of the race.[24]

The education of these Indians also promoted assimilationist goals. Although the commissioner of Indian affairs called for promoting manda-

Seneca Indian School, grades 1–8, 1887, Ottawa County, Indian Territory. Photograph courtesy of the Western History Collections, University of Oklahoma Library.

Seneca Indian School, Wyandotte, Oklahoma, 1902. Photograph courtesy of the Western History Collections, University of Oklahoma Library.

Seneca Indian School, faculty and families, Wyandotte, Oklahoma, 1888. The spring was the watering place for the locality and source of water for the school. Photograph courtesy of the Western History Collections, University of Oklahoma Library.

tory attendance at the Seneca School, Iroquois resistance proved stronger than expected. At a time when more than 40 percent of the school's population were Senecas, the institution's superintendent wrote, in 1881, that the Indian parents were "still inclined to use privilege of the school only as it is profitable to them in food and clothes."[25] The school, which was later taken over by the government and renamed the "Seneca, Wyandot and Shawnee School," had strict military discipline and dress reviews, and, as other boarding schools attended by western Iroquois, forbade the speaking of the Cayuga and Seneca languages. It is not surprising that the school's superintendent reported that twelve of his Seneca students went home during the holidays in the winter of 1881–82, never to return again.[26]

By the 1920s, tribal political disintegration was nearly complete. The functions of leadership within the Iroquois polity had been altered dramatically. The separate Cayuga political apparatus had virtually withered away while the Seneca council, composed of some Cayugas, was described by the Indian agent in the following manner: "Seneca chiefs make formal request for the payment by the State of New York of the Cayuga funds [annuities]. There are practically no other duties performed by these chiefs or council."[27] The growing power of the Bureau of Indian Affairs and especially the local agent or superintendent led one Indian to comment that "we lost our ability to manage because we were so used to the BIA or the Indian agent telling us what to do."[28] One historian has described this condition that most Oklahoma Indians faced in the 1920s:

> The Bureau seemed to base all its actions on a basic premise of Indian ignorance. As proof of this notion's validity, agents pointed to the ease with which whites had stripped away Indian property since allotment. Consequently, Indian finances were closely managed, and when a tribesman wanted something he went to his agent. The agent, arbitrarily making all decisions, approved or rejected the request. Furthermore, when an Indian requested an article which required purchase he was not trusted with the money but was issued a store order. Indeed, it was even difficult for a tribesman to loan money to a member of this family.[29]

The period between 1887 and the 1930s had produced a total economic disaster as well. Besides the loss of almost all of their land, these Indians found themselves hanging onto a tenuous existence. The superintendent of the Quapaw Agency described the conditions of Senecas and Wyandottes in 1922 as "commercially poor Indians living in rough hill country. The majority of the younger members of these tribes were allotted land which is almost worthless as a farming proposition."[30] By the dawning of the New Deal, tribal existence itself was shaky and in great peril of disappearing.

Because Oklahoma contained approximately one-third of America's Indian population, Commissioner Collier soon turned his attention to that state after assuming office in 1933. As a reformer of Indian policies since the 1920s, he was well aware of the terrible conditions of life that the Indians faced. With a new sense of urgency caused by the crisis of the Great Depression, the commissioner visited Oklahoma for the first time in an official capacity in February and March of 1934. In visits to the agencies at Andarko, Miami, and Muskogee, he attempted to generate Indian support for the Wheeler-Howard Bill, then being debated in Congress.[31] Collier faced overwhelming opposition to the bill. He later concluded that this negative reaction was caused by the "many betrayals of past years — betrayals whose consequences were matters of daily experience."[32] It is clear that many Indians agreed with Collier's assessment. Almost universally, the Indians feared that their status as allottees, however meager and poor, would be threatened by new legislation emanating from Washington. Tribal elders remembered that other commissioners and reformers had promised a new day for Indians under the Dawes Act of 1887, one that proved a total disaster for the state's Indians. Moreover, many Oklahoma Indians looked with suspicion on any legislation bearing the BIA's stamp of approval. Doubts about the worthiness of the Indian New Deal were also fueled by the activities of Joseph Bruner, a Creek chief from Sapulpa, head of the National Indian Confederacy and future president of the American Indian Federation, who campaigned against the Indian New Deal right through the 1930s. The white press throughout the state also created fears about the impending legislation, only adding to general misunderstanding and confusion.[33]

On March 24, 1934, the commissioner appeared at Miami before a gathering of Indians from northeastern Oklahoma. In attendance were 550 Indians, including representatives of the Iroquois, the Osages, Ottawas, Peorias, Quapaws, and Shawnees. The transcript of the meeting reveals that the Iroquois representatives who spoke were skeptical of Collier and his program and had little understanding of the meaning of the Wheeler-Howard Bill.[34] After the conclusion of Collier's talk, the two Iroquois chiefs in attendance — William "Stick" Smith, a Cayuga, and John H. Logan, a Seneca — joined the other Indian delegates urging the rejection of the bill. According to their resolution:

That in view of the general uncertainty and the many discrepancies of said bill and the further evident fact that the bill, as a whole, so plainly suggests utter disrespect or disregard for our local State and National Government and tends to revive and urge race prejudice even tho' "the hatchet" of such prejudice and hatred has been buried for years and our Indian people generally are now looked upon as respectable, upright and progressive citizens, the Association of Indian Tribes hereby voices its emphatic DISFAVOR for the passage of or the enactment of the legislation intended by the provisions of the Wheeler-Howard Bill hereinabove referred to and further suggests that the extreme efforts now being extended toward the passage and enactment of such legislation be directed toward more sane, respectful and beneficial accomplishments in the interest of our American Indian citizenship.[35]

As a result of these and other protests and general overall confusion about the bill, Senator Thomas offered an amendment in Congress excluding Oklahoma tribesmen from six sections of the Wheeler-Howard Bill, including provisions dealing with collective landholding and corporate organization of tribal government. Nevertheless, these Indians were to be affected by the bill's official end to the allotment policies of the past and provisions providing for acquisition of land for landless Indians, conservation methods, a revolving fund for economic development, and educational loans for tuition in vocational and trade schools.[36]

Collier was more successful in winning Indian and non-Indian support for his programs on his second official visit to Oklahoma. In October 1934, the commissioner, more aware of the political realities of the state, wrote a series of articles for the influential magazine, *Harlow's Weekly,* to win support and lessen the confusion about his policies.[37] Moreover, realizing that any Indian legislation he wanted had to pass through the Indian affairs committees of the Congress headed by Oklahomans, Senator Elmer Thomas, and Representative Will Rogers, Collier attempted to be more conciliatory to these powerful Oklahoma political leaders. After attending meetings with the two congressmen at Andarko, Concho, Muskogee, Pawhuska, Pawnee, and Shawnee, Collier reached Miami on October 16, where he met with a series of representatives from tribes of the depressed northeastern part of the state. There he heard Chief Thomas Armstrong, an Iroquois leader, describe how his people managed to survive while living in dire poverty in shacks on forty-acre allotments in rough hill country. Armstrong urged Collier to help provide land for landless Indians as well as educational assistance. Armstrong, a member of the Association of Indian Tribes, a Miami-based intertribal organization whose membership also included Iroquois Chiefs Logan and Smith, voiced uncertainty about the merits of applying the now-passed Wheeler-Howard Bill to the nonreservation Indian communities of Oklahoma. Although his organization expressed support for the bill's provision guaranteeing Indian preference in hiring in the Indian Service, they argued against what they believed was a return to reservation status. Hence, they urged special legislation that was specifically written to the realities of Indian communities of Oklahoma in mind and pushed for the building of a much-needed hospital.[38]

Ten days after Collier's appearance at the Miami meeting, an Iroquois council, headed by Armstrong, met at Bassett Springs, Oklahoma, to consider the commissioner's discussions with the tribesmen. In a petition to the commissioner dated October 26, 1934, the Iroquois, already referring to themselves as the "Seneca-Cayuga Tribe of Indians of Oklahoma," indicated their unanimous support for a modified version of the Wheeler-Howard Act, "so that land could be purchased near their present homes for all landless Indians and for those Indians having insufficient land on which to make a living." It added that the tribe wished to be "incorporated as a community and not a reservation" but that it favored the Indian educational provisions of the Wheeler-Howard Act. Importantly, the petition made it clear that there was a tribal group composed of both Senecas and Cayugas who were prepared to advocate the need for tribal reorganization among these Indians.[39]

Out of Collier's October visit to Oklahoma and his new collaborative relationship with Senator Thomas and Representative Rogers came the drafting of the Oklahoma Indian Welfare Act, which was finally passed in congress in June 1936.[40] The act provided, in the manner of the Wheeler-Howard Act, for tribal incorporation, educational assistance, and economic development. As in the earlier legislation, the act gave the secretary of the interior the power to "acquire by purchase, relinquishment, gift, exchange or assignment" restricted land of good quality for the purpose of creating communal ownership of property. This land was to be held in trust for the tribe, band or group of Indians and to be exempt from all taxes except the Oklahoma "gross production tax" on oil and gas not in excess of the rate on similar lands held by private individuals. All Oklahoma tribesmen, except the Osage who were excluded from the act, had the right to organize for their common welfare, adopt a constitution and a charter of incorporation prescribed by the secretary of the interior. Indians had the right, after adopting a charter, to borrow money from a 2 million dollar revolving credit fund. The act stressed the development of cooperative associations for the furtherance of credit, production, marketing, consumer protection, or land management but recognized the right of the State of Oklahoma to regulate these activities. Unlike the Wheeler-Howard Act, the 1936 act never used the word "reservation" or encouraged the reestablishment of Indian reservations. In sharp contrast, the Oklahoma Indian Welfare Act had no controversial section dealing with the referendum procedure that had led to the IRA's rejection in New York. Section 3 of the 1936 act required a referendum on the charter of incorporation that had to be "ratified by a

OZARK PLAYGROUDDS "LITTLE NIAGARA" AT PENSACOLA DAM DISNEY OKLA.

"Ozark Playgrounds — Little Niagara," Grand River Dam Authority's Pensacola Dam, Disney, Oklahoma, April 17, 1941. Photograph courtesy of the Western

majority vote of the adult members of the organization voting" and that would be voided if less than 30 percent of the Indians of a particular tribe failed to cast ballots.[41]

The Seneca-Cayugas became the first tribe to come under the act, the first of eighteen to adopt a constitution and bylaws and the first of thirteen to ratify a charter of incorporation. This process of creating the Seneca-Cayuga Tribe of Indians of Oklahoma was accomplished without the intratribal battle as in Wisconsin and left little bitter aftertaste. After a six-week period of debate, discussion, and little conflict over the merits of tribal reorganization, about 55 percent of the Iroquois went to the polls on May 15, 1937, and voted to accept the new tribal constitution and bylaws by a margin of 186 to 0; one hundred sixty-four eligible voters either failed to participate or boycotted the referendum. One month later on June 26, the first anniversary of the Oklahoma Indian Welfare Act, the Seneca-Cayugas,

History Collections, University of Oklahoma Library.

in similar manner, adopted their corporate charter allowing them full access to the benefits outlined in the legislation.[42]

The question arises as to why the Iroquois in Oklahoma accepted tribal reorganization? The answer is complex and multicausational. As one of the smaller Oklahoma tribes, totaling only 732 persons in 1937, Collier purposefully chose them as his first tribe to push incorporation.[43] In March, April, and May 1937, Collier used every possible means to win support. Perhaps with the memory of the IRA fiasco in New York in mind, he worked closely with H. A. Andrews, the Indian agent for the Seneca-Cayugas, at every turn. Andrews wrote Collier about the importance of this first referendum: "If these 2 tribes ... [Wyandottes and Seneca-Cayugas] are granted charters, the other tribes will see the advantages to be derived from such procedures and will be taking steps for organization."[44]

Collier provided Andrews with Indian Service employees to facilitate

Grand River Dam project, Langley, Oklahoma, June 1939. Photograph courtesy of

the campaign for acceptance. He had Felix Cohen, the assistant solicitor of the Interior Department, and Collier's special assistants, Fred Daiker and A. C. Monahan, draft the constitution and bylaws for the tribe in March 1937, after a formal request for incorporation by Chief Thomas Armstrong and his council. After a month of discussions and redrafting, the constitution and bylaws were approved by Secretary Ickes on April 26.[45] In addition, Collier sent Monahan, his regional coordinator, along with Ben Dwight, an Oklahoma Indian and organizational field agent for the bureau, to Miami to take "every appropriate step" to get "the resident voters to the polls."[46] Andrews, Dwight, and Monahan held public meetings, posted notices, prepared eligibility lists, notified absentee voters, created a tribal election board, and distributed circulars and pamphlets describing the advantages of incorporation under the Oklahoma Indian Welfare Act.[47] Collier's strategy was stated succinctly in a letter to Andrews: "I feel justified in requesting the wholehearted assistance of employees who may be fitted by position or talents to help in this work, and ask that they give their time whole-heartedly even to the extent of giving the work of organization precedence over their own work."[48]

the Western History Collections, University of Oklahoma Library.

The drive for tribal reorganization among the Seneca-Cayugas was not merely a *fait accompli* of the Indian Bureau. The Indians themselves, as has been previously discussed, had urged some form of incorporation since 1934. As in the case of the Wisconsin Oneidas, the Seneca-Cayugas had largely lost their land base under the operations of the Dawes Act and consequently had little to lose by accepting the Indian New Deal. Although in less desperate shape than some of the Plains tribes in Oklahoma, one tribal elder recalled that "everyone among us was poor in the 1930s."[49] Promises of easier credit, educational assistance, and land—all part of Collier's program —were especially appealing to these economically hard-pressed Indians. Moreover, the Seneca-Cayugas, despite their historic divisions, were less politically factionalized than other Indians of northeastern Oklahoma in part because they had more tribesmen with a higher percentage of Indian blood quantum, a fact not lost on bureau personnel.[50]

The Indian New Deal in Oklahoma was to produce significant results. A tribal business committee headed by Chief Thomas Armstrong was soon elected.[51] The newly consolidated tribe operating as a singular entity for the first time began the application process for loans under the provisions of the

Oklahoma Indian Welfare Act.[52] The Seneca-Cayugas began working with Indian personnel in an attempt to rebuild their tribal land base. Though successful in increasing their tribal holdings by tenfold, tribal leaders had no authority to stop Indians who had allotted lands from selling off their allotments or to prevent these lands from falling into non-Indian hands as a result of foreclosure of debt repayment. Moreover, any hopes of recreating any semblance of Iroquois landholdings before the Dawes Act were soon to be washed away. The Seneca-Cayugas were shortly to find themselves facing disaster with the development of the Grand River Dam Authority Project.

Oklahomans had dreamed of harnessing the Grand or Neosho River in the northeastern corner of the state since the late nineteenth century. This project was revived during the 1930s. Powerful Democratic voices in Congress, such as Senator Thomas, rationalized numerous dams by insisting that the state, more economically hard-pressed than others, needed cheap hydroelectric power, flood control as well as reclamation, water, levee, and recreational projects to spur employment. On April 26, 1935, the Oklahoma State Legislature created the Grand River Dam Authority as a governmental agency for the purpose of developing and utilizing the water resources of the Grand River. Spurred on by the political pork-barreling of Senator Thomas and Representatives Wesley Disney and Frank Bailey, Congress passed a bill in October 1937 granting the authority, through the Public Works Administration (PWA), an outright subsidy of 45 percent of their operating budget and a commitment to purchase low-interest bonds issued by the authority up to 11.5 million dollars. As a result, the Grand River Dam Authority began in the early months of 1938 construction of three dams—Pensacola, Markham Ferry, and Fort Gibson. By 1940, the project had created the Grand Lake, also called the Lake of the Cherokees, a huge body of water lying in five counties and two states.[53]

In the process, 1,285.73 allotted acres of Cherokee and 805.25 acres of Quapaw Agency Indian lands, mostly Seneca-Cayuga, were condemned, sold to the Grand River Dam Authority and then flooded. Half of the Seneca-Cayuga ceremonial area along the Elk River was also lost in the process.[54] One Indian elder described her predicament caused by the project's inception: "I do not know how long I can stay here as I am told that the water from the Grand River Dam will come up to the top of the door."[55] Although some of the out-of-work Seneca-Cayugas found employment in work-relief projects related to the construction of the Pensacola Dam, these Indians lost seven tracts of land totaling the 281.33 acres that had just been purchased back by the Interior Department under the provisions of the

Oklahoma Indian Welfare Act. The Grand River Dam Authority condemned and flooded these lands in 1940 with money provided by Congress to the Public Works Administration, an agency headed by Secretary Ickes.[56]

The Congressional pork barrel flooded away any illusions of a return to the better days of the Iroquois past. Nevertheless, the Indian New Deal among these Indians had produced notable changes. Besides an increased tribal land base, the Oklahoma Iroquois, truly confederated for the first time, now had the unified tribal mechanism in the form of a new business committee, however alien to Indian tradition, to operate more effectively in the future. As the dam projects showed, their success in this regard depended on how much Congress allowed this new political body to work.

7

THE BIG DEAL

New Deal Community Action Programs in New York

The drainage project on this reservation [St. Regis] was recommended
and started at a very crucial time, as in the history of the reservation there
were never so many men out of work and the project was a Godsend to
them.

Chief Joseph F. Tarbell (Mohawk)
CCC-ID Timekeeper
May 1938

Under supervision of the WPA, the labor for the handsome structure
[Tonawanda Indian Community House] was performed entirely by the
Indians from the Tonawanda Reservation and the building stands as a
monument to their skill.

Report of the (New York State)
Department of Social Services,
July 1, 1936—June 30, 1937

COMMISSIONER COLLIER'S PLAN for tribal political reorganization was
only one element, however important, of the total Indian New Deal.
The Iroquois benefited by the bureau's creation of the position of "community
worker" in New York, an applied anthropology experiment that
achieved positive results. The Civilian Conservation Corps-Indian Division
administered by the Interior Department helped improve reservation conditions
while providing badly needed work relief. Equally significant were the
myriad of federal programs, indirectly tied or independent of bureau

sponsorship, initiated by the Roosevelt administration in response to the Great Depression, including those administered by the Works Progress Administration and the National Youth Administration. The New York Iroquois, largely neglected by the federal government prior to 1933, also built the first Indian community house for the exclusive use of an Iroquois community and developed an innovative camp counselor training program for Indian youth.

In December 1934, Commissioner Collier, in a speech at Pittsburgh, stressed the need to work closer with anthropologists. For more than a year previously, Collier had sent out questionnaires, held informal discussions with prominent anthropologists, most notably William Duncan Strong of the Bureau of American Ethnology, and had made other overtures to win the profession's support for his program. The commissioner had borrowed this idea from the British Empire's use of social scientists. Moreover, his plan was a conscious effort to employ them in places where missionary influence was previously strongest. Although the experiment was based on a colonial supposition that was resented by many Native Americans and some anthropologists as well, the program that was implemented made significant contributions to Indian life in the period.[1]

In 1935, Collier appointed Strong to head the newly created Applied Anthropology Staff of the BIA. An entire generation of aspiring anthropologists, many of whom were out of work or were unable to secure academic positions because of the Great Depression, received much of their field-work training under the auspices of Collier's program. Through the efforts of Strong, William N. Fenton was appointed as community worker in the Indian Service at Tonawanda, receiving a salary of $2,000 per year, subsidized use of his own automobile, and a small per diem of $3.50 a day for traveling expenses. With a fresh climate of experimentation, money in his pocket, and new mentors at the hustings "down below" (the Longhouse district at Tonawanda), Fenton assumed his position in February 1935.[2]

The young anthropologist was no stranger to Iroquoia. In the two years prior to his appointment, Fenton had conducted field work for his dissertation among the Senecas on Iroquois social structure, ceremonial organization, and medicine for the Institute of Human Relations at Yale University. In the process, he had developed friendships, learned much from the older Indians at the "doings," witnessed the extraordinary sense of cooperation by reservation folk during the difficult times of the Great Depression, and developed acquaintances that played a significant role in his research and scholarship for the next four decades.[3] Fenton's return to Seneca country, as he was well aware, was going to be different this time. When he entered the Tonawanda Reservation in February, he was "wearing a new hat." He was now a "Fed," part of Commissioner Collier's experiment in applied anthropology at the Bureau of Indian Affairs. Fenton, who was cognizant of Iroquois distrust and even open hostility toward United States officials, reflected this concern when he wrote Collier: "I think I will get on better when in an un-official capacity. There is strong feeling amongst the Iroquois about government agents."[4]

In his two and a half years of service, Fenton walked the fine line of survival. He had to contend with a do-nothing Indian agent, federal governmental Indian policies that were often at odds with Iroquois wishes, factional tribal politics, and, most importantly, the severity of reservation poverty intensified by the Great Depression. On occasions, his professional goals as an aspiring anthropologist often ran counter to his official duties. In a society with an historic district of Washington and Washington-directed Indian policies, the more Fenton wore an official hat, the more his ability to gather information for his own research suffered. Yet, if he ignored the bureau's directives altogether, he could easily foresee finding himself unemployed at a time of the nation's worst depression. Consequently, Fenton often felt as though he were "between a rock and a hard place."[5]

Fenton, from the beginning, had to contend with overcoming Iroquois distrust and suspicion about outsiders. One month after he started work, one Seneca, in a questioning tone, wrote Collier inquiring about the stranger who "hangs around in our reservation every day."[6] Collier responded by defining Fenton's role as "community worker at the New York agency to assist the Indians of the Tonawanda Reservation and other communities in organizing enterprises which will meet their social needs." Collier added that Fenton's role was to "promote group meetings, clubs, and classes, especially for adults" and to cooperate with the Indians in all efforts to develop "economic, social and health programs, with the objective of fostering the growth of definite civic and social responsibilities."[7]

Anthropologists working in the Indian service under Commissioner Collier frequently complained about having to work with the old-line bureau personnel. No clearer example of these complaints can be provided than Fenton's relationship with W. K. Harrison, the Indian agent in New York. For more than thirty years, Harrison had survived in his Salamanca post primarily by not rocking the boat. Silent as President Coolidge, Harrison was accepted by the Iroquois largely because he did not bother them. They preferred "a smooth old gentleman who only appears to pay their annuities, attend councils, and is a nice symbol of the government."[8]

The two men, who were separated in age by nearly half a century, were light years apart in their approach to the Iroquois and their problems. From the first days on the job at the New York Agency, the young anthropologist suspected that Harrison was not "convinced of the practicality of the program involved, or what he expects of a community worker."[9] Harrison questioned the necessity of Fenton's frequent travels to Rochester and Buffalo, especially without the agent's prior permission. Outraged, Fenton wrote to the central office in Washington asking for the privilege of exercising his own judgment on the need to travel. He added: "The old gentleman is anxious that I do not play politics, a situation which he can control by keeping me in Akron. I don't happen to be interested in politics, but I am interested in these Indians. While here, I can devote much time to studying them, but I have to go to Buffalo to arrange outside help for them; to get lecturers, to see people, who really listen when you write afterwards."[10] Despite the agent's objections, Fenton continued his travels. The distance between Harrison's Salamanca office and Fenton's work at Tonawanda allowed the community worker some latitude from outside interference.

The debate over the IRA consumed most of Fenton's attention during the first six months in his new position. Acutely aware of the strong opposition to the act, Fenton faced a major dilemma: how to keep the trust of the Indians while associated with promoting an unpopular cause. Fenton later reflected on this experience: "Many of them have expressed their feelings frankly to me about the IRA, which they wholeheartedly doubted and no amount of persuasion would dislodge them, and have told me I may live to regain the status I once enjoyed as participant in their rituals and recreation. My connection with the Government has cast an awful pall upon my presence. They hate to think that their friend, whom they admit they like, is connected with the government."[11] After this crushing defeat, Fenton turned his attention to specific areas of need. The applied anthropologist had now become more aware of the bottomless gulf between official expectations and the realities of Indian life in New York in the period. Consequently, during the remainder of his tenure as community worker, he served the Iroquois as a concerned social problem-solver rather than involving himself in the maelstrom of Iroquois politics. In the process, he regained much of the support he had lost in the referendum debacle. Moreover, he was able to make use of his anthropological training to serve the Iroquois, especially at Tonawanda.

His most significant accomplishments were in the area of education. Fenton organized study clubs at Tonawanda which brought in outside speakers and allowed the younger Indians to learn from their elders on the

H. R. Dane, librarian of the Grosvenor Library in Buffalo, and Inez Blackchief in the library at the Tonawanda Indian Reservation, July 16, 1935. Photograph by William N. Fenton, courtesy of the William N. Fenton Collection, U.S. Indian Service Photographs, 1935–37.

reservation. He handled the necessary paperwork to help promising students on several Iroquois reservations secure educational loans to go to college. He also encouraged several students, who might never have thought of higher education, to enter Cornell, Dartmouth, and St. Lawrence. Quite significantly, he helped organize the first community library at Tonawanda which immediately proved successful.[12]

Fenton also worked to improve health care at Tonawanda. His activities included securing a wheelchair for a disabled old woman, driving Indians to the hospital for check-ups, handling business matters for those seriously ill, lecturing on ways to improve public health on the reservation, and cooperating with state physicians to stem the ravages of disease.[13] He convinced the family of William Gordon, leaders of the Longhouse, to commit their son

Mutual Aid Society Singers at a wood bee, Tonawanda Indian Reservation, March 3, 1935. Photograph by William N. Fenton, courtesy of the William N. Fenton Collection, U.S. Indian Service Photographs, 1935–37.

Theodore, suffering from a serious case of tuberculosis, to a sanitarium, rather than rely solely on native herbal medicines and medicine society rituals. Through his special knowledge of Seneca mores, he "persuaded them that the songs might relieve the individual of conflicts arising out of not fulfilling the requirements of belonging to a certain society, but that Theodore had T.B., a white man's disease, which their most potent rituals would not cure."[14] Fenton's applied anthropology had saved a life. As he subsequently wrote: "The title Community Worker implies a method; one should work with groups rather than cases. The method should be designed to fit the customs of the people."[15]

Throughout his tenure as community worker, Fenton attempted to cut through established procedures and red tape. He acted as an intermediary to secure funds from the New York State Department of Social Welfare for

National Youth Administration project, Seneca boys reshingling the Longhouse at Tonawanda Indian Reservation, September 1936. Chief Henan Scrogg, project supervisor, at right. Photograph by William N. Fenton, courtesy of the William N. Fenton Collection, U.S. Indian Service Photographs, 1935–37.

casket lumber for Longhouse funerals. He then borrowed three Indian laborers, members of the Salt Creek Mutual Aid Society, from the local public works project to dig the graves, all to the chagrin of off-reservation non-Indian funeral directors. He also helped obtain needed improvements for the bridges and roads, secure road signs, shingle the Longhouse, and bring electrification to Tonawanda. Moreover, he worked closely with Arthur C. Parker in Parker's successful efforts in establishing a Tonawanda community center and in reviving Iroquois arts. He also won Seneca

National Youth Administration project, Seneca Boys reshingling the Longhouse at Tonawanda Indian Reservation, September 1936. Photograph by William N. Fenton, courtesy of the William N. Fenton Collection, U.S. Indian Service Photographs, 1935–37.

appreciation for his help in organizing and publicizing field day events for community fund-raising efforts. Part of Fenton's success in these efforts could be attributed to his keen ability to speak the Seneca language, a fact acknowledged by the better Iroquois speakers. Another reason for the apparent success of the community worker experiment was the young anthropologist's admiration for the Iroquois people and their struggle to overcome the serious problems of the Great Depression.[16] As a result of seeing the spirit of cooperation and the productive work of Iroquois singing societies during the crisis of the Great Depression, Fenton attempted to advise both Washington and Albany to incorporate an understanding of Seneca lifeways into any and all programs for these Indians: "Perhaps the modest example of these singing companies suggest a method of meeting

New Deal work-relief project, putting up guide posts along Shady Lane, Tonawanda Indian Reservation, August 1935. Photograph by William N. Fenton,
courtesy of the William N. Fenton Collection, U.S. Indian Service Photographs,
1935–37.

Community worker William N. Fenton, Chief Henan Scrogg (right), and unidentified man and boy before the Tonawanda Longhouse that is being reshingled under
the auspices of the National Youth Administration, September 1936. Photograph
courtesy of the William N. Fenton Collection, U.S. Indian Service Photographs,
1935–37.

social problems. A group of individuals band themselves together for the purposes of joint pleasures and mutual assistance. They elect their native leader and solve the problems which every society has to meet in some traditional manner. Where these societies exist, they should be encouraged. The recognition of native leadership and the delegation of responsibility promotes self respect and independence."[17]

The applied anthropology program in New York ended on August 14, 1937, when Fenton applied for a leave of absence, later changed to resignation, from the Indian Service after accepting an instructorship in the social sciences at St. Lawrence University. The New Deal experiment with anthropologists, although serving the purposes of the Indian Bureau and the anthropologist, was indeed significant well beyond immediate bureau administrative needs and the subsidization of the field work for anthropologists. It often provided concrete and dramatic benefits for those served.[18] It is clear that the gap that often existed between Washington and reservation life in the period was only capable of being bridged when the personnel at the local level were working in the context of tribal cultures and understood the people being served.

Commissioner Collier's New Deal programs achieved positive results in other areas and mitigated the effects of the IRA referendum in New York. The Civilian Conservation Corps-Indian Division (CCC-ID), which was administered directly at the agency level, provided work relief, infused reservation communities with badly needed moneys, and helped rehabilitate and preserve Indian landholdings.[19] Equally important, the CCC-ID and other federally subsidized programs fostered better Iroquois-federal relations in the period. After the failure of the IRA referendum in New York, Harrison acknowledged this fact in a letter to Commissioner Collier: "and the work-out of these projects at this time should help to create a friendly feeling toward the Government, a condition to be greatly desired in New York State reservations at the present time."[20]

Even before Commissioner Collier's nomination and appointment to office, bureau officials had recognized the urgent need to make forestation improvements, control soil erosion, restore grazing lands, and undertake other conservationist policies on Indian lands. After the passage of the Emergency Conservation Work Act in March 1933, intensive lobbying by both J. P. Kinney, chief forester in the Indian Bureau and Secretary Ickes led to the creation of a separate Indian program under Indian Service auspices in late April. Commissioner Collier soon created a special office to administer the program under the direction of Jay B. Nash, head of the physical education department at New York University, a specialist in adult education and outdoor recreation, and member of Collier's American Indian Defense Association. Nash was quickly succeeded in office by Daniel Murphy, a competent career administrator in the Indian Service. Murphy ran the Indian Emergency Conservation Work Program (IECW), which was later renamed Civilian Conservation Corps-Indian Division in 1937, with the aid of Assistant Commissioner William Zimmerman, Jr., until the experiment's demise in 1942. On the technical side of the project, Collier chose Kinney as general production supervisor. The former chief forester, despite this apparent demotion and his numerous running battles with Collier, served ably in the position.[21]

From 1933 to 1942, eighty-five thousand Indian enrollees served in CCC-ID and $72,647,283 was spent on more than seventy reservations. Approximately 60 percent of the amount allocated by the government went for wages, subsistence, and other direct benefits to the Indian enrollees. Although there were limitations to the program, the experiment, besides providing essential work relief, achieved significant results in protecting and improving forest and range lands and developing land resources.[22]

The CCC-ID differed from the regular CCC in several distinct ways. Unlike the CCC, the Indian program was administered by the Bureau of Indian Affairs and directly supervised at the agency level. Although Indians could be enrolled in the CCC, non-Indians, with few exceptions, could not be included in the CCC-ID. Where the CCC required their enrollees to be unmarried and under the age of twenty-five, the CCC-ID had no age or marriage restrictions. Nearly 50 percent of the Indian enrollees were over the age of thirty. Hence, to a significant number of Indians, the CCC was not merely a youth program but their only means of family economic survival. Moreover, unlike the formal and uniform requirements of the regular CCC, the Indian Division had more diversity in its undertakings and its policies, varying from one Indian agency to another depending on local conditions and needs.[23]

The IECW began after mid-June 1933. By year's end, approximately twenty-five thousand Indians had served as enrollees. The enrollee received $30.00 per month or $1.50 per working day since the Indians were allowed to work only twenty days each month. Workers received $1–2 per day if they used their own horses and were given a small commutation allowance if they had to travel to the project. An enrollee could advance to become an assistant leader, leader, subforeman, assistant foreman, or even a group foreman at a top salary of $167.00 per month.[24]

During the first two years, the national focus of the project was on the construction of track trails, telephone lines, lookouts for forest fire protection, the construction of boundary, and drift fences and the development of stock water supplies on range lands. This initial period was followed by a broadening of goals, including educational and recreational features. Eventually, Indians received on-the-job training and vocational classroom instruction in the rudiments of carpentry, stone masonry, road construction, drilling and blasting, and other manual trades. In the process, enrollees were employed for the construction or rehabilitation of irrigation and drainage ditches and for the building of structures for the prevention of soil erosion on agricultural lands; the suppression of forest and range fires; the construction of storage dams for irrigation and smaller reservoirs for recreational use; and pest control projects.[25]

The Iroquois benefited significantly from the CCC-ID program. Between 1933 and 1942, the federal government spent a total of $260,180.61 for land and $4,000.24 for building improvements in New York. After a slow start in the development of projects on the New York reservations, the experiment flourished from late 1935 onward. Under the able direction of Group Foreman Clinton G. Pierce, an Oneida living on the Onondaga Reservation and a graduate of the prestigious New York State College of Forestry at Syracuse University, the program was carefully laid out. By 1935, 10 percent of the Iroquois were employed by the program.[26]

In a special report in February of that year, Pierce described each of the reservations and their topography and outlined the conservationist concerns and problems facing the Iroquois. In his analysis, Pierce suggested programs designed to regulate, protect, and develop Indian forest lands; reduce fire hazards by clearing brush; plant trees for basketry material and watershed protection; build tract trails to enable removal of short, crooked, and bulky wood; fence, post, and mark reservation boundaries to prevent white encroachments; establish fire lanes to prevent spread of fire; begin flood control and soil erosion prevention projects by straightening streams, cleaning channels of log jams and debris; and constructing drainage ditches. As one of a handful of foresters of Indian descent in the country, Pierce pointed out that all IECW projects must take into account the Indian's "strong feeling of independence" and "strong tendency to dictate rather than to be dictated to." He also observed that the Iroquois "are self-governing units over which the Federal Government has exercised little power, the state having assumed the greater administrative service." Obviously aware of past mistakes, he warned that any conservation work must be cleared through the existing tribal council.[27]

Pierce's program was put into practice in 1935. From a paltry allocation of $5,000, the program grew substantially, receiving a total of $82,955.95 before June 30, 1937.[28] Nevertheless, the CCC-ID in New York was plagued by numerous problems. The sizeable distance of some reservations from Salamanca, the seat of the Indian agency, and to each other increased travel time and added expenses to the project. The New York Agency which supervised the program had to secure tools, cars, trucks, tractors, and other equipment by borrowing these items from New York State and county road engineers when and if they were available. Pay was also a problem. Pierce claimed that "the local relief agencies pay a larger wage scale and they pay at the end of each week. Under our regulations it requires two times as much work to earn the same pay and necessitates waiting several weeks for their pay."[29] On several occasions, the New York Agency also had considerable trouble securing the services of a physician for the required examination of each enrollee.[30]

In November 1935, Kinney evaluated the projects, and, on the whole, praised Pierce's and the New York Agency's efforts as well as the Indian enrollee's conscientiousness. The IECW had cleared and straightened Cold-spring Creek on the Allegany Reservation which Kinney judged a "very commendable project and one that was being well-executed and would be of lasting benefit." Nevertheless, on the same reservation, he questioned the value of planting white pine seedlings on hillsides and makeshift efforts at straightening Red House and Bay State creeks. At Cattaraugus, he pointed out the deficiencies in IECW attempts to reconstruct a trail. At Tonawanda, he saw little value in planting trees for there was no prospect of commercial timber operations. Kinney lauded the Indians at Onondaga for improving one of their major roads, recommended that reservation timber land be improved by thinning, and suggested that the straightening of Hemlock Creek be abandoned because of its impracticality. At St. Regis, the general production supervisor agreed with Pierce's earlier assessments that IECW focus its attention on constructing a series of drainage ditches on the reservation.[31] Because of Pierce's excellent work in carefully establishing the IECW program in New York, the Indian Service promoted him by transferring him to the Klamath Reservation in the Pacific Northwest in December 1935.[32]

Despite the loss of Pierce's expertise, the program continued with much success. The New York Agency carried out Pierce's and Kinney's suggestions by establishing the St. Regis Drainage Project on the 14,030-acre reservation. Although the elevation of much of the land was generally high, the reservation contained lowlands and marshes around the center of the reservation which were within the flood plains of the St. Lawrence and St. Regis Rivers. Consequently, spring rains did not run off and delayed planting. Heavy rains in the summer often flooded and ruined crops after planting. Although there were previous attempts by the Mohawks to drain their lands, the Indians "lacked the funds to construct a ditch sufficient to drain off all their lands."[33] Since farming, along with raising dairy cattle, was the leading industry on the reservation at the time, Pierce had earlier concluded that a "project for effective drainage would benefit this reservation and its people more than any other program."[34]

Three drainage projects were implemented, the first beginning in November 1935. These projects were especially timely because of the sharp cutback in Mohawk employment at the aluminum plant at Massena because of the Great Depression.[35] The West Ditch, the first IECW project, entailed cleaning out the natural drain which led to the St. Regis River, removing mud, stones, and branches of trees with shovels, picks, and slush scrapers and the blasting away with high explosive the ledge rock which impeded the flow of water. Applications for work relief far outran the positions available since, in the words of the project timekeeper, there were a "great many men out of work at this time because of the depression, some have not had work for a year, and in desperate circumstances."[36] Men with large families were given job preference for work on this initial $14,000 project. In four months, during the bitter cold of a North Country winter, twenty-three Mohawk men with the aid of two teams completed the two-and-a-half-mile project. The Mohawk timekeeper described the feat:

> These men have worked in every kind of weather, in the cold or wet, so long as they knew they were getting paid for it, some continually worked in water knee deep. The cold weather which set in on November 29, somewhat improved the working conditions, as the water our main problem, lowered so that most of the men were out of water. On December 5 the mercury dropped to ten below zero, and it was the first real weather we had and it lasted for a week but the men came thru in fine spirits. The ground froze to the depth of about a foot, and it was necessary to start some of the men one hour earlier in the morning to break up the ground for the teams that came to work at eight in the morning.[37]

A second project, the Frogtown Ditch, began in November 1936. It proved to be largely an abortive effort caused by factors that affect the reservation to this day. Heeding Clinton Pierce's advice, federal officials and administrators had carefully attempted to make contact with tribal leaders on every reservation. The St. Regis political situation, however, was quite different and more politically explosive than other Iroquois communities. Harrison, Kinney, and Pierce in 1935 had secured the formal approval of the elected Mohawk Council to the St. Regis Drainage Project. Unfortunately, they had not bothered to secure the approval of a rival council, the Mohawks —who never accepted the state-imposed elected system, preferring instead the authority of hereditary leadership. One federal administrator described the factional activity and its effect on IECW work:

> On the St. Regis, a certain group of Indians, being dissatisfied with the present form of Government, which it is understood was established by State law, have revolted and established an organization based on their ancient tribal customs. On the assumption the present tribal council is unconstitutional they have chosen, through their clan mothers, chiefs and sub-chiefs, and claim their organization is the leading body. No decision regarding the matter has been rendered by any court. The new group claims a majority and is objecting to having work done under Emergency Conservation Work on the Reservation.[38]

Because of the strenuous opposition of Frank Terrance, a traditionalist opponent of the elected council who refused to allow the ditch to traverse his land, the Frogtown Project, scheduled to be one-and-a-half miles long on the southern part of the reservation, was only partially completed.[39] Terrance described his objection to the project in a letter to Commissioner Collier. As secretary and clerk of his Mohawk council, he condemned federal administrators coming on the reservation and making agreements with the elected council. He insisted that the Indians were not citizens of the United States but members of foreign nations and hence no agreement could be made by individual Indians with individual white officials; that those Indians who allowed the ditching were seduced by government money or promises of work; that these actions violated treaty rights; and that the Mohawks "are absolutely able to ditch our lands without any aid or assistance by the Federal or State Governments or by the PWA funds."[40]

A third part of the St. Regis Drainage Project, the construction of the East Ditch, began in late 1937. The project had initially been delayed because of failure to reach agreement with Canadian authorities. Since the St. Regis Reservation straddles the border, the Canadians feared that by granting permission for an outlet for drainage on their side of the international boundary, they would be liable for any damages caused by flooding of Mohawk lands on their side. After failing to work out an acceptable compromise over a two-year period, the New York Agency modified its plans by rerouting the ditches. Forty men and seven teams eventually constructed a ditch one-and-a-half miles long from the East Marsh of the reservation with an outlet at the St. Regis River.[41]

Overall, the St. Regis Drainage Project and the CCC-ID programs on the other Iroquois communities both in New York and in the west improved conditions on the reservations. At St. Regis alone, the CCC-ID at its peak employed a total of 130 enrollees in revolving shifts, or nearly one-fourth of the total work force.[42] An Iroquois, who had previously been enrolled at the St. Regis CCC-ID camp near Malone, described with pride his new position as assistant instructor at the Onondaga Reservation: "We are making a road straight over the hill and I am keeping right well. I suppose it's on account of having a fresh air job.... Last week we just completed a log shanty up in the woods so as to keep out of bad weather. It is made without a nail in the whole house and it will benefit the public. It will shelter woodcutters in winter and berry pickers in summer and this morning we are to continue on road work.[43] To him, an adult Onondaga with a family and no employment, as well as to a significant number of other Indians, the CCC-ID and other work-relief projects represented survival during the Great Depression, and importantly, a new deal from past indifference. Despite the objections of some traditionalists at St. Regis and other reservations, the leaders of the Confederacy itself at Onondaga and elsewhere came to accept the community action programs of the Roosevelt administration. No clearer proof of this statement can be found than in focusing on the work of the National Youth Administration (NYA) in Iroquoia.

The programs of the NYA and the WPA were largely independent of the control and supervision of the bureau, although the Indian Service had some impact on each through the cooperative efforts of the Indian agent and the community worker. The NYA, through the leadership of Louis R. Bruce, Jr., the agency's statewide supervisor of Indian programs, designed twenty-six work projects and employed 248 Iroquois youngsters by 1939. Every New York reservation was affected by the size and scope of the undertaking. It consisted of having tribal elders, such as Chief Jesse Lyons, teach Indian youth about their rich cultural heritage. Under the auspices of NYA,

Louis R. Bruce, Jr., commissioner of Indian affairs, 1969–72. Photograph courtesy of Louis R. Bruce, Jr.

youngsters also constructed recreation grounds and community work centers, especially the one at Onondaga, that served the artistic, educational and social needs of the reservations; served as nurses assistants at Indian clinics or as clerks in libraries; and, most successfully, worked as camp counselors specializing in teaching Indian lore.[44]

Bruce, a Mohawk-Sioux who was later appointed commissioner of Indian affairs by President Nixon in 1969, was a capable administrator of the NYA Indian programs. Coming into contact with Eleanor Roosevelt while working as a salesman at Rogers Peet, a clothing store in New York City, Bruce had been invited to the White House to discuss his ideas with President Roosevelt and Aubrey Williams, the head of the NYA. He was soon appointed to head the NYA for Indians in New York State, beginning in March 1936. As an Iroquois, born on the Onondaga Reservation in 1906, and educated at nearby Syracuse University, he was quite familiar with the people and their problems and became a strong advocate of securing better services for Iroquois youth, appealing to government officials throughout the mid- and late 1930s.[45]

Bruce's success was largely based on his ability to deal effectively with the Iroquois themselves. Advisory committees, composed of tribal leaders, screened and selected Indians for the program based upon ability and character. Quite significantly, the most prominent community leaders were well-represented in the programs both as formally hired instructors or as informal resource persons. Both Chiefs Andrew Gibson and George Thomas, two Onondagas who were Confederacy officials, contributed their expertise. Chief Thomas' son, E. Lee, served as an Indian camp counselor and illustrated the NYA's *The Indian Counselor's Handbook of Legends and Information on the Iroquois* while Beatrice Smith, Chief Gibson's granddaughter, also served in the program.[46]

Bruce's success was also based on his ability to build on earlier successful programs. The NYA's most heralded experiment, teaching Iroquois youth job skills to prepare them for employment as camp counselors, is a case in point. The idea for this program was first developed by Ray Fadden at the St. Regis Reservation. Without federal support, Fadden, a science teacher who had previously taught at the reservation school at Tuscarora, had organized the Akwesasne Mohawk Counselor Organization in the mid-1930s. The aim of the organization was to encourage Mohawk youth to participate in outdoor recreation, learn wilderness survival skills, teach Indian lore as well as arts and crafts, and most importantly, to inculcate an overall appreciation of their Indian heritage. After attending a Boy Scout

National Youth Administration Community Center, Onondaga Indian Reservation, 1940. The community center was built by Indian youth workers for the Onondaga Indians and was used for NYA programs and activities. Photograph courtesy of the Franklin D. Roosevelt Presidential Library.

jamboree in Walden, New York, accompanied by his troop of Mohawk scouts and becoming thoroughly embarrassed by the stereotypic portrayal of Indians during a pageant, Fadden resolved to teach his boys to serve as camp counselors in order to undo the ignorance and dispel the false images about Indians held by white youth. Since some of the Indian youngsters had little knowledge of their own culture, Fadden encouraged them to collect stories and learn crafts by listening to and watching their Mohawk elders at St. Regis. He also designed a program in outdoor conditioning and wilderness survival that required the youngsters to climb and hike through rugged parts of the Adirondack Mountains and to endure other physical trials. The success of the program became evident when the boys began to be hired as camp counselors.[47]

Bruce and Karl D. Helsey, the director of NYA in New York State, borrowed Fadden's idea and established similar undertakings for boys and girls on every Iroquois reservation, beginning with an initial model program at Onondaga. By 1937, 101 Indians had already gone through the program and were employed as camp counselors. The program grew rapidly, and, by April 1939, 171 Iroquois youth were "preparing themselves to bring Indian culture to boys and girls in camps this summer."[48] Besides being screened and selected by the Indian advisory committees, the boys and girls had to pass tests arranged by camping authorities, including those designed by Nelson Burris of the camp committee of the Children's Welfare Federation, and plan camp activities. One counselor-in-training patterned his camp government upon the Iroquois Confederacy's political structure with each camper belonging to a different nation of the League. Another wrote a pageant based upon the consolidation of the Six Nations to get camper involvement. In the training process, they acquired new knowledge of their heritage, including artistic styles, dances, herbalism, and songs.[49]

The NYA published a handbook in 1940 that served as a practical guide on the procedures to follow and the responsibilities of Iroquois camp counselors. The guide also contained information gathered by the youngsters from tribal elders in the project about Iroquois crafts, history, and legends. In addition, the handbook contained information on how to make a corn husk doll and recognize the headdresses of the Iroquois. It, as well, versed the youngsters in their treaty rights. Ray Fadden's influence was apparent throughout. The handbook included stories that he compiled such as "How the Mohawks Used the Tobacco Plant," "The Discovery of Fire," "Wampum," "The Creation," and "How Man was Created."[50]

The NYA Indian programs faded into memory with the coming of World War II, although Fadden's independent experiment lived on for several decades. In the process, the tough conditioning of the camp counselor program had not only prepared Indians for leadership responsibilities but had also trained them for service in another white man's war across the ocean. Most importantly, the NYA programs had helped instill pride in Indian youths at the crossroads of their lives.

More than any other work-relief project, the WPA's construction of the Tonawanda Indian Community House, which used virtually all Indian labor, stands as a living legacy of the New Deal. Erected on land adjacent to the reservation boundary nearest Akron, New York, this two-story building in the shape of a huge longhouse is still the focal point of reservation life, housing an auditorium, clinic, club rooms, classrooms for adult and juvenile

Ray Fadden (left) and Iroquois youth of the National Youth Administration project, late 1930s. Photograph courtesy of Louis R. Bruce, Jr.

education, a gymnasium, library, museum, and public showers.[51] Administered by a director who is an employee of the New York State Department of Social Services, this WPA project was built on land purchased by the Indians themselves as the Tonawanda Indian Reservation Library and Community Association. In the process of construction, the Tonawanda Senecas were instructed in masonry and carpentry skills for future employment.

This project was created as a result of the effective lobbying efforts and political savvy of Nameé Henricks, a white woman from Penn Yan, New York. Although the original idea for the project was conceived by Arthur C. Parker, director of the Rochester Municipal Museum, and a small group of Senecas headed by May Spring and Elsina Doctor, the building of the community center would not have been accomplished without Henricks'

May Spring in Seneca woman's costume, Tonawanda Indian Reservation, July 16, 1935. Photograph by William N. Fenton, courtesy of the William N. Fenton Collection, U.S. Indian Service Photographs, 1935–37.

persistence. In all, she made eleven trips at her own expense to Albany to confer with state WPA officials, Governor Lehman, and Commissioner of Social Welfare David Adie and three trips to Washington to confer with Eleanor Roosevelt, Commissioner Collier, prominent congressmen and national WPA administrators.[52]

Henricks, the wife of a minister who occasionally served as a visiting clergyman at Tonawanda, reacted to the poverty on the reservation.[53] Lester W. Herzog, head administrator for WPA programs in New York State, gave the rationale for a federally sponsored Tonawanda Indian Community House at the dedication ceremonies in 1939: "A chicken coop for a library, an unheated frame building for a meeting place and a darkened barn for a workshop seemed out of place in this modern world."[54]

As an individual active in numerous women's organizations as well as the Daughters of the American Revolution, Henricks used her longtime contacts to serve the needs of the Senecas. From the mid-1930s onward, she pressured state and federal officials for talking books for blind Indians, work-relief projects, road repairs, wells, and emergency food supplies during blizzards.[55] Working with the local library association and Parker, she began promoting the idea of a community center in early 1935. By March, the project was well underway. Parker and Henricks, working with a Tonawanda reservation committee headed by Elsina Doctor, May Spring, and Wyman Jemison, held meetings on the project that generated further community support.[56]

A formal proposal and architectural plans were then submitted to the New York State Department of Social Welfare and the Bureau of Indian Affairs with a supporting letter written by Parker commending the "project as a fundamental thing for the betterment of the Indians of the entire area. The Tonawanda band of Senecas is the only group without an adequate building for gatherings."[57] While attending a DAR convention in Washington in April, she did not miss an opportunity to talk about conditions at Tonawanda and the need for a center. She pigeonholed Elmer Thomas, chairman of the Senate Indian affairs committee, W. Carson Ryan, Jr., the director of Indian education, Commissioner Collier, and, most importantly, Eleanor Roosevelt.[58] After spending an hour discussing the project with Collier, the commissioner wrote to Parker insisting that he favored the idea of a community center but that the bureau had no money to fund construction. In a postscript, Collier noted that he was exploring the possibility of financing the building "under the New York Work-Relief 4 billion."[59] Through Ryan, Collier directed Fenton, his New York community worker, to assist Henricks and Parker in every way possible.[60] Collier's feelings about the project were revealed in a later letter to Eleanor Roosevelt. After once more formally endorsing the idea of a WPA-sponsored project, he reflected: "I do know that wherever Mrs. Henricks goes she makes friends for the Indians and for the administration."[61] By May, the promoters of the project named a board of directors headed by Elsina Doctor and incorporated as the "Tonawanda Indian Community House Association" under New York State law.[62]

Eleanor Roosevelt's support was the necessary ingredient for the success of the project. Without her commitment, the Tonawanda Indian Community House would not have been built. She invited Henricks to the White House to explain the needs of the Senecas, inquired about the feasibility of government sponsorship, endorsed the project to federal and state officials, provided Henricks with letters of introduction to key politicians, overcame bureaucratic tape at every turn, and used her position as "First Lady" to politically strong arm acceptance of the work-relief proposal from reluctant administrators.[63]

The project was faced with an uphill battle. A major problem involved the bypassing of the chief's council at Tonawanda, a deliberate move to get the project rolling as fast as possible to secure WPA funding without being held up by intertribal factional political activity. Moreover, because of the need for a group to take the lead and be a responsible sponsoring body or "holding agency" under the laws of the state, traditional Iroquois beliefs about themselves as an independent sovereignty would have emerged to block the council's support for the center.[64] Consequently, when the council learned of the project, some expressed resentment since they had not been consulted and had little control of the project beforehand.[65] Because of the desperate need for a center which was recognized even by the most offended of these Indian leaders, the opposition dissipated when Henricks began to get results. With the added assurance of the well-respected Parker that the community center association would "consult your honorable body wherever possible to secure the best advice," the project became a source of pride and one favored by the community at large.[66] When the cornerstone of the building was laid in May 1937, Chief Aaron Poodry, who initially had been offended by the bypassing of the tribal council, hailed the all-Indian project and hoped it was the "beginning of a new era of self-help."[67]

Another problem involved the location of the building. Both Henricks and Parker believed that they could convince state officials to service and maintain an Indian center but only with concessions. If the state could be allowed to lease the land adjacent but contiguous to the reservation on a tract purchased by the community association, then, they believed, the state would be more willing to undertake the project. Since white leasing arrangements of reservation lands in the past produced unfavorable situations, distrust, and fears of land dispossession, the project organizers hoped to allay these tribal concerns and minimize intratribal political activity at the same time. Moreover, neighboring townspeople from Akron, fearful that a loss of business would accrue if an Indian center, which would be off the tax rolls, was built on or near the reservation and resentful that the Indians were being considered for WPA funding on a project that excluded whites, protested after the formal announcement of the plan. The Tonawanda Indian Community House Association, under Parker's urging, favored a more rural location near Basom, away from the road to Akron that was noted for its liquor traffic. Two potential sites were chosen for construction—one off the reservation near Basom and the other just over the Akron side of the reservation boundary. Largely because the Basom site required more expense in the sinking of costly wells and pumping water a considerable distance, the Tonawanda Indian Community House Association purchased the Akron tract after raising $450 from the reservation community.[68]

The community association faced an even more troublesome problem. David C. Adie, the New York State commissioner of welfare, raised serious objections to the plan almost from its inception partially because of departmental and personal rivalry with Lester Herzog, the WPA head in New York. Largely motivated by departmental budgetary considerations, Adie, at the last minute and just prior to formal WPA approval, insisted that the project was unsatisfactory since the proposal had no adequate description of the lands on which the building would be constructed and no information about who would maintain and be responsible for the center after completion, since the majority of the Senecas were on relief and his department had inadequate funding. In a questioning tone, he added that the project would set an expensive precedent, leading to similar facilities on other Iroquois reservations.[69] The project was rocked by Adie's objections since it required a governmental sponsor, such as the Department of Social Welfare, before WPA approval.[70]

Parker and Henricks attempted to counter Adie's criticism of the proposed project. Angered by the tone of the letter and by the delay in gaining acceptance, Parker responded to Adie's objection point by point, requested a full description of the land to be purchased with a signed option-to-buy statement from the Tonawanda Indian Community House

Association, wrote a formal justification for the project to the WPA office in Albany and forwarded a letter to Eleanor Roosevelt castigating Adie. While in Albany on another lobbying effort, Henricks went over Adie's head. She secured approval for state maintenance and financing of the center after completion from A. S. Weber, New York State budget director, Charles Poletti, then special counsel to Governor Lehman, and Arthur Swartz, a powerful Erie County assemblyman and friend of Adie's. Because of her close ties to Mrs. Roosevelt and the commitment of the WPA to underwrite the entire construction costs of the building, Henricks was able to convince Swartz, Weber, and other Albany politicos of the value of the project.[71] Since the planned WPA project took the burden of home relief off the shoulders of county and state welfare administrators, Adie and local New York officials themselves reluctantly gave their support for the project.[72]

On March 31, 1936, Assemblyman Swartz and State Senator Twomey of Brooklyn introduced a bill, which was largely drafted by Parker, calling for New York State "to provide the maintenance of the Tonawanda Community house under the Supervision of the State Department of Social Welfare" after its erection by the WPA on lands acquired by the Tonawanda Indian Community House Association and leased to the State for ninety-nine years. The building was constructed solely for the use of the "reservation Indian community for the purpose of housing a recreational room and auditorium and space for laboratories, offices, and rooms to be used for a library, museum, clubrooms and space allocation for groups who may be assisted in vocational and industrial guidance," adding that the structure would house "other facilities for adult education which may equip the community for gainful occupation, all of which shall contribute to the social and economic betterment of the Indians of the Tonawanda reservation." The bill also provided $5,000 to the state department of social welfare for the maintenance, operation, and supervision of the center.[73]

On May 15, 1936, the New York State Legislature passed the bill, and work on the project began in November. The WPA expended $60,000 for the construction of the center, improving the grounds around the building and for a second project entailing the extension of the water supply system of Akron to the community house.[74] As a job-training program in carpentry, masonry, and general construction skills, the project had an added significance to the community. Except for two instructors and the architect John T. Carroll of Albany, the WPA hired only Tonawanda Senecas. Mrs. Henricks explained this important feature of the project to Governor Lehman in 1938, calling it the "only trade school for adult education on a single reservation in

To my chosen people, The Tonawanda Senecas
with sincere devotion and affection
Sah-nee-weh
Mrs Walter A. Henricks

Mrs. Walter A. Henricks. Photograph courtesy of the Tonawanda Indian Community House, photograph of original by James Stapleton.

Eleanor Roosevelt. Photograph courtesy of the Tonawanda Indian Community House, photograph of original by James Stapleton.

the state of New York."[75] Even before the completion of the project, some of the Senecas trained were hired as skilled workers in the private sector off the reservation in Buffalo and Batavia.[76]

The Tonawanda Indian Community House was formally dedicated and opened by Eleanor Roosevelt on May 13, 1939. It included a library of ten thousand books collected through the efforts of Parker, Henricks, Fenton, the DAR, Buffalo's Grosvenor Library, and through newspaper and radio appeals that replaced an earlier community library which had burned in a fire in 1937.[77] Despite the initiatives of Henricks, Parker, and Roosevelt and the initial protests of some of the chief's council, the Tonawanda Indian Community House was a community effort, one that is valued by all Senecas to this day.

The myriad of federal government-sponsored programs had accomplished what Collier and Harrison had hoped: they had erased some of the Iroquois bitterness as a result of the IRA referendum of 1935. It was the community worker experiment as well as the CCC-ID, the NYA, and the WPA, rather than the efforts at tribal political reorganization, that were the New Deal for most Iroquois peoples.[78] The community action and work-relief programs, with the Iroquois themselves or with non-Indians who had longstanding ties to them in positions of authority, were the heart of the New Deal for these people. Because of the significant federal responses to the economic crisis facing these Indians, their Iroquois kinsmen from across the Canadian border attempted to secure work relief. Although they were denied employment, the very fact that this occurrence was frequent indicates both the terrible conditions in Canada and the economic attractiveness of Washington's programs to these Indians.[79] These efforts were much more than make-work jobs to the Iroquois. No clearer example of this fact can be found than Arthur C. Parker's WPA Seneca Arts Project.

8

THE SENECA RENAISSANCE
1935–41

It is well to realize, however, that the "relics" within the museum are never greater than the service the museum extends to the public.

Arthur C. Parker
A Manual for History Museums

It is the theory of the Rochester Museum that our Indians need a new teaching, one that will build personal pride, a deeper respect for themselves as a creative people who are capable of producing things that the world admire. The museum wishes to bring back to the Indians a knowledge of the beauty of their ancient arts.

(Rochester) *Museum Service*
January 1936

IN LATE JULY 1941, a fire swept through the old school building on the Tonawanda Reservation near Akron, New York, ending a unique New Deal experiment in reviving Seneca Indian arts and crafts that had begun in 1935. In its own way, the fire equaled in symbolic importance Albany's tragic capitol fire of 1911, for each destroyed a significant body of material relating to Iroquois life and culture. One man provides a link between the two sad events. Arthur C. Parker, then an archeologist at the New York State Museum, witnessed the fire of 1911 and was deeply moved by the loss of a vast quantity of Iroquois materials. The event was one of several factors that influenced Parker's role, three decades later, in conceiving and directing the Seneca Arts Project, some of whose products were then destroyed in the fire of 1941. The Seneca Arts Project was designed by Parker and sponsored by his Rochester Municipal Museum (now the Rochester Museum and Science Center), at Tonawanda and more briefly at the Cattaraugus Indian Reservation. About 100 artists, working at separate times, produced approximately five thousand works of art and reproductions, including wooden false face masks, bowls, cradleboards, ladles and spoons; silver brooches and earrings; woven baskets and burden straps (tumplines); embroidered beadwork, moose hair and porcupine quill work that were used for assorted costume designs; and paintings of Iroquoian life employing pen and ink as well as wash drawing, water coloring, and oil painting. Most significantly, this project provided employment for indigent Indians during the Great Depression, contributed to the fostering of community cohesiveness and pride among the Senecas, and created for the Rochester Museum one of the richest ethnological collections of art in the United States.[1]

The Seneca Arts Project, funded initially by the Temporary Emergency Relief Administration (TERA) and after 1935 by the Works Progess Administration (WPA), was shaped by three major forces: the economic crisis of the Great Depression and its resulting impact on the Indians of New York State; the declining quality of traditional Seneca arts and crafts prior to the project's beginnings; and most significantly, the thought of Parker. Without the economic collapse of the country and the need for relief measures, there would not have been a Seneca renaissance. It is important to note that the WPA's myriad relief measures helped reshape the nation by employing 3 million people and spending 11 billion dollars, and that, in the search for national recovery after 1933, government-sponsored cultural projects, in the words of Alfred Haworth Jones, "furthered an adventure in national rediscovery which represented one of the most far-reaching developments of the Depression decade."[2] Out of economic necessity came the opportunity to develop, revive and experiment.[3]

The setting on New York's Indian reservations further added support to Parker's experiment in combining work relief with artistic revival. Because of the curtailment in factory work and in the construction trades, many Senecas at Cattaraugus turned to subsistence agriculture to survive, while at Tonawanda virtually everyone was out of work except those who had part-time employment in the gypsum mines at Akron, New York. Health conditions were abysmal. Tuberculosis reached epidemic proportions at Cattaraugus while pneumonia struck periodically, seriously affecting life in the Longhouse district at Tonawanda. Moreover, racial discrimination further limited the avenues open to aspiring Indians.[4] Hence, the Seneca Arts Project was

Seneca artists (left to right) Rose Spring, Alice Poodry, Melinda Skye, and Martha Skye making costumes, Tonawanda Indian Reservation, 1930s. Photograph by William G. Frank, courtesy of the Rochester Museum and Science Center, Rochester, New York.

clearly viewed by Indian participants and non-Indian administrators as a means to overcome the worsening situation.

Iroquois art was in a state of crisis in the early 1930s. The Senecas had nearly lost their knowledge of certain art forms or had adopted Plains Indian-styled traits that were not traditionally Iroquois. The weaving of basswood into burden straps and embroidery in moose hair and porcupine quills had virtually disappeared. Moreover, western costume designing was rapidly replacing centuries-old patterns of the Eastern Woodlands. On public occasions most Senecas of the period donned Sioux war bonnets instead of the Iroquois *Gastoweh,* the traditional cap as well as symbol of their unique Indianness. Furthermore, Iroquois art had not only changed under influences from other Indians but also declined in quality to meet the less-than-artistic demand of the tourist.[5] It was this artistic crisis in a time of

William Gordon wearing a *Gastoweh* and carrying a war club, Tonawanda Indian Reservation, 1930s. Photograph by William G. Frank, courtesy of the Rochester Museum and Science Center, Rochester, New York.

governmental experimentation caused by the economic collapse of the country that afforded Parker the opportunity to establish the Seneca Arts Project.

As a nationally recognized archeologist, ethnologist, folklorist, historian, author of children's books, defender of Indian rights, and museum administrator, Parker had dreamed of the possibility of such a project for years.[6] It would not be an overstatement to say that the Seneca Arts Project, as it functioned from 1935–41, was Parker's personal project and that he viewed it as the greatest accomplishment of his life. He conceived it, wrote the necessary proposals, hired all the Indian and non-Indian personnel on the reservations and at the museum directly tied to the project, provided the professional direction, umbrella of sponsorship and material, and quite significantly, was the sole artistic and ethnographic judge of the quality of the work produced. Equally important for the continued survival of the project for six and one-half years, Parker was the master promoter, the brilliant publicist, and speechmaker who helped get the necessary support and funding during the crisis times that occurred on an annual basis from 1935 to 1941.[7]

Parker was motivated by many factors. Although not technically Seneca, his roots, nevertheless, were deeply planted in Iroquois history both at Cattaraugus and Tonawanda reservations.[8] His grandfather was Nicholson H. Parker, a well-educated Seneca farmer on Cattaraugus who served as an interpreter for the United States government; while his great uncle Ely S. Parker, a life chief at Tonawanda and Nicholson's older brother, was the famous Civil War general and later the first Indian to be appointed United States Commissioner of Indian Affairs. It was at Ely S. Parker's home at Tonawanda that Lewis Henry Morgan began his classic ethnological studies of the Iroquois, a fact that was never lost on Arthur C. Parker. Consequently, Parker was always aware of his special intellectual and kinship links to the history of American anthropology as well as to the Seneca peoples.[9]

Parker spent the first eleven years of his life on Cattaraugus until his family moved to White Plains, New York. These formative years helped shape his outlook on life. He was adopted into the Bear Clan and given a Seneca name, *Gáwasowaneh,* "Big Snowsnake." In later years he was an officer in the Society of American Indians and the National Congress of American Indians.[10] In the economic crisis of the 1930s, Parker never forgot his roots and his commitment to the people he had known. Writing less as a museum builder than as an individual concerned with the welfare of the Indians of western New York, Parker clearly revealed his political and

Arthur C. Parker and secretary in his office at the Rochester Museum at Edgertown Park, 1934. Photograph courtesy of the Rochester Museum and Science Center, Rochester, New York.

emotional leaning in an article about the Seneca Arts Project written in 1935: "Long had they [Indians of New York] been taught to imitate all the cultural patterns of the European. Native thinking, native art, native creative ability practically had been crushed out. With this had perished the greater part of the spirit of the people. Formal school education and even religious teaching had served to make the Indians feel that nothing that their ancestors thought or produced was aught but painful evidence of paganism and savagery. The result has been anything but beneficial."[11] The "racial genius" of, what he would refer to as, the "amazing Iroquois" could only be recognized once more through an infusion of pride by means of an artistic renaissance.[12]

Parker's years as archeologist at the New York State Museum in Albany also influenced his later decision about the need for an arts project. As was noted earlier, he witnessed the fire that devastated the west end of the New

York Capitol and State Library. Two-thirds of the Lewis Henry Morgan Collection, the finest ethnographical materials on the Iroquois in the world, and several other smaller collections were destroyed. As he later wrote: "It was an awful experience, I assure you, to see the fruits of one's labors and the results of 60 years by others shrivel up in the merciless flame.... the most discouraging feature of it all is that most of this material can never be replaced."[13] As the self-appointed successor to Morgan, whom he considered almost a spiritual and blood relative, Parker, despite his myriad activities—conducting archeological surveys, writing scholarly ethnological works, and crusading and organizing for Indian rights set about rebuilding the state museum's holdings, soliciting help from well-known collectors.[14] As an avid collector and trader with solid ties to many reservations, he began the impossible task of retracing Morgan's work. Handicapped in his efforts by a parsimonious New York State Legislature, skipped over for promotion, and largely unappreciated, Parker left Albany in 1925 to accept the directorship of the Rochester Municipal Museum.[15]

Parker's preoccupation with Morgan followed him to Rochester, ironically the site of many of Morgan's greatest accomplishments. In writing about the Seneca Arts Project in 1936, he compared his achievement to that of Morgan: "Like the specimens made for Lewis Henry Morgan in 1849, our results are destined to become of historic importance." In this and other writings, the ghost of Morgan appears through the pages. As one of the last great self-taught anthropologists, Parker relived Morgan's amateur route to scholarly respectability, and, in the opinion of William Fenton, had made his most important and scholarly contribution to archeology and ethnology while at the New York State Museum.[16] Now as a museum director in Rochester, the very site of Morgan's work, Parker, the great collector, finally had the opportunity to come full circle in his romantic delusions of being the equal to the "father of anthropology."[17] Writing about the Indian Arts Project in 1936, Parker clearly acknowledged his debt to Morgan:

We are, indeed, deeply interested in the Seneca Indians of western New York. Perhaps this is a Rochester tradition for it was Lewis Henry Morgan who made sociology and ethnology something that could be understood and provided a key to the underlying factors of primitive society. Morgan was a Rochester man. During the period 1845–1881, he made the first real studies of an Indian tribe ever undertaken. In doing so he collected the utensils and craft work of these Indians and deposited them in the State Cabinet (Museum) at Albany, writing careful reports. Later he published

The League of the Iroquois (1851) and *Ancient Society* (1877). These publications were provided with drawings and lithographic prints that illustrated in meticulous fashion the material culture of the New York Indians.[18]

Hence, the Seneca Arts Project, to some degree, was an attempt by Parker to emulate the work of his scholarly model, Morgan. Yet, despite Parker's high standard, the project's ethnographic reproductions could never match the irreplaceable Morgan collection destroyed in Albany in 1911.

Despite the promises of Rochester's men of wealth and politicians to commit themselves to making the city's museum a showplace, Parker soon faced a situation similar to that he had encountered in Albany. Cramped into small quarters in Edgerton Park, the Rochester Municipal Museum in the 1920s had to vie for funds annually and overcome public apathy. Promises of new headquarters for the museum were shelved when the Great Depression hit in force. In one year, the museum's operating budget was sharply cut from $60,000 to $17,000. In disgust, Parker quit in December 1932, only to reassume his duties when the museum's budget was partially restored by the city council.[19] By 1932, his desire to emulate one of Morgan's greatest achievements by building another great Iroquois collection seemed only a fantastic dream, as did his hope of transforming a local museum into a nationally respected center of intellectual activity.

Ironically, Parker's opportunity to achieve both goals—building a great museum and recreating a respectable ethnological collection of Iroquois art — came as a result of hard times, for his ambitions coincided with governmental willingness to sponsor programs to offset the economic crisis. The Temporary Emergency Relief Administration, established in New York in September 1931, had begun its relief program for artists by December 1932, the exact month of Parker's threatened resignation from the Rochester Municipal Museum. Within the next fifteen months, Parker started to draft the plans for what later became the Seneca Arts Project. By April 1934, he already had a detailed proposal that he circulated to New York State agencies outlining his aims.[20] Initially combined with a second proposal devoted to massive archeological surveys of the Genesee Valley, the Seneca Arts Project, by July 1934, had an existence of its own, separate from other objectives of the museum and with its own personnel. In his three-page proposal, Parker clearly specified his goals: "The Rochester Municipal Museum proposes a project by which the almost extinct arts and crafts of the New York Indians may be preserved and put on a production basis in order that such activity and products may contribute to the relief and self-support of the said Indian population."[21]

According to Parker, the plan was to manufacture the articles and record the "activities and general ceremonies of the New York Indians"; the instructors and supervision of the work would be by "native experts"; the Rochester Museum would assume responsibility for the success of the work. He continued by stressing Rochester's proximity to several Iroquois reservations, by mentioning that some Indians had special knowledge to contribute to emphasize the need for grass-roots support; and by emphasizing that "about 40 percent of the Indian population on these reservations" were on relief. He added that the museum would supply tools and raw materials but that all articles produced "will be turned over to the said museum as its property and which it can use for exchange or other distribution with other museums or the public." This key provision enabled the museum, by trading part of the Iroquois materials produced, to acquire a richly diverse North American Indian collection as well as other ethnological exhibits. In conclusion, Parker suggested that the proposed program was largely rehabilitational and would provide the Indians with meaningful employment in hard times.[22]

Parker's singular role in the project was evident from the beginning. His project coordinator at the museum, C. Carleton Perry, suggested, in a letter to TERA, the basic reason for Parker's direct involvement: "May I emphasize the importance of having Doctor Parker assume supervision of the project. He has the right connections with the Indians of Western New York. He also is the best authority on Indians and knows the Indians, particularly of the east, better than any other authority. . . . If this project is going to be successful as the means of rehabilitation, it is necessary that he act as their leader."[23] It is clear from the records of the project and from interviewing staff at the Rochester Museum and Indian participants that Perry had pinpointed the major reason for the project's eventual success, namely Parker's role as leader. Unlike the New Deal tribal reorganization programs fostered from distant Washington by Commissioner Collier and the Department of the Interior, which had limited reservation support and consequently no success among the Iroquois in New York, the Seneca Arts Project was truly a community-based operation on two reservations that Parker had known well since his childhood.

Parker's thirty or more years of friendships, family associations, and field work experiences at Cattaraugus and Tonawanda had brought him into contact with Senecas who had special skills to further the aims of the project.

Seneca Arts Project craftspeople, Tonawanda Indian Reservation, late 1930s. Kneeling, front row: Jesse J. Cornplanter, Jesse Hill, William Gordon. In semicircle, second row: Laura Kennedy, Alice Poodry, unidentified, Martha Skye (holding mask), Ernest Smith (wearing tie), Rose Smith Spring, Sarah Hill, Robert Tahamont, Lillian Blackchief. Back row: Arnold Sundown, Ira Mitten, Jimmy Jonathan, Perry Smith, unidentified, Wayman Jemison, Harrison Ground, Melinda Skye, Elon Webster, Julia Black. Photograph by William G. Frank, courtesy of the Rochester Museum and Science Center, Rochester, New York.

After TERA's acceptance of his application for funding, Parker set about hiring the personnel. He sent out inquiries to educational leaders informing them of the project and asking them to locate competent basket weavers, carvers, quill workers, potters, and silversmiths who might qualify for work relief and contribute to an arts project. Workers not only had to qualify by meeting the requirements of indigency for work relief set by the New York

Jesse Cornplanter at Tonawanda Indian Reservation, 1937 (left) and 1940 (right). Photographs courtesy of the Rochester Museum and Science Center, Rochester, New York, and the National Archives.

State Department of Social Welfare, but also had to meet Parker's discerning standards in Iroquois art. Since his concept of excellence depended on his remembrance of the great Morgan collection destroyed in 1911, much of what he sought from the project could be classified as ethnographic reproduction and not original art. Yet, despite the attempt at reproduction, the Seneca Arts Project materials that remain today in the Rochester Museum exhibit the unique qualities of individual participants, many of whom are considered the foremost Iroquois artists of the twentieth century.[24]

Jesse J. Cornplanter, the famous Seneca raconteur, radio personality, and "show Indian," was one of the artists who was hired by Parker. Cornplanter, the son of the leader of the Longhouse, had first met Parker at the turn of the century. As the renowned "boy artist of Iroquoia,"

Cornplanter had illustrated scenes depicting Iroquois life and legends used in the early *Bulletins* of the New York State Museum, some of which were written by Parker himself. By the 1930s, he had emerged as the finest mask carver in Iroquoia to complement his other artistic talents, and owing to his unique awareness of Seneca mores, music, folktales, and language, he was well respected for his knowledge of the Old Way. In addition, physical disability prevented him from engaging in heavy labor on other work-relief projects.[25] Cornplanter was a natural choice for Parker's project.

At Tonawanda he performed two major functions. As the master woodcarver he produced the finest and uniquely styled false face masks as models for other artists to imitate. More important, he was the major resource person for the oral traditions and legends of the Iroquois, a source of themes, symbolism, and overall artistic inspiration. It was his influence on Ernest Smith, the foremost painter of the project, that helped formulate the traditional scenes that appear in Smith's many paintings for the project. Although a deliberate artist with serious health problems and one who scorned all rules and regulations of administrators, Cornplanter was an important part of the Tonawanda experiment in reviving Iroquois art. Moreover, he and other exceptional mask carvers such as Harrison Ground, William Gordon, and Elon Webster, were to produce hundreds of masks in basswood of every style known that were requested by Parker.[26]

Parker's personal contacts were also reflected in his choice for administrative personnel at the reservation level. Indian supervisors included Cephas Hill and Robert Tahamont at Tonawanda, and Roy Jimerson and Arlene Doxtator at Cattaraugus. The foremen kept the time sheets and handled the everyday problems that arose. Both Hill and Tahamont illustrate Parker's thinking. Tahamont was an educated Abenaki Indian, not Seneca, and a skilled carpenter who had married one of Parker's cousins at Tonawanda. As a member of Parker's family and lacking artistic ability, he was selected for his trustworthiness. More significantly, Hill played a major role on the project. As the "resident intellectual" on the reservation, well traveled, extremely personable and one who understood Seneca, he was the necessary liaison to the community to make the project succeed.[27]

Hill's role can also be seen in other areas. He and William N. Fenton, then working for the Bureau of Indian Affairs as a community worker on Tonawanda, had periodic brainstorming sessions with Parker on the progress and direction of the project. They visited nearly all the museums, historical societies, and galleries in New York that contained Iroquois ethnographic material and photographed collections to serve as models for Indian craftsmen and artists. They also located an old woman, Sarah Hill, who was one of the few surviving Senecas able to weave the old-style baskets, burden straps, and sashes. With string models and Sarah Hill's instruction, the project was able to revive this nearly extinct craft, and Everett Parker emerged as one of the premier weavers of modern Iroquoia. To preserve this extraordinary record of achievement, the project, by then under WPA auspices, made a film documenting the making of burden straps from initial stripping of the basswood tree in the spring to the final completion of the weaving.[28]

Though he delegated day-to-day correspondence and administrative responsibilities to Perry, Parker was involved in every major decision and

Cephas Hill at Tonawanda Indian Reservation, 1939. Photograph courtesy of the Rochester Museum and Science Center, Rochester, New York.

Sarah Hill making a burden strap, Tonawanda Indian Reservation, 1930s. Photograph by William G. Frank, courtesy of the Rochester Museum and Science Center, Rochester, New York.

nearly every piece of work produced in the project. Since few of the artists had any formal training, Parker created, in effect, the "Iroquois School of Art." It was Parker who told Ernest Smith what myth or legend to paint. Smith, an unemployed automobile worker, was soon to achieve national attention. Mrs. Audrey McMahon, the assistant director of the Federal Arts Project of the Works Progress Administration, hailed his scenes of Iroquois life and folklore as "unique" and "the most striking work" on such a project in the country.[29] Smith's numerous canvasses, inspired by Parker and Cornplanter, by Smith's mother, and by the tales told by the old people on the

Everett Parker weaving a burden strap, Tonawanda Indian Reservation, 1937.
Photograph courtesy of the Rochester Museum and Science Center, Rochester,
New York.

reservation, were peopled by fantasies described by William Fenton as
"flapping ears, devouring mouths, long-nosed kidnappers, little people who
painted the strawberries and turned them to ripen, stone-coated giants and
an occasional monster like naked bear, the exploding wren, horned serpents
and flying heads." Encouraged by the well-known painter Roy M. Mason,
n.a. (1886– 1973), on how to do a "wash" with watercolors, Smith's paintings
on charter myths of the Iroquois Confederacy; on Iroquois traditional life;
and Iroquois folklore remain the most important works, ethnologically and
artistically, made on the project.[30]

Parker not only inspired the themes of the works of art, but was also an
exacting critic. To inspire the artists and craftsmen, he frequently brought in
illustrations found in Morgan's writings, or artifacts found in Iroquois
archeological sites by himself or William A. Ritchie, but few items received

Ernest Smith at Tonawanda Indian Reservation, 1938. Photograph courtesy of the Rochester Museum and Science Center, Rochester, New York.

"The Earth, Our Mother (Sky Woman)," painting by Ernest Smith, 1936. Photograph courtesy of the Rochester Museum and Science Center, Rochester, New York.

"Forming the League of the Iroquois (The Council with Tadodaho as the League was Started)," painting by Ernest Smith, 1936. Photograph courtesy of the Rochester Museum and Science Center, Rochester New York.

his total approbation. As an emotionally restrained person by temperament, he rarely expressed himself fully in his usual sign of contentment and glee: "It's a pippin." Most works won token approval from Parker, leading the Seneca artists to work even harder to gain his complete acceptance.[31]

Throughout the operations of the project, Parker was especially concerned with quality and authenticity. As a museum director intending to

Ernest Smith at Tonawanda Indian Reservation, February 4, 1938. Photograph courtesy of the Rochester Museum and Science Center, Rochester, New York.

build a great collection and hoping to acquire art worthy of trading with other institutions throughout the world, he emphasized these conditions. As late as December 1939, Perry wrote to Cephas Hill complaining of the quality of certain works, insisting on orders from Parker that the "costumes are somewhat clownish rather than authentic Iroquois."[32] Furthermore, the correspondence of the project is filled with Perry's attempts to acquire authentic working materials, including animal bones, buckskins, black ash splint, and porcupine quills.[33] The quest for accuracy is revealed in a letter sent by Perry to an Oklahoma Indian trading post in 1937: "Do you have any Indian tanned deer skin? If so, will you kindly quote prices. We are looking for skins as nearer like those used by Indians in the Eastern Woodland Group in the sixteenth century, which are not exactly the same as the buckskin used by the Plains' Indians. However, if the only thing you have available is buckskin, I would appreciate having you send a small sample of skin for examination."[34]

Parker's attempts at quality control also took on other dimensions. He slyly fostered rivalry between the two reservations by telling the artists in each community that their works were less worthy than he had seen at the other one. Nevertheless, the Tonawanda experiment received first priority. Because Tonawanda was only forty miles from Rochester, in contrast to Cattaraugus' 100-mile distance, and was in poorer economic condition, Parker, it is evident, favored the Tonawanda program. Although the Cattaraugus program succeeded in establishing a tribal museum temporarily at the Thomas Indian School and Orphan Asylum, developing mural arts depicting Iroquois life, and encouraging the work of skilled artists including the painter Sanford Plummer, the experiment was the first to succumb to budget cuts.[35]

The success of the project is reflected not only in the quality and quantity of the art produced but also in the Seneca response. Senecas continued to seek employment on the project throughout the life of the program. Sarah Hill, the weaver, in attempting to get back on the project in 1938, asserted that she would willingly give up her pension if she had the opportunity to return. Although economic necessity was the major impetus for application, the spirit of cooperation, the good-natured camaraderie and competition, the festive surroundings, and the instillation of community pride all contributed to the arts project's general acceptance by the Seneca people as a whole.[36] In spite of some grumblings from people excluded from the project or from a few Longhouse people who objected to the secular carving of ceremonial false faces, most would agree with one old Seneca woman who referred to the experiment as a "wonderful and valuable project started from the Indian side of the question."[37] Jesse Cornplanter himself also emphasized the infusion of pride in the work accomplished by the project: "It really is wonderful the way we are doing in this project, [sic] there are some real nice pieces of craftmanship, you would be surprised to see the fine pieces of Silver brooches, Seneca Women's Overdress, and many of the things our people made and used ages ago. It is our own work, our means of earning, our living."[38]

Despite community support, Parker's project was faced with a large number of problems. The major concern was budgetary. Parker had the responsibility of securing necessary funding from three specific sources: the Rochester City Council from 1935–41, TERA in 1935, and WPA from December 1935 to 1941. On at least three separate occasions, he was informed that the program at Tonawanda would be shut down. Until July 1941, partly as a result of his writing and promotional abilities and his ability to work with both Democrats and Republicans as well as Rochester's men of wealth, Parker was able to save the arts project.[39] In a letter to the Rochester

City administration, Perry cited that it was "very good business" for Rochester to partially fund the project, using the rationale that the cost had been minimal even if the museum had been able to purchase the materials made on the project from private traders.[40] Realizing the limitations of appealing to civic pride during the country's worst depression, he added: "There are also a good many hundreds of records and manufactured objects made for us on the project which are priceless due to the fact that they will never be duplicated. There is other material of average quality which through exchange with other museums brings to us much needed material at a minimum of cost. From the viewpoint of ethnologists and anthropologists of other museums, based on our own experience, it is safe to say that this material is easily worth three times its total cost." At a time when other Rochester Museum projects were cut by the exigencies of ward politics and the economic crisis of depression, the Rochester City Council actually increased the program's budget. Although the WPA sharply cut back its funding after 1939, Parker's administrative skill is manifest in the longevity of the project.[41]

One of his tactics was to have the Senecas adopt influential political leaders. Governor Herbert Lehman of New York State was given an Indian name — "Hai-wa-eh-het-tah" or "One who governs with Justice" — while Lester W. Herzog, the WPA director in New York State, was dubbed "Sa-Go-Ya-Da-Geh-Hus" or "He Helps All." Another device was to plant newspaper stories and issue frequent news releases that presented the project's aims and highlighted its accomplishments — in some cases stretching the truth. For example, in news stories on Ernest Smith's accomplishments, he insisted that Smith had never painted before. In addition, Parker promoted the project through his own Rochester radio program, his sponsorship of pageants, and his highly organized outreach program to Genesee Valley schools, clubs, and organizations.[42]

Throughout the tenure of the program, Parker and his administrative staff also had to contend with the problems presented by the complex bureaucratic tangle of federal, state, county, and municipal agencies. He had to wend his way through the maze of administrators of the New York State Department of Social Welfare at Albany and Buffalo; TERA at Albany; the WPA offices in Washington and Albany; county desks of each of these agencies; as well as several city departments in Rochester. Jurisdictional ambiguity complicated matters further since both reservations are located within several counties.

Another thorny matter was the difficulty of arranging prompt payment from TERA and the WPA to the artists on the project. At Tonawanda,

Cephas Hill delivered the work sheets to the New York State Department of Social Welfare offices in Buffalo which would then forward them after processing to the TERA (and after the demise of TERA, to the WPA) office in Albany. Checks would then be forwarded from Albany to the Rochester Museum where Parker himself, Arleigh Hill, or Perry would deliver them personally to the project workers at Tonawanda. Delays in payment occurred, and, in one case, the Indians waited eight weeks for the money.[43]

Combined with these logistical problems was the low pay scale accorded the workers. The Seneca artists received about $.50 per hour, a considerably lower rate than in other work-relief projects.[44] Both the Indians and administrators expressed dismay about wages. In a letter written to TERA in 1935, Perry clearly outlined the problem:

> It is difficult, I realize, to determine what is the prevailing rate in Rochester for such people as artists, researchers, archeologists, entomologists and preparators, for there is no other institution similar to ours doing creative work which calls for a considerable background of training and experience. However, we do feel that those occupations which are unionized are getting better consideration, so far as hourly rate is concerned, than those which are purely professional and not organized. For example, it seems rather out of line to think that an artist of merit should draw $.60 an hour whereas an ordinary house painter is drawing $1.20 an hour. Nevertheless, we do not consider this our own problem and feel that in the main our workers are meeting the situation well and must be brought to realize that it is at present a matter of relief for the needy rather than paying adequate salaries.[45]

And, the artists' own temperament complicated Parker's administrative task. The nine-to-five timeclock regimen of the project proved inconducive to artistic expression. As in other WPA arts projects around the nation involving non-Indians, the Senecas insisted that they were artists, not assembly-line workers. Jesse Cornplanter, responding to criticism for not turning out more masks, asserted that he tried "to do the work as one skilled in his craft should do" and that the artists were "not working on production" but were "craftsmen."[46]

It is also clear that reservation poverty and its resulting impact on the family and the tribal unit affected the Seneca Arts Project significantly. Problems with alcohol, the law, and marital relationships contributed to loss of time, excessive absence, and even suspension from the project. The WPA office in Albany warned project foreman Cephas Hill that his artists' frequent delinquency from work could not be tolerated.[47] It is a tribute to the Indians that they were able to transcend all these problems and the poverty around them to achieve a Seneca renaissance.

After 1939, the federal government sharply reduced funding for the WPA, and budgetary cutbacks undermined the continuance of Parker's efforts at Tonawanda. At about the same time, some of the Indians on the project began to secure employment in western New York factories that had been revived as a result of the country's increased defense spending preceding World War II. By July 1941, a fire, unlike an earlier one that temporarily interrupted work in the winter of 1937, finally ended this long experiment in reviving Indian arts.[48]

The project's demise coincided with the museum's move to its present headquarters, the Bausch estate on East Avenue in Rochester. The coincidence of the two events in a certain sense symbolized the fact that Parker, while stimulating a Seneca renaissance quite consciously fulfilled another goal: with the sizeable collection obtained in the project, part of which was used to trade with other institutions around the world or employed to justify the need for newer and larger quarters, he built a major museum of national reputation.[49] Although he readily admitted that his "main job is the museum I am developing," he never lost sight of wider goals: "I want to make it (Rochester Museum) a University for the common man as well as for the uncommon man — thus our laboratories and studios for those who have talent and genius."[50]

Parker's project achieved other notable results. There is some evidence to suggest that Commissioner Collier used the success of the Seneca Arts Project to justify the creation of the Department of Interior's Indian Arts and Crafts Board.[51] Moreover, major exhibitions of Iroquois art that had been fashioned by the artists were held throughout New York State. From Buffalo to New York City, the Senecas were hailed for their artistry, and non-Indians were becoming educated about the Iroquois. The Seneca Arts Project was featured at the New York World's Fair of 1939. Two cases of Indian art were displayed in prominent fashion on the first floor of the New York State Pavilion; while Ernest Smith's large Indian history map, now on permanent display at the Rochester Museum, was also prepared for the exhibit. Parker, the master promoter, had now achieved international recognition for himself, his museum, his project, his Indians.[52]

Most significantly, Parker's project contributed to the economic and cultural survival of the Senecas. The Great Depression was a time of crisis; extreme poverty threatened not only the arts but also the maintenance of the

Indian Arts Project exhibit, New York State Pavilion, World's Fair, August 10, 1939. Photograph courtesy of the Rochester Museum and Science Center, Rochester, New York.

Indian Arts Project exhibit, New York State Pavilion, World's Fair, August 10, 1939. Photograph courtesy of the Rochester Museum and Science Center, Rochester, New York.

Ernest Smith painting the Indian history map of New York, New York State Pavilion, World's Fair, January 3, 1939. Photograph courtesy of the Rochester Museum and Science Center, Rochester, New York.

very fabric of Seneca existence. To this day, the Senecas who were interviewed consider the project to be the most important accomplishment of their lives. According to Cephas Hill, "The project brought pride and community cooperation and cohesiveness to the reservation."[53]

The Seneca Arts Project was less than successful in one major aspect. Despite Parker's hopes, the artists trained on the project could never make a living in art when the support of the WPA ended. Ernest Smith continued to paint but worked full-time making blueprints. Jesse Cornplanter, Elon Webster, Kidd Smith, and Harrison Ground continued to carve. But without a market for their art, which was too expensive for the tourist and less desirable to the collector than southwestern pottery or silver work, many of the artists turned to other forms of work to earn a living. Though Iroquois art survived as a distinct genre because of Parker's project, the goal of creating a permanent profession for Indians as artists never materialized.[54]

In the process of organizing, administering, and promoting the project, Parker had helped to revolutionize museum work. His concept of a "doing

Kidd Smith at Tonawanda Indian Reservation, 1939. Photograph courtesy of the Rochester Museum and Science Center, Rochester, New York.

museum" called for museums to work with the community to assume a greater role than that of merely storing and cataloging archeological relics and ethnographic materials. In a Deweyian sense, he believed that the museum was an educational institution, a "peoples' college." Consequently, he encouraged untutored Indians to appreciate their rich heritage, as in the

Kidd Smith. Photograph courtesy of the National Archives.

Seneca Arts Project, or offered his museum's services to amateur archeologists, lay groups, schools, as well as to the Boy Scouts. Just as he, as a youngster, was encouraged by the staff at the American Museum of Natural History to pursue his intellectual curiosity by granting him permission to go behind the exhibits, Parker replicated his own exciting experiences of childhood by creating a "doing museum."[55] Writing in 1936 about the Seneca Arts Project, he elaborated on the nature of the museum's service to communities: "And, so when we say, 'It ought to be in a museum' let us consider what the modern museum is doing for mankind in a social way, in a way that increases social values. Perhaps as the museum emerges from the Twentieth Century and its greatest contribution to creative education we shall indeed say in a more enlightened sense, when we consider the administration of social projects 'It ought to be in a museum,' for then we shall know museums for what they do for mankind instead of what they visibly store-up on glass shelves."[56]

9

THE ONEIDA LANGUAGE AND FOLKLORE PROJECT
1938–41

It's quite funny having a white man come here and teach us how to write our own language. But it's interesting. And I think it will be a good thing for the tribe. My little grandson here can't speak any Oneida. We older people don't like to see them forget all about their heritage.

Stadler King (Oneida)
"Tribal Myths will be Saved"
Milwaukee Journal
January 1939

PARKER WAS NOT THE ONLY ANTHROPOLOGIST WORKING with the Iroquois attempting to combine research with meeting the social needs of an Indian community. The Oneida Language and Folklore Project, originated by Professor Morris Swadesh at the University of Wisconsin and supported by the Works Progress Administration's Federal Writers' Project, was one of the first modern in-depth scientific studies of an Iroquoian language and had a long-range impact on Wisconsin Oneida existence. The project, which attempted to teach the Oneidas to write their language, helped spawn interest in future work in applied linguistics among the Iroquois, helped to develop an Oneida orthography and a hymnal, and helped preserve tribal history and folklore. At the same time, the project also contributed to a furthering of community cooperation and pride and created employment for the project's workers during the economic crisis of the

Great Depression. Although the experiment was entirely composed of adult speakers of the language and its objectives were much more limited than present day bilingual, bicultural programs, the Oneida Language and Folklore Project set the basis for further language programs among these Indians. It is significant to note that several of Lounsbury's students built on their mentor's earlier studies and training to develop a bilingual, bicultural program for school children at Oneida in the 1970s. Furthermore, much of the history and folklore preserved in story form by the earlier project of the late 1930s has been incorporated into the learning lessons of the present.[1]

As in the case of the Seneca Arts Project, the Swadesh-Lounsbury experiment grew largely out of the economic crisis of the Great Depression and the opportunity to innovate through federally funded New Deal programs. The Federal Writers' Project was established in 1935 primarily to provide work relief for writers and other white-collar personnel caught in the throes of the Great Depression.[2] Nevertheless, as was true of the Federal Arts Project, the experiment was to go far beyond subsidizing professionals. It produced as its magnum opus the famous American Guide Series; promoted regionalism and the growing interest in minority groups and socioethnic studies through the significant efforts of folklorists John Lomax, Benjamin Botkin, and its very active Folklore Section; and was responsible for collecting the former-slave narratives, one of the most important primary sources dealing with the Afro-American past. In similar vein, Grant Foreman, the director of the Oklahoma Historical Society, directed an oral history project, "the Indian-Pioneer History," in the late 1930s to preserve much of Oklahoma history, especially the interaction of Indian and white.[3] In the process of spending nearly $27 million from 1935 to 1943, the Federal Writers' Project had subsidized a generation of Americans, including Conrad Aiken, Saul Bellow, Ray Allen Billington, John Cheever, Jack Conroy, Loren Eiseley, Ralph Ellison, Studs Terkel, Richard Wright, and Frank Yerby. According to Jerre Mangione, former staff member under Project Director Henry G. Alsberg:

> it was a freak enterprise, a strange creature of the Depression created by a special breed of men and women known as New Dealers whose motive was more political than cultural. The hope that a writer's project could somehow enhance the nation's culture was a fragile one in the minds of those who fathered it. Before the Project began to show what it could, Harry Hopkins considered it "fantastic" for the government to dare play the role of author. And fantastic it was; but the writers and non-writers on

the Project somehow managed to play their role well, so that in spite of all the administrative blunders, the political imbroglios, and the congressional salvos, they produced more good books than anyone dreamed they could.[4]

Besides these national forces and trends, the idea for an Oneida Language and Folklore Project evolved from the realities of Indian life in the 1930s. The need for work relief caused by the Great Depression at Oneida allowed for the project's inception. By 1939, 86 percent of all Oneida tribesmen were receiving some form of public assistance.[5] In addition to the grim realities of Oneida economic existence, these Indians were rapidly losing their ability to use their native language, a situation that was prompting concern both by linguists and Indians themselves. Swadesh reflected on the declining ability of Oneidas to speak their language in an article in 1941:

> Oneida is the sole language of a few old people; English is the sole language of many children and a certain number of young and middle-aged adults. Perfect bilingualism (knowing both English and Oneida well) and graded bilingualism (knowing English well and Oneida partly or Oneida well and English partly) applies to the large majority of the people. There is a continuous series from Oneida monolinguals through different grades of bilinguals to English monolinguals. The present state of the community is the interim manifestation passing from a purely Oneida-speaking community to a purely English-speaking community.[6]

The movement for Indian assimilation had not only led to the Dawes Act and tribal land loss but also to loss of language ability in the native tongue. Indians who attended government-subsidized schools at Carlisle, Chilocco, Flandreau, Hampton, and Oneida were punished for speaking Oneida.[7] Mrs. Stadler King, the wife of a participant on the Oneida Language and Folklore Project, recalled that she had been reprimanded for speaking Oneida in school by having "a rag tied around my mouth all one day."[8] Moreover, the substantial out-migration of Indians from Oneida to the cities of the Midwest also contributed to loss of language. Hence, the creation of a language project, one that ran counter to past assimilationist policies, was viewed by the Oneida community with a great deal of enthusiasm.

The state of Indian language study in the 1930s contributed to the possibility of establishing a program at Oneida. By the mid-1930s, Commissioner Collier and Bureau of Indian Affairs personnel were pushing in this direction. The Office of Indian Education under the directorship of Willard W. Beatty developed pamphlets in Indian languages, bilingual texts, and inservice bilingual training programs for the first time. The bureau and its Office of Indian Education had set the climate needed for the government's sponsorship, under WPA, of an Oneida Language and Folklore Project.[9]

The state of Iroquois language study by the 1930s also contributed to the Oneida Project. As early as the spring of 1935, Professor Edward Sapir of Yale University suggested the idea of an Iroquois linguistic research project in which Morris Swadesh, Stanley Newman, and William Fenton and their Indian informants would be supported by the Indian Bureau.[10] The idea was subsequently considered by William Duncan Strong of the Office of Applied Anthropology of the Indian Bureau and dismissed because of the lack of funds. Nevertheless, Strong and his successor Scudder MeKeel in their roles as applied anthropologists did not dismiss the idea altogether and asked field agents and anthropologists their opinion "as to the practical value of applied linguistics, that is, teaching of interpreters, or teaching the Indians, on your reservations, to write their own languages."[11] Although a New York-based project never materialized in the 1930s, it is important to note that MeKeel, after leaving his post as a government-applied anthropologist, returned to the University of Wisconsin. There at Madison, he was one of the several directors of WPA funded projects at the University that supervised the Swadesh-Lounsbury Federal Writers' Project at Oneida.[12]

Linguistic research on Native American languages had been significantly on the rise since 1927, the year the Committee on American Native Languages of the American Council of Learned Societies was founded. Professor Franz Boas of Columbia University headed the original committee which was composed also of Leonard Bloomfield and Edward Sapir. Its emphasis was scientific, its objective being "to secure an adequate record of Indian languages and dialects, and ... to take such further steps as seem desirable and practicable for the furthering the study of the native American languages."[13] The committee, during its greatest period of activity, 1927–37, sponsored the collection of and publication of linguistic materials. Significantly, Swadesh, the originator of the Oneida project, was one of the later members of this committee. Swadesh, one of Sapir's students, wrote his doctoral study of Nootka language structure under his mentor's guidance.[14] Through his work with his Nootka pupil Alex Thomas, Swadesh had successfully learned the practice of teaching Indians to write their languages.[15] This style of collaborative camaraderie with Indians in the scientific study of Native American languages was the basis of his later plan for the Oneida Indian Language and Folklore Project.

Swadesh was heavily influenced by Sapir's teachings. As a member of the "first Yale School" of linguistics, Swadesh was inculcated with Sapir's concern about rescuing disappearing languages and relating the "results and methods of linguistic inquiry to other things."[16] While serving as a Research Fellow of the Institute of Human Relations at Yale from 1932 to 1937, Swadesh was not only formulating his own ideas about the relatively new field of structural linguistics, but was also looking to apply his theoretical concerns to public policy issues, which was a distinct component of his entire professional career until his death in 1967.

In the fall of 1937, Swadesh accepted a position as assistant professor of anthropology and sociology at the University of Wisconsin, Madison.[17] The following year, he began to consider the possibility of working on an Iroquoian language. The proximity of the Oneida community to Madison along with the setting at the University of Wisconsin provided him with the opportunity to work with the Oneidas. The university, suffering through the throes of the Great Depression, aggressively began to seek out federal government subsidies in the form of WPA projects to help meet its financial needs. The university's Social Research Office submitted twenty project proposals to the WPA between March 1938 and February 1939. Nineteen were funded, totaling approximately $343,000, including "Project Sub-Unit 7," Swadesh's Oneida experiment, a Phonetic Vocabulary of the Oneida Indian Language and the accumulation of native folk lore." The project was described in one university report in the following manner: "The data gathered on this field survey in the Oneida Indian Reservation will be exceedingly valuable for future analyses by students in the field of Indian anthropology."[18] Starting with seed money in the form of an emergency allotment of $200 in July 1938, the project was granted an appropriation of $10,728 in December to begin operations at Oneida in January 1939.[19]

As Swadesh was preparing the project and making contact with the Oneida community, three fateful occurrences came about that changed his plans. In late 1938, he was informed that his contract at the University of Wisconsin would not be renewed. Almost concurrently, he was offered a position by Mexico to head that government's Tarascan literacy project. A third event proved to be his most important contribution to the future success of the Oneida project. Committed to the language experiment but having little desire to remain to fulfill the last semester of his contract at the university, Swadesh selected Floyd Lounsbury, an undergraduate then major-

Floyd Lounsbury (left) and class, Oneida Language and Folklore Project, Oneida, Wisconsin, 1939. Photograph by Robert Ritzenthaler, courtesy of the Robert Ritzenthaler Collection, Milwaukee Public Museum.

ing in mathematics at Madison, to carry out the project. Lounsbury, a twenty-five year old student from Waukesha, Wisconsin, jumped at the opportunity given to him by the slightly older linguist. Lounsbury had previously taken courses in structural linguistics as well as philology with Professor Freeman Twadell and had audited Swadesh's courses in Indian languages and field methods at the University. In the months prior to the formal inception of the project, Swadesh assigned readings and brought Oneidas to meet with him and his prized student in Madison to gain acceptance in the community and obtain a familiarity with the sounds and pronunciation of the language.[20]

The Oneida Language and Folklore Project began formally in January 1939 and continued for nineteen months. Approximately two dozen Oneidas were put in a two-week training session with the understanding that the best

Esther and Oscar Archiquette in front of their home, Oneida, Wisconsin, 1939.
Photograph by Robert Ritzenthaler, courtesy of the Robert Ritzenthaler Collection,
Milwaukee Public Museum.

writers of the language would be selected at the end of the period. The
Oneidas were amenable to the idea, in part because most were transferred
from outdoors WPA projects during the cold winter. Others reflected the
sentiments of one participant who believed it was an essential first step in
teaching the young about their Oneida heritage. The project personnel were
informed that their primary aim was to write texts in their native language.
The initial screening period trained these Indians in phonemic spelling
essential for the task at hand. Keenly aware that they were attempting to
preserve their language for future generations, the classroom situation was
quite businesslike. They would meet weekdays for about eight hours a day

and receive $.50 per hour or $45 per month for their efforts, approximately the same rates as other WPA "white-collar" projects.[21]

Community acceptance was further encouraged by the active participation of Oscar Archiquette, the youngest and most enthusiastic Oneida associated with the project. As a major political leader at Oneida, he had the necessary contacts needed by the project directors. Despite his lack of formal education, he was extremely knowledgeable about tribal history and the best native speaker on the project. Largely through Archiquette's efforts, first Swadesh and then Lounsbury won acceptance by the Oneidas. His lifelong devotion to the promotion of the Oneida language continued until his death in 1971.[22]

Oneida approval of the project was also furthered by their admiration for the skill of Lounsbury. The young linguist with a remarkable ear would correct them, especially for certain imprecisions in language and would point out Mohawk words that had been incorporated into their speech patterns. Lounsbury also gave insights about language, rules to guide in selecting most effective comparisons, and the techniques of marking off a variable from a consonant. He taught them, people with little formal education, about pronominal and prepronominal prefixes. Using the blackboard, the extraordinary linguist clarified pronunciation by atomizing the Oneida language as a skilled surgeon. Ideas that only existed in the Oneida's subconsciousness were now verbalized; the science and sophistication of language was slowly being revealed to them.[23] When he insisted that their language contained voiceless syllables, the Oneidas responded by maintaining that "we've been speaking this language all our lives and we've never realized we did this." Out of these sessions, Lounsbury developed a nineteen-letter Oneida written alphabet which the Indians practiced writing and speaking.[24]

The training sessions, with Swadesh initially in attendance, first met in the parish hall of the Methodist church in DePere but were soon moved to the north wing of the Episcopal church at Oneida because of heating problems. A class of thirteen Oneidas was selected to continue throughout the project. Eight speakers were to remain as participants for the entire nineteen months: Archiquette, Andrew Beechtree, Guy Elm, LaFront King, Alec Metoxen, David Skenandore, John Skenandore, and Louis Webster. Other participants included Tillie Baird, Ida Blackhawk, Stadler King, Eddie Metoxen, and Rachel Archiquette Smith Miller. These Indians, most of whom were over fifty years of age, were tested after a half day of explanation. Less than 50 percent were accurate to Lounsbury's satisfaction. Consequently, the young linguist repeated the work in the afternoon. By the end

Oneida Language and Folklore Project participants, Oneida, Wisconsin, 1939. Left to right: David Skenandore, Floyd Lounsbury, Lawrence Kerstetter, Tillie Baird, John Skenandore, Rachel Smith Miller, Oscar Archiquette, Ida Blackhawk, Andrew Beechtree, Guy Elm, Eddie Metoxen, Emerson King, Alec Metoxen, Stadler King. Photograph by Robert Ritzenthaler, courtesy of the Robert Ritzenthaler Collection, Milwaukee Public Museum.

of the first day, the Oneidas had achieved 75 percent accuracy, and, two and a half days later, they were 98 percent accurate in their Oneida writing abilities.[25]

Lounsbury was well aware of other contemporary linguistic programs among the Indians. Language materials were sent from the famous Navajo experiment under Bureau of Indians Affairs' auspices. However, since the Navajo bilingual texts were not only on a different linguistic group but were designed for teaching children, they proved virtually worthless in their application at Oneida.[26]

The work on the orthography was the first aim and took the immediate attention of the group. The class would often break up into smaller groups and Lounsbury, using lesson worksheets, would do language drills. Next, the Oneidas would go out into the community and collect brief stories, usually varying in length from a paragraph to a page, which they would write down in their new written alphabet. The stories then would be typed in the WPA office in Green Bay by a typist assigned to the project. The stories were typed in triplicate, forty words per page, and one of the copies was returned to the Indians who provided an interlinear literal translation to each story. The Indians would also provide a free translation version which would be typed separately.[27]

The stories collected are a monumental achievement of the project. The subjects range from lists of place names to every important aspect of Oneida history and culture. They include Iroquois animal symbolism, herbalism, games, proper names, and recipes; ghost and trickster stories; Indian school experiences; major turning points in Oneida history such as the American Revolution, removal and resettlement in Wisconsin and the Kansas Claim; and reactions to contemporary events including the New Deal.

Community involvement in the collection of the stories was apparent from the beginning. Skits employing the stories were put on for the Oneida's enjoyment. Moreover, nearly every adult member of the community contributed a story to the project.[28] Elders recalled special recipes for many different varieties of Iroquois corn soup, cracked dried corn and pumpkins and Indian hominy.[29] Others told of Indian salves that were good for sore throats, rheumatism, and sprains.[30] Many of the stories were devoted to moral lessons discouraging Indian laziness, blind obedience, greed, and promoting family responsibilities to the elderly.

Josephine Webster, an old Oneida lacemaker, recalled with pride how a group of women philanthropists from New York City introduced this skill among the tribe in 1898. By the second decade of the twentieth century, 60 to 100 Oneida women, in their new economic role in the community, were producing bobbin pillow laces, tablecloths, and handkerchiefs which the New York women marketed until their organization folded in 1926.[31]

Oneida life at Indian schools received much attention in the stories. The lasting pride that Oneidas experienced in attending these institutions contrasts to the sobering reality of the detribalization process occurring at the schools. One of the early stories collected reveals the reality of assimilationist teachings at the old Oneida Indian school at the turn of the century. Jonas Elm insisted: "I didn't learn anything during that time. As a matter of fact I knew less than when I first got there."[32] Others recalled endearingly the other side of these schools. Moses Elm emphasized the great Oneida athletes at Carlisle, who had made the school a football power-house.[33] Albert Webster described life at Hampton Institute where the Oneidas first became versed in Gospel music, later becoming well known on Wisconsin radio.[34] Ida Blackhawk, who attended Lincoln and Hampton Institutes as well as Carlisle, recalled her training in home economics and domestic science as well as the "outing system" at these schools that placed Indians in the homes of the "best wealthy white people" to learn by example.[35]

Others had more chilling stories to tell. The level of education at the schools in the 1880s among the Oneidas was revealed by a student who ran away from Carlisle after ten months: "I was 17 years old when I went to Carlyle [sic] Indian School, I was in the 3rd grade when I went. I had been going to school at Aswabenon here, they put me in 2nd grade when I got there. I went to school 10 months then I ran away, I was caught in Pittsburgh and I ran away again."[36] Archiquette remembered his experiences at Flandreau in South Dakota, a place he was sent to as a fifth-grade student at the age of fifteen in 1915. He was accused of writing his name in a dictionary, one that had been given to him by his sister, and was physically punished for it. Reacting to the unfortunate situation, Archiquette punched the principal and was summarily dismissed from the school.[37]

In a lighter and more carefree manner, Andrew Beechtree, in one story using inversion as a device, poked fun at the oft-held white belief that the Indians were one of the lost tribes of Israel. Beechtree insisted that the lands south of Lake Ontario contained the Garden of Eden, that it was great apple country, and that the Jews were descendants of the Iroquois, not the reverse.[38] Ida Blackhawk told a story about an Oneida and a white who were talking and suddenly a third man passed by. The white man, startled, insisted that the man looked like the devil. The Oneida man responded: "I don't know the devil."[39]

The project's stories also recorded the concerns and aspirations of contemporary Oneidas of the 1930s. "Willie Fat" Skenandore told Andrew Beechtree, a project participant and former member of Skenandore's faction, that the Oneida claims issue must be pressed, indicating to him that the United States government was obligated to help the Indians for their support in the American Revolution.[40] Another Oneida recalled how he and other Indians had been fleeced by Minnie Kellogg in pursuing the New York claim.[41] Archiquette, in one story, described the significant changes wrought by the coming of the Indian New Deal to Oneida:

The Indian Reorganization Act was approved in Washington. From it the Government is buying land for the Oneidas. We are very fortunate to get or have our homes again. We Indians have had hard times because the United States Government did not fulfill its promises with us Oneidas and because we are not acquainted with the pale face laws. Through this new act for the Indians, the Government is buying land what we lost to the white people and there is a revolving fund set up for us, where we can borrow money to buy stock and farm implements. We pay three percent on a dollar interest. We can go into any business we want but I think most of us is going to farm. The Government has bought 1200 acres up-to-date. There are a few Indians now living on this land, so it is very pleasing to see that we will all own homes again some day.[42]

The project was beset with only one of the major problems that most other WPA programs faced, namely how to justify its existence to congressional critics. Senator Alexander Wiley, the Republican from Chippewa Falls, Wisconsin, and a constant critic of the WPA, saw the project as a financial boondoggle wasting the taxpayer's money.[43] In response, the WPA had several articles published containing promotional photographs in Milwaukee newspapers justifying the project. Other problems were less apparent than in other projects, undoubtedly owing in part to the proximity of Oneida to the WPA regional office in Green Bay.[44]

The project's funding came to an end during the summer of 1940. Unfortunately, a revised edition of the Oneida hymnal which had been put together as part of the project remained unpublished.[45] The original manuscript of the hymnal written in blank notebooks obtained from a five-and-ten cent store in Green Bay had proven to be an immediate sensation and was copied by project participants for other community members. Nevertheless, the demand far outweighed the handwritten supply. The new edition of the hymnal had been revised by Lounsbury, typed on mimeographed stencils, run off in the sociology department at the university, and sent to the WPA bookbinding project at Waupaca where it remained unpublished because of the end of the project's operating funds. Archiquette, who was largely responsible for the transliteration of the hymnal into the new alphabet, retrieved the manuscript in 1941. To raise money for publication, the Oneidas put on one-act plays; while the Northern Paper Mills Company of Green Bay, Wisconsin, donated the needed paper for the printing.[46] This revised hymnal, which is still used by the famous Oneida Singers today, is viewed by the Oneidas themselves as a major accomplishment of the Oneida Language and Folklore Project.[47]

In assessing the significance of the Oneida Language and Folklore Project, it is important to note that the experiment did not produce an overnight language turnaround at Oneida. Even by 1939, a large percentage of Oneidas had already lost their language. With the coming of war and in the postwar climate that followed, teaching Indians their own languages became out of step with American society's increasing emphasis on assimilating Indians. Even to the Oneidas, the preservation of language became less important than economic survival in the white man's world. The youthful enthusiasm of Swadesh, Lounsbury, and Archiquette had to be recaptured and the country had to be reawakened to the old social consciousness of the 1930s. This new awareness was to be rekindled and was to result in a contemporary language program at Oneida in the 1970s.

The achievements of the Oneida Language and Folklore Project were nonetheless impressive. A vast body of linguistic data was accumulated on an Iroquoian language for the first time. Although Lounsbury was later to modify the orthography, his research and scientific approach virtually founded the contemporary interest in Iroquoian linguistics through his writings and techniques on the subject over the next forty years. The published hymnal and morphology are in themselves a worthy monument to the project.[48] The project's books of stories are one of the better all-Indian archival repositories in the United States describing Indian life of the nineteenth and early twentieth centuries. It is quite different from other WPA Federal Writers' Projects. Grant Foreman's Indian-pioneer history had whites interviewing Indians. Moreover, whites interviewed blacks in accumulating the famous former-slave narratives. At Oneida, Indians listened to other Oneidas, all while attempting to learn to properly write their language.

The Oneidas benefited in other ways. David Skenandore, the last surviving Oneida project member, recalled: "It put bread on the table and we were glad to have a paying job."[49] Earning a dollar attending school was an easier form of work relief than road-building in the middle of the winter in Wisconsin. Quite significantly, the Oneida Language and Folklore Project provided enjoyment to a small group of Indians and gave them a sense of mission during the nation's worst depression. According to Skenandore: "We all realized that we were attempting to preserve and pass on the language for the future."[50] Although that lofty goal has not yet been fully achieved, Floyd Lounsbury's Indian language class at Oneida was the first to make this attempt.

10

CONCLUSION

B Y THE TIME OF UNITED STATES ENTRY into World War II, New Deal programs had changed the very face of Iroquoia. Although there were flaws in Commissioner Collier's and the Roosevelt administration's overall approach to the Six Nations, the work of the 1930s significantly affected the Iroquois, culturally, economically, and politically. In New York, the Iroquois firm insistence on federal recognition of their sovereignty, however unreal to Washington policy-makers, had to be understood and dealt with before any progress could be made. Since Iroquois concepts of sovereignty clashed by their very definition with Collier's aims at tribal reorganization, governmental officials had to find other responses to meet the needs of Indians in New York. Those programs which were less directly tied to the Indian Service, an agency viewed by many Iroquois as historically corrupt, inefficient, and superfluous, and those which had fewer overtones of political interference in tribal affairs, but with strong community-based involvement, succeeded in New York.

Because of the largely landless nature of Indian existence in Oklahoma and Wisconsin, Iroquois concepts of sovereignty, although important, did not preclude Seneca-Cayuga and Oneida acceptance of changes in their tribal structure. Prior to the IRA referendum, political factionalism at Oneida had produced a situation verging on anarchy and one filled with corruption. The historic amalgamation in Oklahoma of peoples of diverse Iroquois backgrounds and the gradual withering of the separate Cayuga tribal structure before the New Deal led to the emergence of a united

council composed of both Senecas and Cayugas at the time of the passage of
the Oklahoma Indian Welfare act and its referendum.

Commissioner Collier and his immediate circle of associates in Indian
policy-making — Willard Beatty, Felix Cohen, Allan Harper, Nathan Margold, William Zimmerman, Jr., and others — brought into office a sincere
commitment to improving the lives of American Indians in the United
States. They were truly dedicated men and extremely sympathetic to the idea
of helping Indians. They had to deal with problems caused by the failures of
past policy-makers and local Indian agents described so graphically in the
Meriam Report; tribal factionalism of horrendous proportions as found at
Oneida, Wisconsin, in 1934; and with the nearly total Indian distrust of all
promises and motives emanating from Washington.

Unfortunately, Collier's inflexibility, paternalistic nature, vindictiveness,
and past life experiences, on occasion, interfered with his emotional
attachment to improving the conditions of Indian life. His superb staff,
assembled at the top echelon level of the Indian Service, as well as the
community workers and applied agents in the field, all-too-frequently were
put on the defensive by justifying Collier's insistence on tribal reorganization
long after it was viewed by Indian nations as a dead issue. Collier did not
heed his own sound advice propounded to his superintendents in the Indian
Service. Ironically, in a memorandum on March 6, 1935, quoting from *The
Constitution of 5 Nations* as translated by the chiefs of the Six Nations Council
and edited by Arthur C. Parker, Collier urged his Indian Service employees
to be sensitive to the wishes of all Indian peoples during the difficult period
of voting, drafting constitutions, and incorporating tribal political structures
under the IRA. He insisted:

> You shall now become a mentor of the people. ... The thickness of your
> skin shall be seven spans — which is to say that you shall be proof against
> anger, offensive actions and criticism. Your heart shall be filled with peace
> and good will and your mind filled with a yearning for the welfare of the
> people. ... With endless patience you shall carry out your duty and your
> firmness shall be tempered with tenderness for your people. Neither anger
> nor fury shall find lodgment in your mind and all your words and actions
> shall be marked with calm deliberation. In all of your deliberations ... , in
> your efforts at lawmaking, in all your official acts, self-interest shall be cast
> into oblivion. Cast not over your shoulder behind you the warnings of the
> nephews and nieces should they chide you for any error or wrong you may
> do, but return to the way of the Great Law which is just and right. Look
> and listen for the welfare of the whole people and have always in view not

only the present but also the coming generations, even those whose faces
are yet beneath the surface of the ground — the unborn of the future
Nation.[1]

In defense of Collier, the commissioner had to contend with the
significant diversity of Indian America, in aspirations, needs, and problems.
Moreover, in order to improve conditions, he had to defend the Indian
Bureau, an agency of government he had mercilessly attacked during the
1920s and 1930s, before an often hostile Congress. Hence, his credibility was
frequently questioned by Capitol Hill politicians as well as their Indian
constituents. By developing a uniform and national Indian policy, the IRA,
and packaging it before Congress to meet the political needs of American
politics, he was exposing himself and his staff to relentless salvos from Indian
nations, such as the Iroquois in New York, whose peculiar circumstances did
not fit the model cast in the legislation. Furthermore, to Iroquois people of
rural conservative values, Collier represented yet another hurdle to clear in a
long series of threats to order and stability. Although Collier was largely
miscast as a villain, his liberal civil rights approach did not adequately
embrace, to the Iroquois, the constancy of federal-Indian treaties of the
1780s and 1790s, thus resulting in the bitter clashes of 1934 and 1935. Once
Collier failed to secure tribal reorganization in New York and realized both
the strength of the opposition and the nature of his tactical mistake, the
Indian New Deal changed direction. By working behind the scenes and
indirectly encouraging local leadership and community projects such as the
construction of the Tonawanda Indian Community House, it becomes clear
that he had learned a lesson.

Iroquois inconsistencies were revealed at every turn during the New
Deal era. While maintaining and insisting that they had full autonomy as
sovereign nations, the Iroquois, because of the economic crisis, sought and
accepted substantial federal and state funds that required accountability and
supervision by outsiders. Even in New York, where their assertions of
sovereignty were the staunchest and criticism of governmental bureaucracy
substantial, the Iroquois accepted both federal and state aid at an unpre-
cedented level. Even leaders of the League gave their formal endorsement to
this policy. This trend toward dependence on and seeking out federal grants
or money became a feature of Oneida (Wisconsin), Seneca Nation, and
Seneca-Cayuga existence in the post– World War II period. Today, in sharp
contrast to the New Deal years, the Confederacy's position at Onondaga,
reflected at some of the other New York reservations, is to avoid this route.

Significantly, the New Deal did not permanently reverse trends that were underway prior to 1933. Although no new allotments were permitted after 1933, tax sales and alienation of Indian allotments continued in Oklahoma. The factional intratribal political behavior at St. Regis that limited the CCC-ID program there continues today at an even higher emotional level. Land claims assertions, a most important feature of the Iroquois polity in the 1920s, reemerged in the 1960s and 1970s after its nadir during the New Deal. Religious revitalization movements and other manifestations of cultural regeneration and solidarity, encouraged by the Kellogg party in the 1920s, once again have become vital forces among the Iroquois. Furthermore, the establishment of the Longhouse religion at Oneida, Wisconsin, and its rekindling at St. Regis in the past two decades stands as an example of this trend, as well as the increasing communication between geographically separate Iroquois communities.

The Indian New Deal programs in Iroquoia, which had been winding down in scale since 1939, came to a complete halt soon after American entry into World War II. Within a year after the attack on Pearl Harbor, Congressional funding for CCC-ID, WPA, NYA and other work-relief projects ceased to exist because of the war effort. Rather than solely overseeing Indian affairs, the Indian Bureau was shifted to Chicago with Collier and his staff increasingly concerned with the administration of islands in the South Pacific liberated from the Japanese Empire.

Despite significant protest about being drafted as American citizens under the provisions of the Selective Service Act of 1940, Iroquois did enlist in large numbers serving with distinction in all theatres of the war. The Seneca language, as was true of Navajo, was used to foil the Japanese in the South Pacific. One Seneca-Cayuga family contributed five sons to the war effort. Another Oklahoma Iroquois, Chief James Allen, was held by the Germans as a prisoner-of-war for twenty-two months after being captured during the Sicilian campaign in 1943. Nine Mohawks from St. Regis were killed during the conflict, while numerous Iroquois received military commendations for their wartime heroism.[2]

After their active participation in and triumphant return from the war, the Iroquois, nevertheless, faced new and major threats to their existence. Without federal programs as provided during the Indian New Deal, Iroquois survival became tougher to deal with. Out-migrations to cities once again increased because of economic pressures. Educational programs of the New Deal that promoted Indian cultural retention such as the NYA and WPA projects previously discussed became vague memories in the postwar world. Assimilationist values were reintroduced in Indian educationalist circles during these conservative budget-cutting times. The new age of federal withdrawal required Indians to become less culturally separate. The closing of many Indian reservation schools and the Thomas Indian School and Orphan Asylum in the mid 1950s, following the Supreme Court decision of *Brown* v. *Board of Education of Topeka, Kansas* which sought racial integration of black and white schools, led to busing of more Indian children to day public schools off the reservation and discouragement of New Deal cultural enrichment type programs until the late 1960s.

Threats to Iroquois existence were manifested in other ways. After World War II, Congress handed over criminal and civil jurisdiction of the Iroquois to New York State, despite strong Indian opposition to the move. Most importantly, the Iroquois have lost significant acreage in the East in the post-war period: a dam at Onondaga, the Kinzua Dam's flooding of the entire Cornplanter Tract, the New York State Power Authority's condemnation of the Southwestern corner at Tuscarora, and the St. Lawrence Seaway Project that took Mohawk lands. Moreover, in spite of their aforementioned insistence on the sanctity of federal-Iroquois treaties, the Senecas in New York, Oneidas in Wisconsin, and Seneca-Cayugas in Oklahoma faced the serious threats of termination of treaty obligations during the 1950s and 1960s.

Deskaheh's example of the 1920s continued to affect Iroquois life and led them to react in distinct ways to these threats against them. Chief Clinton Rickard, and his organization, the Indian Defense League of America, aside from annually commemorating Indian guarantees under the Jay Treaty, appealed to the United Nations in 1949. During the fights against the New York State Power Authority and the Army Corps of Engineers, they sought national and international recognition for their causes. Although once again receiving the assistance of Eleanor Roosevelt, their appeals proved fruitless. Nevertheless, to this day, Deskaheh's words and tactics are still employed by the Iroquois in their determined effort to conserve and protect their existence. Consequently, Six Nations chiefs as delegates of the League traveled to Geneva, Switzerland, under Iroquois-issued passports to make an appeal before an agency of the United Nations on behalf of all Native Americans.

In similar vein, Alice Lee Jemison's politically activist journalistic tradition continues today. *The First American* which ceased publication in the mid-1950s was in some ways the harbinger of *Akwesasne Notes* in its watch-dog role over congressional legislation as well as in its agitation against the Indian Service and its continued role in Indian affairs. Despite the far right-wing rhetoric of Jemison and her publication and the Marxist-radical style of *Akwesasne Notes,* one should realize that Indian political movements take on the style in vogue, but not necessarily the substance of, the non-Indian world's politics. Both should be seen as publications attempting to conserve Iroquois identity, not as vehicles attempting to challenge or even overthrow a non-Indian governmental order. Although *Akwesasne Notes* is larger and more international in character, its insistence on treaty obligations parallels the earlier periodical. Hence, the old Indian movement of the 1930s has more in common with red power militancy than generally believed. To many Iroquois, whether in the 1930s or 1980s, the past is still a present reality.

For a more complete understanding of the Indian New Deal, historians should be aware that the period had a largely intangible nature that can best be appreciated through undertaking field work and oral history. To Iroquois elders, despite the suffering they faced during the economic crisis of the 1930s, the era is viewed with nostalgia. The excitement of cooperating together in much-needed tribal projects, not simply "make-work relief," ranging from constructing community centers to reviving near lost artistic styles was the New Deal to most Iroquois. Being funded on a significant scale for the first time, the Iroquois were encouraged to maintain their cultural traditions. In sharp contrast with the past, the non-Indian world gave the Iroquois, for less than a decade, the opportunity to be "Indian." Hence, the Iroquois New Deal, as was true of the New Deal as a whole, was a vast effort in community building that succeeded, however, limited in time, more than it failed.

In retrospect, the New Deal, with all its faults, was a more positive interlude, however brief, between the age of allotment and the age of termination. Although the tribal business committees as well as the charters, constitutions, and bylaws were foreign models to most of these Indians, today's critics of the New Deal should keep in mind the existing conditions of life in the 1930s that spurred acceptance by some Native Americans and prompted Indian Bureau interest in tribal reorganization and other programs. The period, 1933 to 1941, was an era in which abler policy-makers than in the past administered, socially responsible anthropologists experimented, and concerned philanthropists contributed their energies for the betterment of the Iroquois. They overcame the near-chaotic nature of the Iroquois polity caused by historic forces and especially the Kellogg turmoil of the 1920s and their own somewhat distorted perceptions of the Iroquois and their problems to produce a New Deal for these Indians. Although at times there resulted an inevitable clash between two cultures, neither of which completely understood what motivated the other, these years, when judged by federal policies and programs before and since, can at least be considered a better deal for the Iroquois.

NOTES

Preface

1. The best monographic treatments of the Indian New Deal are the following: Donald L. Parman, *The Navajos and the New Deal* (New Haven, Conn., 1976); Kenneth R. Philp, *John Collier's Crusade for Indian Reform, 1920–1954* (Tucson, Ariz., 1977); Graham D. Taylor, *The New Deal and American Indian Tribalism: The Administration of the Indian Reorganization Act, 1934–1945* (Lincoln, Nebr., 1980).

2. Robert Burnette (Rosebud Sioux) and John Koster, *The Road to Wounded Knee* (New York, 1974), pp. 115, 117, 132, 168–69, 182–87; Joseph DeLaCruz (Quinault), "On Knowing What is Good for the American Indian," Letter to the editor, *New York Times*, Aug. 2, 1978, p. 20; Interview of Rupert Costo (Cahuilla), April 20–21, 1979, Geneva, N.Y.

3. American Indian Policy Review Commission, *Final Report* (Washington, D.C., 1977), 1: 309–310.

4. Although there are other writings on the Six Nations in the twentieth century, the sole major contribution to Iroquois historiography in the period is Barbara Graymont's edited *Fighting Tuscarora: The Autobiography of Chief Clinton Rickard* (Syracuse, N.Y., 1973).

5. Bernard S. Cohn, "History and Anthropology: The State of Play," *Comparative Studies in Society and History* 22 (April 1980): 216.

6. Ibid., p. 221.

7. Ibid.

8. Vine Deloria, Jr., "The Twentieth Century," in *Red Men and Hat Wearers: Viewpoints in Indian History*, Daniel Tyler, ed. (Boulder, Colo., 1976), p. 163.

1 —Iroquois Concepts of Sovereignty

1. James W. Clute, "The New York Indians' Rights to Self-Determination," *Buffalo Law Review* 22 (Spring 1973): 985–1019.

2. For the origins of the Longhouse religion, see Anthony F. C. Wallace, *The Death and Rebirth of the Seneca* (New York, 1970).

3. Edmund Wilson, *Apologies to the Iroquois* (New York, 1959), pp. 254–55.

4. Quoted in Kinzua Project Indian Committee, *The Kinzua Dam Controversy* (Philadelphia, 1961?), p. 10.

5. William N. Fenton, "The Iroquois Confederacy in the Twentieth Century: A Case Study of the Theory of Lewis H. Morgan in 'Ancient Society,'" *Ethnology* 4 (July 1965): 258.

6. Norman B. Wilkinson, "Robert Morris and the Treaty of Big Tree," *Mississippi Valley Historical Review* 60 (Sept. 1953): 257–78; Henry S. Manley, "Buying Buffalo from the Indians," *New York History* 28 (July 1947): 313–29; William Chazanof, *Joseph Ellicott and the Holland Land Company: The Opening of Western New York* (Syracuse, N.Y., 1970), pp. 18–24; Wallace, *The Death and Rebirth of the Seneca*, pp. 179–83, 323–24.

7. Laurence M. Hauptman, "Senecas and Subdividers: Resistance to Allotment of Indian Lands in New York, 1875–1906," *Prologue: The Journal of the National Archives* 9 (Summer 1977): 105–116.

8. Lewis Cooper (Seneca) to E. B. Meritt (assistant commissioner of Indian affairs), Sept. 2, 1924, BIA Central Files, 1907–1939, #66455-1924-128 New York, Record Group 75, National Archives (Hereafter cited as RG75, NA).

9. Ernest Benedict (Mohawk) to the American Civil Liberties Union, March 27, 1941, American Civil Liberties Union Archives, Princeton University, 2287: 221–25.

10. Congressman C. E. Hancock (Syracuse, N.Y.) to Commissioner Charles J. Rhoads, Nov. 17, 1931, BIA Central Files, 1907–1939, #64489-1931-128 New York, RG75, NA.

11. Onondaga Historical Association, *Official Record of Indian Conference Called to Determine the Status of the Indians of the Six Nations...March 6–7, 1919* (Syracuse, N.Y., 1919), pp. 62–63.

12. *Fighting Tuscarora*, p. 53.

13. George P. Decker, "The New York Iroquois and State Game Laws," typescript, 1908, New York State Library, Albany. Decker was a former deputy attorney general and an attorney for the Six Nations. *U.S.A. ex. rel. John D. Lynn v. Frederick Hamilton and Others* (1915).

14. For a full discussion of this law [*United States Statutes at Large*, 44 (1927): 932] and Iroquois reaction to it, see United States, Senate, Committee on Indian Affairs, Hearings on S.5302: *Fish and Game Within the Allegany, Cattaraugus, and Oil Spring Reservations*, 72nd Cong., 2nd Sess. (Washington, D.C., 1933); Ray W. Jimerson (president, Seneca Nation of Indians) to Senator Burton K. Wheeler, Feb. 6, 1934, Senator Robert F. Wagner MSS., Legislative File, Box 224, File 1544 "Indians," Georgetown University;

Robert P. Galloway (attorney for the Seneca Nation) to Governor Herbert Lehman, Jan. 28, 1933, Governor Herbert Lehman MSS., Microfilm Reel 86, "Seneca Nation of Indians," Columbia University; *People v. Redeye*, 358 NYS 2d 632 (1974).

15. Felix Cohen, *Handbook of Federal Indian Law* (Washington, D.C., 1942; Reprint edition, Albuquerque, N. Mex., 1972), p. 419.

16. Gerald Gunther, "Governmental Power and New York Indian Lands — A Reassessment of a Persistent Problem of Federal-State Relations," *Buffalo Law Review* 7 (Fall 1958): 1–14.

17. United States Congress, House Committee on Indian Affairs, Hearings on H.R. 9720: *Indians of New York*, 71st Cong., 2nd Sess. (Washington, D.C., 1930), p. 1.

18. Ibid., p. 19–20.

19. Ibid., p. 199.

20. Ibid., pp. 154–65.

21. *United States v. Forness*, 125 F 2d 932 (1942).

22. New York State Legislature, Legislative Document No. 51: *Report of Joint Legislative Committee on Indian Affairs* (Albany, N.Y., 1945), p. 4; "Indian Group Fights State Authority," *Syracuse* (N.Y.) *Herald Journal*, March 11, 1948, p. 4; *United States Statutes at Large* 42 (1948): 1224; 44 (1950): 845.

23. Joshua Jones (Onondaga) to John Collier, Feb. 26, 1934, #4894-1934-066 Part 2-A, Sec. I, Box 2, Records Concerning the Wheeler-Howard Act, RG75, NA.

24. Mohawk Petition, Jan. 31, 1934, Senator Robert F. Wagner MSS., Legislative File, Box 224, File 1544, "Indians," Georgetown University.

25. See the following articles in the *Syracuse* (N.Y.) *Post-Standard*: "Iroquois Indians Declare War on Enemies of U.S.," June 11, 1942, p. 1; "Chiefs of Iroquois Leave for Capital With War Papers," June 13, 1942, p. 6; "Six Nations Chief Speaks on Radio," June 15, 1942, p. 14; "Indians to Honor Heroic Dead," Sept. 13, 1945, p. 23.

26. Joseph Keppler to Oliver LaFarge, April 18, 1941, American Civil Liberties Union Archives, Princeton University; Ernest Benedict to American Civil Liberties Union, March 27, 1941; Interviews of Chief Leon Shenandoah (Tadodaho), May 15, 1979, Onondaga Indian Reservation, and Chief Corbett Sundown (Seneca), Tonawanda Indian Reservation, May 22, 1980; United States Department of the Interior, *Annual Report of the Commissioner of Indian Affairs*, 1942 (Washington, D.C., 1942), p. 240; for Iroquois draft resistance, see the following articles in the *New York Times*: "Indians Seek Draft Test," Oct. 10, 1940, p. 14; "Mohawks Resist Draft," Oct. 12, 1940, p. 14; "Say 1794 Treaty Exempts Indians," Feb. 22, 1941, p. 8; "Indian Loses Draft Plea," May 15, 1941, p. 14; "Indian Drops Selectee Fight," Aug. 5, 1941, p. 22; "Indians on the 'Warpath' Over Selective Service Act," Oct. 21, 1941, p. 25; "Nation is Still 'Paleface,' but its Defense is Given Back 'Reluctantly' to the Indians," p. 27. See also "5 Indians Fight Draft as Threat to Sovereignty," *New York Herald Tribune*, Oct. 21, 1941, p. 11.

27. *Fighting Tuscarora*, p. 127.

28. *Ex Parte Green* 123 F 2d. 862 (1941); Interview of Chief Leon Shenandoah, May 15, 1979; "How it is With Us," *Akwesasne Notes* 6 (Late spring 1974): 2.

29. *Akwesasne Notes*, ed., *Voices From Wounded Knee* (Rooseveltown, N.Y., 1974), p. 96.

See also "Buying the Brooklyn Bridge: Mohawks Refute Land Claims," *Akwesasne Notes* 10 (Early spring 1978): 35.

30. New York State Assembly, (unpublished) *Report of the Indian Commission to Investigate the Status of the American Indian Residing in the State of New York Transmitted to the Legislature, March 17, 1922* (Albany, N.Y., 1922), p. 2 (Hereafter cited as the Everett Report).

31. *Official Record of Indian Conference,* March 6–7, 1919 (Syracuse, N.Y., 1919); *United States v. Boylan,* F 165 (1920).

32. Arthur C. Parker, the noted anthropologist and reformer of Seneca ancestry was the representative from the New York State Department of Education who served on the Everett Commission. For an analysis of the commission, see Helen Merritt Upton, "History of the State Administration of the New York Indians." (Master's thesis, Syracuse University, 1959), pp. 53–64. Upton's thesis has recently been published as *The Everett Report in Historical Perspective: The Indians of New York* (Albany, N.Y., 1980).

33. *Everett Report,* p. 324.

34. Ibid., pp. 303–304.

35. *Deere et al. v. State of New York et al.,* 22 F. 851 (1927).

36. "Looking for an Indian Booker T. Washington," *New York Tribune,* Aug. 27, 1911, Sec. II, p. 3; Hazel W. Hertzberg, *The Search for an American Indian Identity: Modern Pan-Indian Movements* (Syracuse, N.Y., 1971), pp. 36, 60–61, 65, 97; Ramona Herdman, "A New Six Nations: Laura Cornelius Kellogg Sees the Old Iroquois Confederacy Re-established on a Modern Business Basis," *Syracuse* (N.Y.) *Herald,* Nov. 6, 1927, p. 11; Interview of Melissa Cornelius, Oct. 21, 1978, Oneida, Wis.

37. Herdman, "A New Six Nations" *Syracuse Herald,* Nov. 6, 1927.

38. Laura Cornelius Kellogg, *Our Democracy and the American Indian* (Kansas City, Mo., 1920).

39. The early part of the Kellogg episode in Iroquois history can be traced by reading the Warren H. Norton Scrapbooks, "Indians, 1916–1927," pp. 88–288, Onondaga Historical Association, Syracuse, N.Y. "Final Notice: To All Oneidas who May Participate in the New York Claim," Dec. 31, 1925, BIA Central Files, 1907–1939, #9788-1923-26, Part I, New York, RG75, NA.; "Many Indians on this reservation lost money to the Kelloggs." Interview of Chief Irving Powless, Sr., May 15, 1979, Onondaga Indian Reservation. Similar conclusions about the Kelloggs' activities were expressed on the Oneida (Wis.), Tonawanda and Cattaraugus reservations. See the photograph of receipt given by the Kelloggs.

40. *Hearings on S. Res. 79* 12: 4858.

41. Freeman Johnson (Tonawanda Seneca) to commissioner of Indian affairs, April 7, 20, 1927; Jonas Schuyler (Oneida) to Commissioner of Indian Affairs Charles Burke, Jan. 7, 1927; William Skenandore (Oneida) to commissioner of Indian affairs, July 9, 1926, BIA Central Files, 1907–1939, #9788-1923-260, Part II, New York, RG75, NA.

42. F. G. Tranbarger (clerk, Indian Office) Report to Commissioner Burke, Nov. 2, 1927, (Report on *King v. Kellogg* trial, 1927) BIA Central Files, 1907–1939, #9788-1923-260, Part II, New York, RG75, NA; "Three to Go on Trial in Six Nations Case,"

New York Times, Oct. 4, 1927, p. 5; *Deere et al. v. State of New York et al*. James Deere, the plaintiff, an enrolled St. Regis Mohawk, brought suit on behalf of himself and his tribe and members of the Iroquois Confederacy for land loss that he contended were in violation of the Treaty of Fort Stanwix (1784). John Collier Circular Letter on "Activities of O. J. and L. C. Kellogg," undated (1933?), J. N. B. Hewitt MSS., #4271, Box 2, National Anthropological Archives, Smithsonian Institution, Washington, D.C.; Collier to Mrs. Charles E. Reynolds (Mohawk), Oct. 7, 1933; Collier to Senator F. Ryan Duffy, May 19, 1933, BIA Central Files, 1907–1939, #40728-1933-051 New York, RG75, NA.

43. "Cayuga Indian Nation to Ask U.S. for Lands," *Buffalo* (N.Y.) *Courier-Express*, Aug. 23, 1935, p. 1. Howard Vernon, "The Cayuga Claims: A Background Study," *American Indian Culture and Research Journal* 4 (Fall 1980): 21–35; "Cayuga Suing to Regain 100 Square Miles in State," *New York Times*, Nov. 23, 1980, p. 42; United States Department of the Interior, Office of Indian Affairs, News Release, Nov. 30, 1939; "On the Warpath," *New York Times*, Dec. 18, 1939, p. 22, c. 4.

44. Plaintiffs' Post-Trial Memorandum on the Issue of Liability, *The Oneida Indian Nation of New York State … v. The County of Oneida, New York and the County of Madison, New York v. the State of New York*, Civil No. 70-CV-5 (1975); William Skenandore, *Brief: U.S. Court: Statement of the Case of the Oneida Tribe* (n.p., n.d.), Milwaukee County Public Library; Mary Winder to Charles H. Berry (superintendent of New York Agency), April 15, 1943, Records of the New York Agency, 1938–49, RG75, NA; *Oneida Indian Nation v. County of Oneida*, 414 U.S. 661 (1974).

45. Sally M. Weaver, "Six Nations of the Grand River, Ontario," in (Smithsonian) *Handbook of North American Indians*, Bruce Trigger and William Sturtevant, eds. (Washington, D.C.), 15: 525–36; Maxwell Jacobsen, "Who Rules the Valley of the Six Nations," *McGill Law Journal* 00 (1976): 130–47; *Richard Isaac v. Ackland Davey* 2 R.C.S. 897 (1977) (R.C.S. = Canada Supreme Court Records).

46. Deskaheh, *Petition to His Most Gracious Majesty King George V* with attached *Memorandum on the Relation of the Dominion Government of Canada with the Six Nations of the Grand River*, Sept. 23, 1921; *Fighting Tuscarora*, pp. 58–65; Carl Carmer, *Dark Trees to the Wind: A Cycle of York State Years* (New York, 1949), pp. 105–117.

47. Deskaheh Radio Broadcast, WHAM, Rochester, N.Y., March 10, 1925.

48. *Fighting Tuscarora*, pp. 69–89. The case was *McCandless, Commissioner of Immigration v. United States ex. rel. Diabo*, 18 F (2d) 282; 25 F (2d) 71 (1927); Interview of Beulah Rickard Lillvick, June 6, 1978, Tuscarora Reservation.

49. Ernest Benedict to American Civil Liberties Union, March 27, 1941.

50. Mary E. Fleming Mathur, "The Jay Treaty and the Boundary Line," *Indian Historian* 3 (Winter 1970): 37–40; and "A Borderline Case," *Akwesasne Notes* 10 (Early spring 1978): 14.

51. U.S. House of Representatives, Subcommittee of the Committee on Indian Affairs, Hearings on H. R. 7781: *Indian Conditions and Affairs*, 74 Cong., 1st Sess., Feb. 11, 1935 (Washington, D.C., 1935), p. 48.

52. *Lonewolf v. Hitchcock*, 187 U.S. 553 (1903).

2 —John Collier and the Iroquois

1. National Resources Board, Land Planning Committee, *Indian Land Tenure, Economic Status, and Population Trends* (Washington, D.C., 1935), pp. 56–57; D. S. Otis, *The Dawes Act and the Allotment of Indian Lands*, Francis Paul Prucha, ed. (Norman, Okla., 1973), pp. 92–93.

2. Lewis Meriam and Associates, *The Problem of Indian Administration* (Baltimore, 1928), p. 7.

3. Ibid., pp. 447–48.

4. Ibid., pp. 3–51.

5. Ibid., p. 22.

6. D'Arcy McNickle, *They Came Here First: The Epic of the American Indian*, rev. ed. (New York, 1975), p. 242.

7. National Resources Board, *Indian Land Tenure*, pp. 27–38.

8. The Iroquois in New York were exempted from the Dawes Act because of questions relating to the Ogden Land Company's claims to Indian lands. Loring Benson Priest, *Uncle Sam's Stepchildren: The Reformation of Indian Policy, 1865–1887* (New Brunswick, N.J., 1942), p. 237; see also my "Senecas and Subdividers," pp. 105–116; and my "Governor Theodore Roosevelt and the Indians of New York," *Proceedings* of the American Philosophical Society, 124 (Feb. 1975): 1–7.

9. Eva Smith (Seneca) to Joseph Keppler, Aug. 27, 1930, Joseph Keppler MSS., Museum of the American Indian Library.

10. Ray Lyman Wilbur to Senator Lynn J. Frazier (chairman, Senate Committee on Indian Affairs), Sept. 30, 1929; Frazier to Wilbur, Sept. 30, 1929; A. A. Grorud (counsel to Senate Committee on Indian Affairs) to Frazier, Sept. 30, 1929, John Collier MSS., "Matters to be Investigated," Nov. 25, 1929, Box 18, Folder 43, Yale University.

11. Quoted in *Hearings on S. Res. 79, 12:* 4865.

12. *Fighting Tuscarora*, pp. 100–101.

13. Collier notes, "Matters to be Investigated," Nov. 25, 1929. The Onondaga factional dispute is recorded in the Warren H. Norton Scrapbooks, "Indians, 1916–1927," pp. 88–265, Onondaga Historical Association, Syracuse. The rivalry continued well into the 1930s, and both Jones and Thomas continued to refer to themselves as head of the Six Nations. Ernest Benedict to American Civil Liberties Union, March 27, 1941; Archie Phinney (field agent of BIA), "A Study of Tribal Government of the St. Regis Indians (Mohawk Tribe) of the State of New York," July 31, 1942, #9506-1936-066 New York, General Records Concerning Indian Organization, 1934–56, RG75, NA. This Mohawk factional dispute continues right up to the present day. "'Besieged' Mohawk Faction Resists Tribal Majority," *New York Times*, June 2, 1980, Sec. II, p. 3. For the Oneidas, see Chapter 5.

14. *Fighting Tuscarora*, pp. 78, 85, 87; John Collier, *From Every Zenith* (Denver, 1963), p. 144; Philp, *John Collier's Crusade*, pp. 76–86; "Matters to be Investigated," Nov. 25, 1929.

15. John Collier, "America's Handling of its Indigenous Indian Minority," *Indians at Work* 7 (Jan. 1940): 11–18 (NBC radio network speech of Dec. 4, 1939); and especially his "United States Indian Administration as a Laboratory of Ethnic Affairs," *Social Research* 7 (Sept. 1945): 265–303.

16. McNickle, *They Came Here First*, pp. 246–47.

17. Collier, *From Every Zenith*, pp. 201–202.

18. Christopher Lasch, *The New Radicalism in America, 1889–1963: The Intellectual as a Social Type* (New York, 1965), pp. 104–140. For Collier's view of Lawrence, see Edward Nehls, ed., *D. H. Lawrence: A Composite Biography* (Madison, Wis., 1938), 2: 197–99. For Lawrence's view of Collier, see Diana Trilling, ed., *The Selected Letters of D. H. Lawrence* (New York, 1958), p. 211. Richard Frost, "The Romantic Inflation of Pueblo Culture," *The American West* 17 (Jan.–Feb. 1980): 4–9, 56–60.

19. Philp, *John Collier's Crusade*, pp. 4–5, 9–22.

20. Collier, *From Every Zenith*, p. 93.

21. Ibid., pp. 9–22, 25, 216–26, 345–51; Stephen J. Kunitz, "The Social Philosophy of John Collier," *Ethnohistory* 18 (Summer 1971): 224–25.

22. Philp, *John Collier's Crusade*, pp. 24–25.

23. John Collier, "The Red Atlantis," *Survey* 49 (Oct. 1922): 15–20.

24. John Collier, *Indians of the Americas* (New York, 1947), p. 10.

25. Collier, *From Every Zenith*, pp. 93–94, 126.

26. Robert F. Berkhofer, Jr., *The White Man's Indian: Images of the American Indian From Columbus to the Present* (New York, 1978), p. 178.

27. Collier, *From Every Zenith*, p. 126.

28. See for example, Collier, "The Red Atlantis," pp. 15–20; "Plundering the Pueblo Indians," *Sunset* 50 (Jan. 1923): 21–25; "The Pueblos' Last Stand," *Sunset* 50 (Feb. 1923): 19–22; "Pueblos' Land Problems," *Sunset* 51 (Nov. 1923): 51; "Persecuting the Pueblos," *Sunset* 12 (July 1924): 53. *The Selected Letters of D. H. Lawrence*, p. 211.

29. U.S. Department of the Interior, Press Release, March 9, 1932, J. P. Kinney MSS., Box 29, #1791A, Cornell University.

30. McNickle, *They Came Here First*, p. 242.

31. Berkhofer, *The White Man's Indian*, p. 185.

32. "Threat to Seneca Land Averted," *Indians at Work* 4 (April 15, 1937): 46; John Collier to W. K. Harrison, March 4, 1935, William Zimmerman, Jr. (assistant commissioner) to Charles H. Berry, June 26, 1942, Records of the New York Agency, 1938–49, RG75, NA; Collier Circular Letter on "Activities of O. J. and L. C. Kellogg," undated (1933?); Collier to Mrs. Charles E. Reynolds, Oct. 7, 1933; Collier to Duffy, May 19, 1933; John Collier, "The Indians of New York State and the New Federal Indian Policy," Speech at Niagara Falls, Sept. 4, 1934, John Collier MSS., Box 48, Folder 47, Yale University.

33. Interview of Genevieve Plummer, July 28, 1977, Allegany Indian Reservation. Mrs. Plummer was a former surrogate of the Seneca Nation and helped count the ballots during the referendum on the IRA.

34. Quoted in "First Citizens of Syracuse — The Red Men of the Onondagas — Perilously Approach New Deal," *Syracuse* (N.Y.) *Herald*, July 27, 1933, p. 13.

35. Quoted in Arthur T. Weil, "Collier Plans to Build Up Indian Agency in New York," *Buffalo* (N.Y.) *Evening News*, Sept. 20, 1933, p. 18.

36. U.S. Department of the Interior, *Annual Report of the Commissioner of Indian Affairs, 1934* (Washington, D.C., 1934), pp. 78–91.

37. Collier, "The Indians of New York State and the New Federal Indian Policy."

38. Quoted in "First Citizens of Syracuse."

39. "Six Nations Cite Grievances Against Government Bureau," *Buffalo Evening News*, Feb. 4, 1933.

40. Quoted in First Citizens of Syracuse"; "Six Nations Cite Grievances Against Government Bureau," *Buffalo Evening News*, Feb. 4, 1933; Weil, "Collier Plans to Build Up Indian Agency."

41. Collier, *Indians of the Americas*, pp. 117–21.

42. Ibid., p. 117.

43. Ibid., pp. 120–21.

44. Collier, "The Indians of New York State and the New Federal Indian Policy."

45. Kunitz, "The Social Philosophy of John Collier," p. 225. It is clear that Collier snubbed important Iroquois leaders by not making direct personal contact with them. He failed to heed the warning of one powerful traditionalist leader by ignoring his request to come to New York to explain the IRA. Joshua Jones to John Collier, May 3, 1934, #4894-1934-066, Part 5B, Records Concerning the Wheeler-Howard Act, Box 5, RG75, NA.

46. McNickle, *They Came Here First*, p. 244.

47. William Duncan Strong to William N. Fenton, Aug. 27, 1934, Fenton MSS., Indian Service Correspondence, 1935–37, State University of New York, Albany (in Dr. Fenton's possession).

48. J. N. B. Hewitt to Chief William Chew, Dec. 13, 1934, Hewitt MSS., #4271, Box 2, National Anthropological Archives, Smithsonian Institution, Washington, D.C.

49. William N. Fenton to Laurence M. Hauptman, Oct. 6, 1978, letter in the author's possession; *Fighting Tuscarora*, pp. 81–82, 92.

50. J. N. B. Hewitt to *Gonya da'we* [Chief Chew], June 9, 1935, Hewitt MSS., #4271, Box 2, National Anthropological Archives, Smithsonian Institution, Washington, D.C.

51. William N. Fenton, "This Island, the World on the Turtle's Back," *Journal of American Folklore* 75 (Oct.–Dec. 1962): 286.

3 — The Only Good Indian Bureau is a Dead Indian Bureau

1. "Mrs. L. Lee Jemison," (obituary notice), *Buffalo* (N.Y.) *Evening News*, March 10, 1964, p. 39; FBI Main File on Alice Lee Jemison, FOIPA #60,431, released Aug. 17, 1978; U.S. Congress, House Committee on Indian Affairs, *Hearings on S. 2103:*

Wheeler-Howard Act—Exempt Certain Indians, 76th Cong., 3rd Sess. (Washington, D.C., 1940), pp. 68–82, 92, 98–110; Harold Ickes, *The Secret Diary of Harold Ickes* (New York, 1954), 2: 506–507; U.S. Department of Interior News Release, Nov. 23, 1938, Office File of Commissioner John Collier, Box 6, File: "Alice Lee Jemison," RG75, NA; John Collier to Oliver LaFarge, May 10, 1939, Association on American Indian Affairs Papers, Box 200, Princeton University. Besides Collier and Ickes, some Justice Department personnel continued to repeat these unwarranted accusations for another two decades. O. John Rogge (assistant attorney general), *The Official German Report: Nazi Penetration, 1924–1942: Pan-Arabism, 1939–Today* (New York, 1961), p. 315; John Roy Carlson (pseud. of Arthur Derounian, FBI agent), *Under Cover: My Four Years in the Nazi Underworld of America—The Amazing Revelation of How Axis Agents and Our Enemies within Are Now Plotting to Destroy the United States* (New York, 1943), pp. 145–46, 150–52, 218.

2. Interviews of Francis Kettle, (former president, Seneca Nation), July 27, 1977, June 4, 1978; Winifred Kettle, July 27, 1977; Edna Parker, June 4, 1978; Florence Lay, June 4, 1978; and Pauline Seneca, June 4, 1978, Cattaraugus Indian Reservation. The above are either contemporaries of Jemison or leading elders of the Seneca Nation of Indians. It should be noted that Jemison had close contact with the leaders of all the Six Nations throughout the interwar period, including Clinton Rickard, Ray Jimerson, Aaron Poodry, Jesse Lyons, and Joshua Jones. Joshua Jones, Jesse Lyons, and Alice Lee Jemison to Senator Robert Wagner, June 10, 1934, Robert Wagner MSS., Legislative File, Box 224, File 1544 "Indians," Georgetown University Library. Both Jones and Lyons were members of the American Indian Federation. Jones, Lyons, and Poodry held offices on the Six Nations Confederacy Council during the interwar years, while Jimerson and Rickard were tribal leaders among the Iroquois during the same period.

3. Interviews of Jeanne Marie Jemison, Aug. 26, 1977, Herndon, Va.; Robert Galloway, June 3, 1978, Silver Creek, N.Y. Ms. Jemison is Alice Lee Jemison's daughter. The late Mr. Galloway, the former attorney for the Seneca Nation, was Jemison's classmate, close friend, and employer.

4. Ray Jimerson to Congressman James Mead, Jan. 28, 1933, with attached resolution of Seneca National Tribal Council and vita of Alice Lee Jemison, Indian Collection, Buffalo and Erie County Historical Society; Ray Jimerson to John Collier, March 26, 1934, with attached resolutions of Seneca Nation Tribal Council dated Jan. 28, 1933 and Dec. 30, 1933, BIA Central Files, 1907–1939, #19086-1934-162 New York, RG75, NA.

5. Interviews of Jeanne Marie Jemison, Aug. 26, 1977, Herndon, Va.; May 2–4, 1978, New Paltz, N.Y.; Aug. 23, 1978, Tyson's Corners, Va. Jemison was employed in the early 1930s in the law offices of Robert Codd, Jr., a man who later attempted to discredit her. Attorney Codd, a man of questionable virtues, was on several occasions an attorney for the Six Nations. Interview of Francis Kettle, July 27, 1977; William N. Fenton to Laurence M. Hauptman, May 22, 1978; *Fighting Tuscarora*, pp. 78–88. Collier and Ickes employed Robert Codd, Jr., to discredit Mrs. Jemison before congressional committees. "Attorney for Six Nations Contradicts Dies Witness," *Buffalo* (N.Y.) *Courier-Express*, Nov. 23, 1938, p. 1.

6. *Woodin v. Seeley* 252N.Y.S. 818 (1931); Interview of Pauline Seneca, June 4, 1978. Mrs. Seneca was Jemison's aunt and the wife of the late Cornelius Seneca. Jimerson to Mead, Jan. 28, 1933; Jimerson to Collier, March 26, 1934.

7. Jimerson to Mead, Jan. 28, 1933.

8. *Fighting Tuscarora*, pp. 98–100, photographs and caption p. 98 passim. The Buffalo newspaper accounts of the case can be followed in *Buffalo Local Biographies* 22, MA, Local History Desk, Buffalo and Erie County Public Library. The murder occurred on March 6, 1930; by March 23, the trial had already begun. "Marchand Jury is Completed," *Buffalo Evening News*, March 24, 1930, p. 1. BIA Central Files, 1907–1909, #14169-1930-175 General Services, RG75, NA.

9. *Fighting Tuscarora*, pp. 98–100, Interview of Beulah Rickard Lillvick, June 6, 1978, Tuscarora Indian Reservation; Newsclippings, Folder B7.1, Joseph Keppler MSS., Museum of the American Indian; see also "Nancy Bowen, called "Witch, Dead," *Buffalo Courier-Express*, Jan. 24, 1960, sec. B, p. 1; "Nancy Bowen Dies; 'Witch' Believer in Famed WNY Trial," *Buffalo Evening News*, Jan. 23, 1960, sec. A, p. 1; "Henri Marchand Dies at 73; Figured in Famous Trial Here," *Buffalo Evening News*, June 1, 1951, p. 26; "Jules Henri Marchand, Painter, Sculptor, Dies," *Buffalo Courier-Express*, June 1, 1951, p. 26; Ann Matthews, "Old Murder Case Figure, Lila Jimerson, Dies," *Buffalo Courier-Express*, Jan. 21, 1972, p. 23.

10. Interview of Robert Galloway, June 3, 1978. Mr. Galloway was Lila Jimerson's attorney. L. E. H. Smith to President Herbert Hoover, May 2, 1930; L. E. H. Smith to commissioner of Indian affairs, May 1, 1930, BIA Central Files, 1907–1939, #14169-1930-175 General Service, RG75, NA; C. J. Rhoads (commissioner of Indian affairs) to Vice-President Charles Curtis, March 26, 1930; Curtis to Rhoads, May 6, 8, 14, 19, 1930, BIA Central Files, 1907–1939, #14169-1930-175 General Service, RG75, NA; Alice Lee Jemison to Mrs. E. Claudia Handley, May 5, 1930; Handley to Senator Robert F. Wagner, May 10, 1930; Wagner to Handley, May 17, 1930, Senator Robert F. Wagner MSS., Legislative File, Box 193, Folder 588, "Indian Affairs," Georgetown University.

11. Alice Lee Jemison, "Present Crime Poor Example of Real Indian," *Buffalo* (N.Y.) *Evening Times*, March 23, 1930, found in *Buffalo Local Biographies* 17, HOX-JIM, 240–41, Local History Desk, Buffalo and Erie County Public Library.

12. Interview of Jeanne Marie Jemison, Aug. 23, 1978, Tyson's Corners, Va.; Alice Lee Jemison, "Civilization and the Indian," *Washington Star*, April 4, 6, 1932, found in J. N. B. Hewitt MSS., #4271, Box 2, File: Kellogg Newsclippings, et al., National Anthropological Archives, Smithsonian Institution, Washington, D.C. In 1939, she and Congressman Usher L. Burdick of North Dakota attempted to remove a group of statues in the East Portico of the Capitol on the ground that it was offensive to American Indians. Horatio Greenough's "Rescue Group" (1853) depicted an American Indian with a tomahawk in hand about to kill a white woman and her child but saved by a heroic pioneer. Jemison and Burdick suggested it be ground into dust and replaced by a statue of Sacajawea. Alice Lee Jemison, "H. J. Res. 276," *The First American* 1, no. 5 (1939): 1–3.

13. For the career of Montezuma, see Peter Iverson, "Carlos Montezuma," In *American Indian Leaders*, W. David Edmunds, ed. (Lincoln, Nebr., 1980), pp. 206–221. "The Bureau Indians," *Wassaja* 3 (March 1919): 1; "Aim-Fire! Shoot Straight," *Wassaja* 7 (Oct. 21, 1921): 1–2; *Let My People Go*, Pamphlet of Speech before Society of American Indians, Sept. 30, 1915 (n.p., n.d.); *Abolish the Indian Bureau* (n.p., n.d.).

14. "The Difference Between the Indian Bureau and Other Bureaus of the Government," *Wassaja* 8 (Oct. 1922): 3.

15. For a study of Montezuma's impact see Hazel Hertzberg, *The Search for an American Indian Identity: Modern Pan-Indian Movements* (Syracuse, N.Y., 1971), pp. 44–45.

16. Latimer quoted in Alice Lee Jemison, "Freedom for the Indian," *Washington Star*, April 24, 1933, Office File of Commissioner John Collier, Box 6, File: "Alice Lee Jemison," RG75, NA.

17. "A Shameful Neglect," *The Six Nations* 1 (Nov. 1, 1926): 40; "Indian Education," *The Six Nations* 1 (Nov. 1, 1926): 39; "Boundary Crossing Question," *The Six Nations* 1 (Oct. 1927): 2; "Bureau of Indian Affairs to Stand Investigation," *The Six Nations* 2 (April 1928): 9.

18. "Federal Indian Bureau About to be Deprived of its Tyrannical Power Over Indians," *The Six Nations* 1 (Nov. 1, 1926): 25.

19. "Six Nations Cite Grievances Against Government Bureau," *Buffalo Evening News*, Feb. 4, 1933; "Indians Ask Collier to Outline Policies," *Buffalo Evening News*, April 18, 1933, p. 23; "Naming of Collier Ends Long Battle," *Buffalo Evening News*, April 18, 1933, p. 23; "Demand for Hearing is Made by Indians," *Buffalo Evening News*, April 19, 1933, p. 6; "Indians Want Some Voice in Selecting Commissioner," *Buffalo Evening News*, April 20, 1933, p. 27; "Collier Confirmed for Indian Bureau," *Buffalo Evening News*, April 21, 1933, p. 38.

20. "Six Nations Cite Grievances." Collier had some support for the commissionership among the Iroquois, although it was limited in nature. Chief Edgar H. Rickard to John Collier, April 28, 1933; Cephas A. Watt to John Collier, April 21, 1933, John Collier MSS., Box 16, Folder 347, Yale University. Watt later broke with Collier over the IRA. Fenton Travel Report, May 30–June 12, 1935, Fenton MSS.

21. Alice Lee Jemison, "Indians Want Some Voice in Selecting Commissioner," *Buffalo Evening News*, April 20, 1933, p. 27. The Intertribal Committee for the Fundamental Advancement of the American Indian was headed by Norman Ewing (Flying Iron), a noted musician and prominent speaker against the Indian Bureau who was an urban Indian residing in Buffalo and later Detroit.

22. Jemison, "Indians Want Some Voice in Selecting Commissioner." The other *Buffalo Evening News* articles written by Jemison that were syndicated were "Indians Plan United Drive for their Racial Freedom," April 18, 1933, p. 23; "Indian Freedom Set Forth as Real Economy Measure," April 19, 1933, p. 6; "Indians Seek End of Bureau Control," April 21, 1933, p. 38.

23. Hoover's appointments to head the BIA (C. J. Rhoads and J. Henry Scattergood) were active in the Indian Rights Association. Jemison, "Indians Want Some Voice in Selecting Commissioner."

24. Jemison, "Indians Plan United Drive for Their Racial Freedom."

25. U.S. Congress, Senate, Committee on Indian Affairs. *Hearings on S. 5302* (Washington, D.C., 1933), p. 7; William Zimmerman, Jr., to Alice Lee Jemison Dec. 17, 1936, Records of the Bureau of Indian Affairs, New System, 1936, File No. 84524, RG75, NA. Ray Jimerson to John Collier, Jan. 27, 1934, #4894-1934-066, Records Concerning the Wheeler-Howard Act, Box 4, RG75, NA.

26. Harold Ickes to John Collier, Aug. 31, 1933, John Collier MSS., Box 8, Folder 153, Yale University.

27. Alice Lee Jemison to President Franklin D. Roosevelt, June 20, 1935, President Franklin D. Roosevelt MSS., OF 296, FDR Library, Hyde Park, N.Y.

28. Collier frequently challenged Jemison's right to testify as a representative of the Seneca Nation of Indians; while Ickes refers to her in his diaries as that Jemison "dame." She produced notarized letters from the Seneca Nation Tribal Council to prove her authority before congressional committees. W. K. Harrison to John Collier, March 26, 1935; Collier to Harrison, March 13, May 2, 1935, BIA Central Files, 1907–1939, #14474-1935-054 New York; Harrison to Collier, March 14, 18, 1935; Collier to Robert M. Codd, Jr., Sept. 20, 1934, Office File of John Collier, Box 6, File: "Alice Lee Jemison," RG75, NA; U.S. Congress, House of Representatives, Committee on Indian Affairs, Hearings on H.R. 7781 and other matters: *Indian Conditions and Affairs*, 74th Cong. 1st. Sess. (Washington, D.C., 1935), pp. 29–30; Ickes, *Secret Diary* 2: 506–507; Jemison to Roosevelt, June 20, 1935; *Hearings on S. 5302*, pp. 6–10.

29. Jimerson to Collier, Jan. 27, 1934.

30. Jemison to Roosevelt, June 20, 1935.

31. See, for example, Philp, *John Collier's Crusade*, pp. 172, 200–203; Parman, *The Navajos and the New Deal*, pp. 70–72.

32. Interview of Joseph Bruner, Feb. 28, 1938, (WPA) Indian-Pioneer History, 87, 271, Indian Archives Division, Oklahoma Historical Society, Oklahoma City; for Bruner's ideas, see his "The Indian Demands Justice," *National Republic* 20 (March, 1935): 23–24. Bruner to Collier, May 19, 28, June 30, 1934, #4894-1934-066, Part 5B, Records Concerning the Wheeler-Howard Act, Box 5, RG75, NA; "Collier Attack Made by Bruner," *Tulsa* (Okla.) *Daily World*, May 3, 1934, p. 16. Chandler had been dismissed as the superintendent of the Quapaw Agency for alleged kickbacks and for many years sought vindication. Le Flore sought a political patronage job in the Indian Service but was turned down because he was informed his quantum of Indian blood was insufficient for job preference; he argued that he was more than a one-eighth Choctaw. Interview of Charles Banks Wilson, Aug. 18, 1979, Miami, Okla. Mr. Wilson, a famous artist, remembered Chandler and his activities. O. K. Chandler to Senator Elmer Thomas, May 8, 1935, Thomas MSS., Box 65; Thomas to Harold Ickes, June 13, 1935, Box 69; E. K. Burley to Thomas, July 2, 1935, Western History Collection, University of Oklahoma; Angie Debo, *And Still the Waters Run: The Betrayal of the Five Civilized Tribes* (Princeton, N.J., 1940), p. 343; W. David Baird, *The Quapaw Indians: A History of the Downstream People* (Norman, Okla., 1980), p. 196.

33. Interviews of Rupert Costo, April 20–21, 1979, Geneva, N.Y.; Catherine Bauer (Mrs. Fred Bauer), April 6, 1978, Cherokee, N.C.; Hertzberg, *The Search for an America Indian Identity*, pp. 46–47 (Sloan); Fred Bauer, *Land of the North Carolina Cherokees* (Brevard, N.C., 1970); U.S. Congress, Senate, Subcommittee of the Committee on Indian Affairs, Hearings on S. Res. 79: *Survey of Conditions of the Indians in the United States*, 76th Cong. (Washington, D.C., 1940), 37: 20786–860 (Bauer), 21436–41 (Castillo), 21466–539 (Black Hills Treaty Council). J. C. Morgan was actually the first vice-president of the AIF, and his name appears on the masthead of AIF's stationary from 1934–37. AIF Memorial sent by Joseph Bruner to John Collier, Dec. 21, 1934; BIA Central Files, 1907–1939, #747-1935-155 General Service; Bruner to Collier, Sept. 6, 1935, Office File of Commissioner John Collier, Box 1, File: "American Indian Federation," RG75, NA; Alice Lee Jemison to Collier, March 13, 1937, BIA Central Files,

1907–1939, #29207-1932-417 Colorado River, Part I, RG75, NA. Chiefs Joshua Jones and Jesse Lyons of the Onondaga Nation vehemently opposed the IRA and were members of the AIF in 1934 and 1935. See AIF Petition of Jones, Lyons, and Alice Lee Jemison to Senator Robert F. Wagner, June 10, 1934, Senator Robert F. Wagner MSS., Legislative File, Box 224, File 1544, "Indians," Georgetown University. The Black Hills Treaty Council, an anti-IRA Sioux group, included among its membership fullbloods opposed to elected systems.

34. John L. Freeman, "The New Deal for Indians: A Study in Bureau-committee Relations in American Government," (Ph.D. diss., Princeton University, 1952), p. 329; *The First American* 1 (April 8, 1937): 2–4; (July 1, 1937): 1, 6, 8; (Aug. 14, 1937): 1–4.

35. Alice Lee Jemison to President Franklin D. Roosevelt, Aug. 11, 1937, BIA Central Files, 1907–1939, #747-1935-155 General Service, RG75, NA. Interview of Catherine Bauer, April 6, 1978; Fred Bauer, *Land of the Cherokees*, pp. 34–53; *Hearings on S. Res. 79*, 37: 20457–670; "Those on Qualla Reservation Refuse to Grant Federal Government Right-of-Way for Blue Ridge Parkway; Legend cited," *New York Times*, Aug. 27, 1939, p. 23; "Cherokee Eastern Band Grants Right-of-Way for Road Across Reservation," *New York Times*, March 3, 1940, p. 1.

36. *Hearings on S. Res. 79*, 36: 21466–877; *Hearings on H.R. 7781*, pp. 436–81; Interview of Rupert Costo, April 20–21, 1979; Alice Lee Jemison to William Sherman Walker, Aug. 31, 1936, Office File of Commissioner John Collier, Box 6, File: "Alice Lee Jemison," RG75, NA.

37. Alice Lee Jemison, "Another View of Treatment of the Indian," *Washington Times*, Aug. 8, 1935, found in Office File of Commissioner John Collier, Box 6, File: "Alice Lee Jemison," RG75, NA, p. 15.

38. Speech of Alice Lee Jemison before Black Hills Treaty Council, Kyle, S.D., July 27, 1938, found in Office File of Commissioner John Collier, "Alice Lee Jemison," RG75, NA.

39. *Hearings on S. Res. 79*, 20527 (Jenckes); Congressman James B. Duffy to Arthur C. Parker, July 5, Aug. 6, 1935; Parker to Duffy, Aug. 7, 1935, Arthur C. Parker MSS., Box 1, File 7, University of Rochester (Beiter); *Hearings on H.R. 7781*, 43–58 (Burdick and McGroarty); Roger Baldwin to John Collier, Dec. 23, 1937, John Collier MSS., Correspondence, 1933–45, Vol. I, Part 2, Series I, Box 2, Folder: Roger Baldwin, Yale University (Wheeler); John Collier Memorandum for Secretary Ickes, May 17, 1940, Collier MSS., Box 8, Folder 155, Sterling Memorial Library, Yale University (Grorud).

40. Alice Lee Jemison and O. K. Chandler, *Now Who's Un-American? An Exposé of Communism in the United States Government* (Washington, D.C., 1937?); U.S. Congress, House of Representatives, Special Committee on Un-American Activities. *Hearings* (Nov. 19–Dec. 14, 1938); Jemison Testimony Reprinted in U.S. Congress House of Representatives, Committee on Indian Affairs, Hearings on S. 2103: *Wheeler-Howard Act –Exempt Certain Indians*, 76th Cong., 3rd Sess. (Washington, D.C., 1940), pp. 196–259; "Indian Bureau Linked to Civil Liberties Union," *Buffalo Courier-Express*, Nov. 23, 1938, p. 1; "Civil Liberties Union Indorsed by Ickes, Dies Group Told," *Washington Star*, Nov. 22, 1938, found in Harold Ickes MSS., Scrapbooks, Box 490, Library of Congress; "Williams of WPA Assailed by Dies," *New York Times*, Nov. 23, 1938, p. 15.

41. Mildred W. Leach to John Collier, March 30, 1939, Office File of Commissioner

John Collier, Box 6, File: "Alice Lee Jemison," RG75, NA; Leach to Harold Ickes, March 6, 1939, BIA Central Files, 1907–1939, #14320-1939-155 General Service, RG75, NA. Mrs. Leach was an officer in the DAR. The DAR sponsored Jemison's investigative tours of western Indian reservations in 1938. Interview of Robert Galloway, June 3, 1978. Pelley made extremist capital out of Jemison's and Bauer's exposes of the conditions on the Eastern Cherokee Reservation. *Indians Aren't Red: The Inside Story of Administration Attempts to Make Communists of the North Carolina Cherokees* (Asheville, N.C., 1939); Alice Lee Jemison, "The Indians are Coming," *Christian Free Press* (Sept. 1938), reprinted in *Hearings on S. 21303* (1940), pp. 78–81. See also pp. 154–57 of these hearings. Geoffrey S. Smith, *To Save a Nation: American Countersubversives, the New Deal and the Coming of World War II* (New York, 1973), pp. 143–44; Robert Marshall to John Collier, Nov. 23, 1937, with attached form letter from the James True Associates to Americans Everywhere, Oct., 1937, Office File of Commissioner John Collier, Box 6, File: "Alice Lee Jemison," RG75, NA. For an analysis of True, see George Wolfskill and John Hudson, *All But the People: Franklin D. Roosevelt and His Critics, 1933–1939* (New York, 1969), pp. 68–70.

42. *Hearings on S. 2103*, p. 165.

43. Ibid., p. 110. Collier produced a chart before the House Committee that allegedly linked Jemison to every major fascist in the country. The FBI file on Alice Lee Jemison reveals that the leadership in the Justice Department believed the charges were circumstantial and mere heresay. Interestingly, Jemison was also accused of being a communist. FBI File, FOIPA #60, 431. The accusation of communism was made also in *Hearings on S. 2103*, 165. For Jemison's antidraft stance, see William Zimmerman, Jr., to Clarence A Dykstra (director of Selective Service), Nov. 27, 1940, Office File of Commissioner John Collier, Box 6, File: "Alice Lee Jemison," RG75, NA.

44. *Hearings on S. 2103* (1940), pp. 102–111; FBI File, FOIPA #60, 431; Philp, *John Collier's Crusade*, pp. 200n2, 201, 202; *The First American*, 1937–40 and later 1953–54, was until 1939 the official newsletter of the American Indian Federation. With 1, no. 5 (1939), Jemison officially announced that the newsletter represented her views only. Another AIF magazine, *The American Indian*, was published in the earlier period of the Indian New Deal.

45. James T. Patterson, *Congressional Conservatism and the New Deal* (Lexington, Ky., 1967), pp. 77–249; Philp, *John Collier's Crusade*, pp. 198–99.

46. "Name-Calling Led by Ickes and Dies," *New York Times*, Nov. 24, 1938, p. 1; "Ickes Calls Dies a Zany," *Baltimore* (Md.) *Sun*, Nov. 24, 1938, found in Ickes MSS., Scrapbooks, Box 491, Library of Congress; U.S. Department of the Interior News Release, Nov. 23, 1938, Office File of Commissioner John Collier, Box 6, File: "Alice Lee Jemison," RG75, NA; FBI File, FOIPA #60, 431.

47. She resigned from the American Indian Federation on July 10, 1939 because she disagreed with the AIF leaders abandonment of their original goals—repealing the IRA, removing Collier and abolishing the BIA altogether. *Hearings on S. 2103*, pp. 166–67. Collier and Ickes called the Settlement Bill, the "Oklahoma Indian Racket." The bill (H.R. 5921) was introduced by Congressman Burdick on April 20, 1939, and called for authorizing payment to certain individual Indians or the heirs of Indians in the sum of $3,000; in return, these Indians would give up all claims against the United States

government. The bill could be found in Office File of John Collier, Box 2, File: "Joseph Bruner," RG75, NA. Although there is no written record of Jemison's attitudes toward the Settlement Bill, it appears that she might have objected to it as an Iroquois committed to upholding of the Treaty of Canandaigua of 1794, which the bill superseded.

48. Ibid., pp. 173–265.

49. U.S. Senate, Subcommittee of the Committee on Interior and Insular Affairs, Hearings: *New York Indians*. 80th Cong., 2nd Sess. (Washington, D.C., 1948), pp. 21–27.

50. Although she favored the end of the BIA's role in Indian affairs, she objected to several features of the termination bills of the Eisenhower administration and predicted: "The present proposals will accomplish only one thing with any certainty — the termination of federal expenditures for the benefit of the Indians," *The First American* 2 (Feb. 3, 1954): 3.

51. *Hearings on H.R. 7781*, pp. 35–36.

52. Ibid., p. 48.

4 —Raw Deal

1. Melvin Patterson, "Attacks Indian Bill," *Buffalo* (N.Y.) *Courier-Express*, June 11, 1935, Letter to the Editor, found in Howard Gansworth MSS., Newsclippings, Box 7, Folder 1935, Buffalo and Erie County Historical Society, Buffalo, N.Y.

2. Theodore H. Haas, *Ten years of Tribal Government Under I.R.A.* (Washington, D.C., 1947), p. 18. No official referendum was held among the homeless Iroquois — the Cayugas living at Cattaraugus and the Oneidas, most of whom living at Onondaga. The Oneidas in New York later attempted to come under the IRA in the 1940s. A referendum was held at the Cornplanter tract in Pennsylvania on June 15, 1935. Twenty-three voted for and 17 against the IRA; however, of the 40 votes cast, 17 were cast by Onondagas and Senecas from other reservations. The Cornplanter Seneca leaders protested coming under the IRA because, of what they claimed, was an illegal referendum. Despite Collier's wish to apply the act to the Cornplanter Tract, this legal confusion appeared to stymie his efforts. Merrill Bowen to John Collier, June 18, 1935; Mitchell S. Pierce to Harold Ickes, June 17, 1935; Collier to W. K. Harrison, July 30, Nov. 18, 1935; Holst Memorandum for Cornplanter Files, Oct. 18, 1937; Kirgis Memorandum, May 24, 1937; Shipe and Faris Report, Oct. 14, 1936, #9562-1936-066 New York, General Records Concerning Indian Organization, 1934–56, RG75, NA.

3. *United States Statutes at Large* 47: 984–88.

4. John Snyder to Alice Lee Jemison, June 12, 1935, Office File of Commissioner John Collier, Box 6, File: "Alice Lee Jemison," RG75, NA.

5. Ibid.

6. *Hearings on H.R. 7902*, p. 389; Frank D. Williams to John Collier, Sept. 27, 1934, Records Concerning the Wheeler-Howard Act, #48622-1934-066, RG75, NA. Williams was out of step with majority thinking at Tuscarora. Interview of Beulah Rickard

Lillvick, June 6, 1978, Tuscarora Indian Reservation. Mrs. Lillvick was the wife of the late Chief Clinton Rickard, one of the most respected of Iroquois leaders of the twentieth century. Edgar Rickard to John Collier, April 28, 1933, Collier MSS., Box 16, Folder 347; John Collier, "The Indians of New York State and the New Federal Indian Policy," Address on Indian Day at the Four Nations Celebration at Niagara Falls, N.Y., Sept. 4, 1934, Collier MSS., Box 49, Folder 47, Yale University.

7. *Fighting Tuscarora*, p. 126.

8. See Chapters 5 and 6.

9. Hauptman, "Senecas and Subdividers," pp. 105–116.

10. Quoted in Carl Carmer, *Listen for a Lonesome Drum* (New York, 1936), pp. 110–111.

11. George F. Newton to John Collier, Oct. 28, 1934, #4894-1934-066, Part 12A, Records Concerning the Wheeler-Howard Act, Box 9, RG75, NA.

12. Quoted in Carmer, *Listen for a Lonesome Drum*, pp. 110-111.

13. *Fighting Tuscarora*, p. 126. There is much evidence to confirm Rickard's claims of racial prejudice. Petition of the Onondaga Indians to Governor Herbert Lehman, May 24, 1934, Governor Lehman MSS., Microfilm Reel 73, Columbia University; Ray Jimerson to John Collier, Jan. 27, 1934, #4894-1934-066, Records Concerning the Wheeler-Howard Act, Box 4, RG75, NA.

14. Harry M. Hirsch, "New York State Indians," *Social Welfare Bulletin* 7 (Jan.–Feb. 1936): 1; New York State Board of Social Welfare, *70th Annual Report* for the year ended June 30, 1936 (Albany, N.Y., 1937), p. 24.

15. Jesse Lyons and Joshua Jones to Governor Herbert Lehman, Feb. 7, 1934, Lehman MSS., Microfilm Reel 73, Columbia University.

16. Works Progress Administration Report, *Social and Economic Survey of the New York Indian Reservations* (Dec. 1939); C. H. Berry, "Report on New York Indian Situation," March 1939, #9506-1936-066 New York, General Records Concerning Indian Organization, 1934–56, RG75, NA.

17. *Fighting Tuscarora*, pp. 49–50.

18. Lulu G. Stillman to John Collier, March 4, March 29 (with attached signed petition against Wheeler-Howard and postscript on Stillman's evaluation of the Everett Report), #4894-1934-066, Part 7, Records Concerning the Wheeler-Howard Act, Box 7, RG75, NA; Stillman to Collier, April 10; Stillman to Senator Burton Wheeler, Jan. 29, 1934, BIA Central Files, 1907–1939, #17799-1934-051 New York, RG75, NA. Stillman's petition gained full acceptance at St. Regis. Petition of the Mohawk Nation Against the Wheeler-Howard Act, Jan. 31, 1934, Senator Robert F. Wagner MSS., Legislative File, Box 224, File 1544, "Indians," Georgetown University.

19. Lulu G. Stillman to all the Six Nations, April 16, 1934, attached to letter from W. K. Harrison to commissioner of Indian affairs, May 15, 1934, #4894-1934-066, Part 7, Records Concerning the Wheeler-Howard Act, Box 7, RG75, NA.

20. Interview of Beulah Rickard Lillvick, June 6, 1978, Ray Fadden, July 15, 1980, Onchiota, N.Y.; *Fighting Tuscarora*, p. 49.

21. *Fighting Tuscarora*, pp. 95–96.

22. Arthur T. Weil, "Collier Plans to Build Up Indian Agency in New York," *Buffalo* (N.Y.) *Evening News*, Sept. 20, 1933, p. 18.

23. Interview of Genevieve Plummer, July 28, 1977.

24. William N. Fenton to John Collier, April 24, 1935; John Collier to Freeman Johnson, June 10, 1935; Fenton Travel Report, May 30— June 12, 1935, William N. Fenton MSS., Indian Service File, 1935—1937 (in Dr. Fenton's possession). It is clear individuals not on tribal rolls saw the IRA as means to be recognized. Non-enrolled Indians of Seneca ancestry saw the IRA as beneficial. Assistant Commissioner of Indian Affairs William Zimmerman specified the new rights of this group on Nov. 16, 1934: "Your admission to membership under this act gives you no right to share in tribal property, funds, etc. *You can only share in such property as may be acquired and assigned to the tribe through the provisions of the act.*" Zimmerman to Patterson, Nov. 16, 1934, #4894-1934-066, Part 12A, Records Concerning the Wheeler-Howard Act, Box 9, RG75, NA. For Brunel Patterson's views, see Patterson to John Collier, April 23, June 18, and Oct. 11, 1934, #4894-1934-066, Part 12A, Records Concerning the Wheeler-Howard Act, Box 9, RG75, NA.

25. *Hearings on H.R. 7781*, p. 32; see also "Indians to Vote Next Week on New Reorganization Act," *Buffalo Courier-Express*, June 8, 1935, p. 1. This concern was also expressed by the Tuscaroras about the large number of Onondagas and non-enrolled Iroquois living on their reservation. Fenton Travel Report, May 30— June 12, 1935; William N. Fenton to John Collier, June 17, 1935, Fenton MSS.

26. "Indians to Vote Next Week on New Reorganization Act." For the Iroquois matriarchate, see Martha C. Randle, "Iroquois Women, Then and Now," Bureau of American Ethnology, *Bulletin* 149 (Washington, D.C., 1951): 167—80; Cara B. Richards, "Matriarchy or Mistake: The Role of Iroquois Women Through Time," in *Cultural Stability and Cultural Change*, Verne F. Ray, ed. (Seattle, Wash., 1951), pp. 36—45; Judith K. Brown, "Economic Organization and the Position of Women among the Iroquois," *Ethnohistory* 17 (1970): pp. 151—67. For a modified view of the Iroquois matriarchate, see Elisabeth Tooker, "Women in Iroquois Society," paper presented at Conference on Women in the Era of the American Revolution, George Washington University, July 25, 1975.

27. *Hearings on S. 2103*, p. 448.

28. Ray Jimerson to Congressman Edgar Howard, April 12, 1934, Arthur Parker MSS., Box 1, File 5, University of Rochester; William N. Fenton to John Collier, June 17, 1935, Fenton MSS.; Interview of Chief Corbett Sundown, May 22, 1980, Tonawanda Indian Reservation.

29. United States, House of Representatives, Committee on Indian Affairs, *Hearings on H.R. 7902* (Washington, D.C., 1934), 9: 389; Ray Jimerson to Edgar Howard, April 12, 1934, Arthur C. Parker MSS.

30. Jesse Cornplanter to C. Carleton Perry, Dec. 18, 1940, Indian Arts Project Correspondence, Rochester Museum and Science Center (hereafter cited as RMSC).

31. Jesse Cornplanter to John Collier, June 12, 1940, Office File of Commissioner Collier, Box 6, File: "Alice Lee Jemison," RG75, NA.

32. *Fighting Tuscarora*, pp. 58—65; Ray Fadden, *Deskaheh: Iroquois Statesman and Patriot* (Onchiota, N.Y.,?); *Akwesasne Notes, A Basic Call to Consciousness* (Rooseveltown, N.Y.,

1978), p. 29; Carl Carmer, *Dark Trees to the Wind: A Cycle of York State Years* (New York, 1949), pp. 105–117.

33. Joshua Jones to John Collier, Feb. 26, 1934, Joshua Jones and Jesse Lyons, Telegram, June 19, 1934, #4894-1934-066, Part 5B, Records Concerning the Wheeler-Howard Act, Box 5, RG75, NA; Fenton Travel Report, May 30–June 12, 1935, Fenton MSS. This argument was also used by the St. Regis Mohawks and Tonawanda Senecas. Petition of the Mohawk Nation to Harold Ickes, Jan. 31, 1934; Head Sachem of Tonawanda Senecas Freeman Johnson to John Reeves, Feb. 6, 1934, #4894-1934-066, Part 2a, Records Concerning the Wheeler-Howard Act, Box 2, RG75, NA.

34. William N. Fenton to John Collier, April 24, 1935, Fenton MSS.

35. Alice Lee Jemison to Congressman Alfred Beiter, June 18, 1935, Arthur C. Parker MSS., Box 1, File 7, University of Rochester; Fenton Travel Report, May 30–June 12, 1935, Fenton MSS.

36. *Fighting Tuscarora*, pp. 125–26.

37. Interview of Genevieve Plummer, July 28, 1977.

38. Ibid.; Interviews of Francis Kettle, July 27, 1977, June 4, 1978, Winifred Kettle, July 27, 1977, Cattaraugus Indian Reservation. Interview of Reverend W. David Owl, Versailles, N.Y., July 28, 1977. Ms. Kettle, the former director of the Seneca Women's, Infant's, Children's Community Health program, remembered the turmoil of the IRA referendum at Cattaraugus. Owl, a Cherokee Indian, was a highly respected Baptist-Presbyterian missionary on the reservation and was integrally part of Seneca life in the 1930s.

39. William N. Fenton to John Collier, April 24, 1935, Fenton MSS.

40. Harrison Farmer (Onondaga Tribal Council secretary) to John Collier, May 3, 1934, #4874-1934-066, Records Concerning the Wheeler-Howard Act, Box 4, RG75, NA; Interview of William N. Fenton, Sept. 28, 1977, Albany, N.Y.

41. Harrison Farmer to John Collier, May 3, 1934.

42. *Fighting Tuscarora*, p. 125.

43. John Collier to Senator Royal S. Copeland, June 12, 1934, Senator Robert F. Wagner MSS., Legislative File, Box 224, File 1544, "Indians," Georgetown University.

44. Ibid.; William N. Fenton to John Collier, April 24, 1935, Fenton MSS.; Ray Jimerson to President Roosevelt, Telegram, June 20, 1934; Joshua Jones to John Collier, Feb. 26, May 3, 1934; Jason Snow to commissioner of Indian affairs, March 30, 1934, #4894-1934-066, Part 5B, Records Concerning the Wheeler-Howard Act, Box 5, RG75, NA; *Hearings on H.R. 7781*, p. 37; Interview of William N. Fenton, Sept. 28, 1977, Albany, N.Y.

45. William N. Fenton to John Collier, May 10, 1935, Fenton MSS.

46. W. K. Harrison to William N. Fenton, May 28, 1935, Fenton MSS.

47. William N. Fenton Travel Report, May 30–June 12, 1935, Fenton MSS.; William N. Fenton to William Duncan Strong, Sept. 2, 1934, Fenton MSS; Interviews of William N. Fenton, Sept. 28, 1977, Albany, N.Y., Ray Fadden, July 15, 1980, Onchiota, N.Y., Louis R. Bruce, Jr., Dec. 11, 1980, Washington, D.C.; Weil, "Collier Plans to Build Up Indian Agency in New York."

48. Alice Lee Jemison to Senator Robert F. Wagner, April 15, 1934, Senator Robert F. Wagner MSS., Legislative File, Box 224, File 1544, "Indians," Georgetown University.

49. *Hearings on H.R. 7781*, p. 483.

50. Fenton Travel Report, May 30–June 12, 1935, Fenton MSS.

51. Ibid.

52. William N. Fenton to John Collier, June 17, 1935, Fenton MSS.

5 – A Revolution at Oneida

1. Interviews of Norbert Hill, Sr., Oct. 17, 1978; Frank Danforth, Oct. 20, 1978; Jim Schuyler, Oct. 20, 1978; Anderson Cornelius, Oct. 21, 1978, Oneida, Wis.; Ruth Baird, Oct. 20, 1978, Green Bay, Wis. There are 3 separate communities of Oneida Indians: one near London, Ontario; another near Green Bay, Wisconsin; and a third, in the vicinity of Oneida, New York. For the best and most complete studies of the Oneida Tribe of Wisconsin, see Jack Campisi, "Ethnic Identity and Boundary Maintenance in Three Oneida Communities," (Ph.D. diss., Albany, State University of New York, 1974); and his "Oneida," in *Handbook of North American Indians* 15: 481–90. See also Harry W. Basehart, "Historical Changes in the Kinship System of the Oneida Indians," (Ph.D. diss., Harvard University, 1952).

2. Campisi, "Ethnic Identity and Boundary Maintenance," pp. 105–110, 133–34; Basehart, "Historical Changes in the Kinship System," pp. 159–60.

3. Robert Ritzenthaler, "The Oneida Indians of Wisconsin," *Bulletin of the Public Museum of the City of Milwaukee* 19 (Nov. 1950): 26–28; Robert Ritzenthaler, Oneida Field Notes, 1939, Milwaukee Public Museum; Campisi, "Ethnic Identity and Boundary Maintenance," p. 154.

4. United States Department of the Interior, *Annual Report of the Commissioner of Indian Affairs, 1875* (Washington, D.C., 1875), p. 369.

5. For a useful summary of the Dawes Act, its origins and its impact, see Wilcomb E. Washburn, ed., *The Assault on Indian Tribalism: The General Allotment Law (Dawes Act) of 1887* (Philadelphia, 1975).

6. William Parsons (U.S. special Indian agent) to commissioner of Indian affairs, Aug. 18, 1887, BIA Central Files, 1907–1939, #7276-1908-3043, RG75, NA; Otis, *The Dawes Act and the Allotment of Indian Lands*, pp. 92–93.

7. J. M. Stewart (director of lands) Memorandum to Commissioner Collier, Aug. 11, 1937, BIA Central Files, 1907–1939, #51350-1934-1752 Tomah, RG75, NA; United States Department of the Interior, *Annual Report of the Commissioner of Indian Affairs, 1918* (Washington, D.C., 1918), pp. 15–33, 66, 195, 197; *Annual Report of the Commissioner of Indian Affairs, 1919* (Washington, D.C., 1919), pp. 3–14, 183, 185.

8. See for example, United States Department of the Interior, *Annual Report of the Commissioner of Indian Affairs, 1896* (Washington, D.C., 1896), p. 322.

9. United States Congress, Senate Subcommittee of the Committee on Indian Affairs, Hearings on S. Res. 79 (70th Cong.): *Survey of Conditions of the Indians in the United States*, 76th Cong. (Washington, D.C., 1940), 37: 21250.

10. National Resources Board, *Indian Land Tenure*, pp. 28–35.

11. Basehart, "Historical Changes in the Kinship System," p. 218. Interviews of Jim Schuyler, Oct. 20, 1978, Anderson Cornelius, Oct. 21, 1978, Oneida, Wis.; Jack Campisi, Field Notes, 1972 (In possession of Professor Jack Campisi, State University of New York, Albany, N.Y.).

12. Campisi insists that there were only 84.8 acres of land held in common by the tribe, while J. P. Kinney claims there were 89 acres of tribal lands by the New Deal era. The Oneidas, according to Kinney, had 692 acres of land owned individually in allotments. Basehart insists there were 733 acres held as allotments. Campisi, "Ethnic Identity and Boundary Maintenance," p. 158; J. P. Kinney, *A Continent Lost—A Civilization Won; Indian Land Tenure in America* (Baltimore, 1937), pp. 355–56; Basehart, "Historical Changes in the Kinship System," p. 218.

13. Cara E. Richards, *The Oneida People* (Phoenix, Ariz., 1974), pp. 77–78.

14. United States Office of Indian Affairs, Annual Statistical Report, Keshena Agency, Oneida Reservation, 1932, p. 15, found in Annual Reports from the Indian Agencies in Wisconsin, 1909–1939, Microfilm Reel #5, State Historical Society of Wisconsin, Madison, Wis.

15. United States Congress, Senate Subcommittee on Indian Affairs, Hearings on S. Res. 79 (70th Cong.): *Survey of Conditions of the Indians in the U.S.* 71st Cong., 1st Sess. (Washington, 1930), 5: 1930.

16. Ibid., 1932.

17. W. F. Dickens to Senator Robert LaFollette, Jr., Senator Robert LaFollette, Jr., MSS., Box 412, Series C, File: Indian Affairs, July 1–9, 1929, Manuscript Division, Library of Congress.

18. Ritzenthaler, "The Oneida Indians," 14.

19. Ibid., 25; Interview of Anderson Cornelius, Oct. 20, 1978; Robert Ritzenthaler, "The Cultural History of the Wisconsin Oneidas." (Master's thesis, University of Wisconsin, Madison, 1940), pp. 10–11; Alfred W. Briggs (Wisconsin director of unemployment relief) to John Collier, May 5, 1934, BIA Central Files, 1907–1939, #14504-1934-723 Keshena, RG75, NA.

20. Ralph Fredenberg to Commissioner of Indian Affairs, April 18, 1935, BIA Central Files, 1907–1939, #803-1934-310 Keshena, RG75, NA.

21. For the best analysis of the Kelloggs, see Campisi, "Ethnic Identity and Boundary Maintenance," pp. 441–43. Interviews of Ruth Baird, Oct. 20, 1978; Jim Schuyler, Oct. 20, 1978; Interview conducted by Robert W. Venables of Oscar Archiquette, July 9, 1970, Shell Lake, Wis. The author would like to thank Dr. Venables of the Museum of the American Indian for allowing me to use this transcribed interview that he conducted with Oneida Tribal Chairman Archiquette. Undated (1933?) circular letter sent by John Collier, "Subject-Activities of O. J. Kellogg and Laura C. Kellogg," J. N. B. Hewitt MSS., #4271, Box 2, National Anthropological Archives, Smithsonian Institution; Hewitt to M. W. Stirling, June 25, 1932, Bureau of American Ethnology Letters

Received, 1909–1950, Box 45, "J. N. B. Hewitt, 1929–1937," National Anthropological Archives, Smithsonian Institution, Washington, D.C.; *Hearings on S. Res. 79*, 12: 4894–95. Archiquette claimed the Kelloggs pilfered $60,000 from the Oneidas, while Hewitt maintained that at Six Nations Reserve in Ontario, the Kelloggs solicited $80,000 for the claim.

22. Campisi, "Ethnic Identity and Boundary Maintenance," pp. 441–43.

23. Ibid., p. 443.

24. William Skenandore to Senator Robert M. LaFollette, Jr., May 27, Aug. 26, 1929, Senator Robert M. LaFollette, Jr., MSS., Box 412, Series C, File: Indian Affairs, Sept.–Dec., 1929, Manuscript Division, Library of Congress; Skenandore to Senator George W. Norris, June 23, 1934, with attached letter to commissioner of Indian affairs, Senator George W. Norris MSS., Box 213, File: Indian Affairs, 1934–38, Manuscript Division, Library of Congress; Skenandore to commissioner of Indian affairs, July 8, 1930, BIA Central Files, 1907–1939, #7276-1908-3043, RG75, NA.

25. Basehart, "Historical Changes in the Kinship System," p. 249.

26. Interviews of Norbert Hill, Sr., Oct. 18, 1978; Frank Danforth, Oct. 20, 1978; Jim Schuyler, Oct. 20, 1978; Robert Ritzenthaler, Oneida Field Notes, 1939, Milwaukee Public Museum; William Skenandore, *Brief: U.S. Court: Statement of the Case of the Oneida Tribe* (n.p., n.d.). Commissioner Collier, later Skenandore's foe, was impressed by his legal abilities. Collier to John Reeves, Memorandum, Dec. 18, 1933; Collier to Congressman James Frear, Feb. 28, 1934, John Collier MSS., Box 5, Folder 101, Part 2, Series I, Yale University.

27. William Skenandore to John Collier, Dec. 24, 1933; Skenandore to Congressman James A. Frear, Feb. 8, 1934, John Collier MSS., Box 5, Folder 101, Part 2, Series I, Yale University; Skenandore to commissioner of Indian affairs, Nov. 28, 1933, BIA Central Files, 1907–1939, #52895-1933-155 Keshena, RG75, NA.

28. Oscar Smith to Senator Robert M. LaFollette, Jr., May 18, 1933, BIA Central Files, 1907–1939, #22817-1933-155 Keshena, RG75, NA.

29. Morris Wheelock to John Collier, Oct. 17, 1933, BIA Central Files, 1907–1939, #46567-1933-155 Keshena, RG75, NA.

30. Morris Wheelock to John Collier, Nov. 10, 1933, BIA Central Files, 1907–1939, #46567-1933-155 Keshena, RG75, NA.

31. Printed Minutes, Testimony taken at Hayward, Wis., April 23–24, 1934, to discuss the Wheeler-Howard Bill of Indian Rights, pp. 64–68, 72, John Collier MSS., Box 43, Folder 78, Part 2, Series III, Yale University.

32. P. J. Powlas (from Milwaukee) to commissioner of Indian affairs, Nov. 21, 1934, #4894-1934-066, Part 12A, Records Relating to the Wheeler-Howard Act, 1933–1937, Box 9, RG75, NA; Oscar Archiquette to John Collier, June 6, 1934, #4894-1934-066, Part 5a, Records Relating to the Wheeler-Howard Act, 1933–37, Box 5, RG75, NA; Archiquette to Collier, July 18, 1934, #4894-1934-066, Part 12c, Records Relating to the Wheeler-Howard Act, 1933–37, Box 10, RG75, NA; Archiquette to Collier, Oct. 4, 1934, BIA Central Files, 1907–1939, #50724-1934-054 Tomah, RG75, NA.

33. The case was *William Skenandore, et al., v. the United States*. J. M. Stewart (director of Lands, Department of the Interior) to Commissioner Collier, Memorandum, Aug.11,

1937, BIA Central Files, 1907–1939, #51350-1934-1752 Tomah, RG75, NA.

34. William Skenandore to commissioner of Indian affairs, Oct. 17, 1934, BIA Central Files, 1907–1939, #42251-1928-155 Keshena, RG75, NA.

35. Ibid.

36. William Skenandore to commissioner of Indian affairs, July 21, Nov. 19, 1934, #4894-1934-066, Part 12A, Records Relating to the Wheeler-Howard Act, 1933–37, Box 9, RG75, NA.

37. William Zimmerman, Jr., to William Skenandore, Dec. 6, 1934, #4894-1934-066, Part 12A, Records Relating to the Wheeler-Howard Act, 1933–37, Box 9, RG75, NA.

38. Oscar Smith to secretary of the interior, Dec. 20, 1934, with Petition dated Dec. 1, 1934, #4894-1934-066, Part 12B, Records Relating to the Wheeler-Howard Act, 1933–37, Box 10, RG75, NA.

39. Theodore H. Haas, *Ten Years of Tribal Government Under IRA* (Lawrence, Kans., 1947), p. 20; "Oneida," *DePere* (Wis.) *Journal Democrat*, Dec. 20, 1934, p. 9.

40. Petition to Indian Bureau, dated received Dec. 27, 1934, BIA Central Files, 1907–1939, #803-1934-310 Keshena, RG75, NA.

41. William Skenandore, "Indian's Plaint," *Washington Post*, Aug. 11, 1937, Letter to the Editor. See also "Oneida Indians and Their Lands," *New York Herald Tribune*, Nov. 29, 1936, p. 12, Letter to the Editor; United States Congress, Senate Subcommittee of the Committee on Indian Affairs, *Hearings on S. Res. 79*, 37: 21227–61; Chief Jonas Schuyler to commissioner of Indian affairs, Aug. 28, 1936, BIA Central Files, 1907–1939, New System, 1936, #81192, RG75, NA.

42. Ritzenthaler, Oneida Field Notes, 1939.

43. Ralph Fredenberg to commissioner of Indian affairs, April 18, 1935, BIA Central Files, 1907–1939, #803-1934-310 Keshena, RG75, NA.

44. Richards, *The Oneida People*, pp. 85–86; Ritzenthaler, "The Oneida Indians," pp. 14–15.

45. Constitution and By-Laws for the Oneida Tribe of Indians of Wisconsin, Approved Dec. 21, 1936 (Washington, D.C., 1937). These documents can be found in George E. Fay, comp., *Charters, Constitutions and By-Laws of the Indian Tribes of North America* (Greeley, Colo., 1967), 2: 72–89. Theodore Haas, *Ten Years of Tribal Government Under IRA*, p. 26. Frank Christy (superintendent Tomah Indian School) to commissioner of Indian affairs, Feb. 4, March 20, 1937; Peru Farver (field agent of Great Lakes Indian Agency) to Morris Wheelock, March 1, 19, April 14, 1937, Oneida Tribal Records, Oneida Indian Historical Society (OIHA). [Copies in possession of Dr. Jack Campisi, State University of New York, Albany].

46. *Hearings on S. Res. 79*, 37: 21250.

47. Ibid., 21254.

48. Morris Wheelock to Peru Farver, April 26, 1938, Oneida Tribal Records, OIHA.

49. Interview conducted by Robert W. Venables with Oscar Archiquette, July 9, 1970; Ritzenthaler, "The Oneida Indians," 15; Campisi, "Ethnic Identity and Boundary Maintenance," p. 158.

50. For example, Oneida Tribal Business Committee, Minutes, Dec. 4, 1939, Oneida Tribal Records, OIHS.

51. Morris Wheelock, "Credit at Oneida," undated, Oneida Tribal Records, OIHS.

52. "Trust Agreement for Rehabilitation Grant to Organized Tribe," Jan. 14, 1938, Oneida Tribal Records, OIHS.

53. Ritzenthaler, "The Oneida Indians," p. 15.

54. Ibid.

55. Ibid., 25.

56. Interview of Anderson Cornelius, Oct. 20, 1978.

57. United States Department of the Interior, *Statistical Supplement to the Annual Report of the Commissioner of Indian Affairs, 1940* (Washington, D.C., 1940), p. 16.

6 – Something Old/Something New

1. The historical literature on the Seneca-Cayugas is quite thin. The best surveys are William C. Sturtevant, "Oklahoma Seneca-Cayuga," in *Handbook of North American Indians*, 15: 537–43; and Ermine Wheeler-Voegelin, "The 19th and 20th Century Ethnohistory of Various Groups of Cayuga Indians," MSS. in (Smithsonian) National Anthropological Archives, Washington, D.C. The historical narrative of this chapter is largely drawn from Sturtevant and Wheeler-Voegelin and from Grant Foreman's (WPA) oral history project among these Indians in 1937. The invaluable tribal testimony in this Federal Writers' Project, usually referred to as the "Indian-Pioneer History," is housed at the Oklahoma Historical Society and the University of Oklahoma. The author consulted the following interviews: Alex and Grover Splitlog, Dec. 3, 1937, Miami, Okla., 48: 56; Annie Young Bumberry, Nov. 4, 1937, Seneca, Mo., 18: 316–23; Eva Spicer Whitetree Nichols, April 21, 1937, Miami, Okla., 7: 492–98; Mary Virginia Spicer Whitecrow, May 3, 1937, Miami, Okla., 11: 345–51.

2. Kinney, *A Continent Lost–A Civilization Won*, pp. 355–56.

3. Interview of Chief James Allen, Seneca-Cayuga Tribe of Oklahoma, Aug. 17, 1979, Miami, Okla.

4. Interview of William H. Parcell, Aug. 17, 1979, Miami, Okla. Mr. Parcell was the Employment Assistance Officer at the BIA Miami Indian Agency at the time; Kinney, *A Continent Lost*, pp. 355–56.

5. Linda Parker, "Indian Colonization in Northeastern and Central Indian Territory," in *America's Exiles: Indian Colonization in Oklahoma*, Arrell Gibson, ed. (Oklahoma City, Okla., 1976), pp. 104–108.

6. Under this treaty the United States government provided Kansas lands for New York Indians. About 200 Indians accepted these lands in exchange for their lands and claims to lands in New York and Wisconsin. Nearly half died in the resettlement (removal) process. Most of the rest returned to their tribesmen, complaining of government indifference, hostile western Indians, climate, and poor lands in Kansas. They later sued and won for the loss of these lands which occurred during the settlement of Kansas. Some of these Indians, however, became incorporated into other Iroquois populations in the West. Grant Foreman, *The Last Trek of the Indians* (Chicago, 1946), pp. 332–35.

7. Ibid., p. 336; I. V. Gilkison (Indian superintendent at Six Nations Reserve, Brantford, Ontario) to D. B. Dyer (Indian agent, Quapaw Agency), Jan. 27, 1881, Oct. 10, 1882, Quapaw Agency Records, Microfilm Reel 7, Indian Archives Division, Oklahoma Historical Society (IAD, OHS); Gilkison to Dyer, July 7, 1884, Quapaw Agency Records, Microfilm Reel 12; IAD, OHS, Gilkison to Dyer, Feb. 25, March 28, April 15, 1885, Miami Agency Records (Old Quapaw-Seneca Agency), Misc. Corresp. 1871–97, FRC#437724, Federal Records Center, Fort Worth, Tx.

8. John Winney to D. B. Dyer, April 29, 1881, Quapaw Agency Records, Reel 12, IAD, OHS; Winney to Dyer, Aug. 25, 1880, Quapaw Agency Records, Microfilm Reel 12, IAD, OHS; and Jeremiah Hubbard, *Forty Years Among the Indians* (Miami, Okla., 1913; Reprint edition, Knightstown, Ind., 1975), p. 61.

9. Wheeler-Voegelin, "19th and 20th Century Ethnohistory of Various Groups of Cayuga Indians," pp. 92–126; Interview of Chief James Allen, Aug. 17, 1979; James H. Howard, "Cultural Persistence and Cultural Changes as Reflected in Oklahoma Seneca-Cayuga Ceremonialism," *Plains Anthropologist* 6 (1961): 21–30; and his "Environment and Culture: The Case of the Oklahoma Seneca-Cayuga," *Oklahoma Anthropological Society Newsletter* 18 (Sept. 1970): 5–13; (Oct. 1970): 5–19.

10. Baird, *The Quapaw Indians*, p. 110; see also H. Craig Miner and William E. Unrau, *The End of Indian Kansas: A Study of Cultural Revolution, 1854–1871* (Lawrence, Kans., 1978).

11. John Whitetree to O. Delano (secretary of the interior), Aug. 26, 1873, Quapaw Agency Records, Microfilm Reel 12, IAD, OHS; Wheeler-Voegelin, "19th and 20th Century Ethnohistory of Various Groups of Cayuga Indians," pp. 92–126; Sturtevant, "Oklahoma Seneca-Cayuga," p. 540; John Winney to D. B. Dyer, Aug. 25, 1880.

12. H. W. Jones to Enoch Hoag, June 19, 1872, Aug. 20, 1873; Jones to Major Ingalls, Feb. 19, 1875; A. Blipshaw (acting commissioner) to J. V. Summers (Quapaw Indian agent), Dec. 7, 1885; Hiram Price (commissioner of Indian affairs) to D. B. Dyer, Undated, Quapaw Agency Records, Microfilm Reel 12, IAD, OHS; Baird, *The Quapaw Indians*, p. 139.

13. Thomas J. Morgan (commissioner to John V. Summers (Quapaw Agent), July 19, 1889, Quapaw Agency Records, Microfilm Reel 12, IAD, OHS.

14. United States Department of the Interior, *Annual Report of the Commissioner of Indian Affairs, 1888* (Washington, D.C., 1888), p. 109; *Annual Report, 1890* (Washington, D.C., 1890), p. 83; *Annual Report, 1891* (Washington, D.C., 1891), p. 234; *Annual Report, 1892* (Washington, D.C., 1892), p. 243; *Annual Report, 1901* (Washington, D.C., 1901), p. 218; *Annual Report, 1902* (Washington, D.C., 1902), pp. 188–89; *Annual Report 1903* (Washington, D.C., 1903), p. 161; *Annual Report, 1904* (Washington, D.C., 1904), pp. 181–82.

15. For the mining history of this region, see Arrell M. Gibson, *Wilderness Bonanza* (Norman, Okla., 1972); for its impact on the Indians, see Baird, *The Quapaw Indians,* pp. 149–207.

16. United States Department of the Interior, *Annual Report of the Commissioner of Indian Affairs* (Washington, D.C., 1897), pp. 134–35.

17. (Advertisement), "A New Town With Great Prospects," Miami Agency Records

(Old Quapaw-Seneca Agency), Misc. Corresp., 1871–97, FRC#437724, Federal Records Center, Fort Worth, Tx.

18. A. Blipshaw (acting commissioner) to John V. Summers, May 21, 1888; D. M. Browning (commissioner) to George S. Doane (Quapaw Indian agent), March 25, 1897; Thomas Ryan (acting secretary of the interior), May 8, 1901; Ryan to commissioner of Indian affairs, May 9, 1901, Quapaw Agency Records, Microfilm Reel 12, IAD, OHS.

19. The historical record reveals corruption at this agency from the 1880s through the New Deal. Commissioner of Indian Affairs Hiram Price warned Quapaw Agent D. B. Dyer about tampering with the Seneca annuity moneys long before the Dawes Act. Price to Dyer, undated, Quapaw Agency Records, Microfilm Reel 12, IAD, OHS. H. A. Andrews, the agent during the New Deal years, was himself accused of shaking down Indian employees for kickbacks in the 1930s. Senator Elmer Thomas to Clarence W. Winney (Seneca-Cayuga) April 8, May 21, 1935; Thomas to John Collier, April 8, 1935; John Collier to Thomas, April 13, 1935; William Zimmerman, Jr., to Thomas, May 20, 1935, Elmer Thomas MSS., Box 65, Western History Collection, University of Oklahoma. Interviews of Velma Nieberding, Aug. 17, 1979, and Charles Banks Wilson, Aug. 18, 1979, Miami, Okla. Nieberding, an non-Indian, is a local historian, author of *The Quapaws* (Miami, Okla., 1976), and keen observer of Indian-white relations in northeast Oklahoma for more than forty years. Mr. Wilson, the well-known artist of western America, is a lifelong resident of Miami, local historian of Indian life and perspicacious observer. He is the author of *The Quapaw Agency Indians* (Miami, Okla., 1947), reprinted in 1956 as *The Indians of Eastern Oklahoma*.

20. Otis, *The Dawes Act and the Allotment of Indian Lands*, p. 150.

21. Paul A. Ewert (special assistant to the attorney general of the United States) to Judge Quigley, May 31, 1909, Quapaw Agency Records, Microfilm Reel 1, IAD, OHS.

22. United States Department of the Interior, *Annual Report of the Commissioner of Indian Affairs, 1896* (Washington, D.C., 1896), pp. 149–50.

23. Hubbard, *Forty Years*, pp. 30, 50; Interview of Alex and Grover Splitlog, Dec. 3, 1937, (WPA) Indian-Pioneer History, 68: 56–65; D. B. Dyer, (Seneca) Annual Report, 1882, Quapaw Agency Records, Microfilm Reel 1, IAD, OHS.

24. Hiram Price to D. B. Dyer, Aug. 22, 1883 with attached petition to Indian Agent Dyer, July 7, 1883, Miami Agency (Old Quapaw Agency), Misc. Corresp., 1871–97, FRC#437724 Federal Records Center, Fort Worth, Tx.

25. (Charles Kirk) superintendent, Seneca School Monthly Report, May 2, 1881, Quapaw Agency Records, Microfilm Reel 23, IAD, OHS.

26. Interviews of Mamie Turkey Long (Seneca-Cayuga), Turkey Ford, Oklahoma, Feb. 19, 1970, T-623-3, 52: 4–8; Kenneth Oyler (Cayuga), Commerce, Okla., April 3, 1970, T-572-3, 10: 9–10, Doris Duke American Indian Oral History Project, Western History Collection, University of Oklahoma. Long attended the Seneca Indian School while Oyler attended Chilocco. (Charles Kirk) superintendent, Seneca School Monthly Report, Feb. 1, 1882, Quapaw Agency Records, Microfilm Reel 23, IAD, OHS.

27. Superintendent's Annual Narrative and Statistical Report, the Seneca School, 1920, Quapaw Agency Records, Microfilm Reel 131, p. 5, Federal Records Center, Fort Worth, Tx.

28. Interview of Ruby Diebold, Aug. 18, 1979, Bassett Springs, Okla. Mrs. Diebold is a Seneca-Cayuga traditional leader and wife of the late Chief Charlow.

29. B. T. Quinten, "Oklahoma Tribes, the Great Depression and the Indian Bureau," *Mid-America* 49 (Jan. 1967): 29–43.

30. Superintendent's Annual Narrative and Statistical Report, 1922, Quapaw Agency Records, "Seneca," Microfilm Reel 112, p. 5, Federal Records Center, Fort Worth, Tx.

31. Philp, *John Collier's Crusade*, pp. 153–54.

32. Collier, *From Every Zenith*, p. 174.

33. For reaction to Collier's visit, see *Harlow's Weekly* 42 (Feb. 17, 1934): 11; (March 3, 1934): 12; (March 10, 1934): 15; (March 17, 1934): 17; (March 24, 1934): 9.

34. Minutes of Meeting Held at Miami, Oklahoma, March 24, 1934, to discuss the Wheeler-Howard Bill, pp. 50–52, John Collier MSS., Box 43, Folder 76, Part II, Series II, Yale University.

35. Ibid., p. 93.

36. Philp, *John Collier's Crusade*, p. 176.

37. John Collier, "Present Status of Oklahoma Indians," *Harlow's Weekly* 43 (July 14, 1934): 14–15; (July 28, 1934): 13; (Aug. 4, 1934): 12–13; (Aug. 11, 1934): 14–15; (Aug. 25, 1934): 15.

38. Philp, *John Collier's Crusade*, p. 178; "Changes in Wheeler-Howard Act Agreed Upon," *Harlow's Weekly* 43 (Oct. 20, 1934): 4–5; Homer Chandler (Association of Indian Tribes) to Elmer Thomas, Dec. 31, 1934, March 4, April 17, 1935; Thomas to Chandler, March 6, 1935, Elmer Thomas MSS., Box 66, Western History Collection, University of Oklahoma.

39. Resolution of Seneca-Cayuga Tribe of Indians of Oklahoma, Oct. 26, 1934, #4894-1934-066, Part 12A, Records Concerning the Wheeler-Howard Act, 1933–37, Box 9, RG75, NA.

40. For the legislative history of this act, see Peter Wright, "John Collier and the Oklahoma Indian Welfare Act of 1936," *Chronicles of Oklahoma* 50 (Autumn 1972): 347–71.

41. *U.S. Statutes at Large* 49: 1967–68.

42. Haas, *Ten Years of Tribal Government Under IRA*, p. 28; Corporate Charter of the Seneca-Cayuga Tribe of Oklahoma, June 26, 1937; H. A. Andrews to John Collier, May 17, 1937; Ben Dwight to A. C. Monahan, May 10, 1937, File: Seneca-Cayuga — Constitution and By-laws, Miami Agency, Miami, Okla. The author wishes to thank Mr. William Parcell for allowing me access to these agency records.

43. "Seneca Tribe" Census Roll, dated May 15, 1937, File: Seneca-Cayuga — Constitution and By-laws, Miami Indian Agency, Miami, Okla. The Seneca-Cayugas were the fifth smallest tribe to accept incorporation. Haas, *Ten Years of Tribal Government Under IRA*, p. 28.

44. H. A. Andrews to John Collier, April 24, 1937, File: Seneca-Cayuga — Constitution and By-laws, Miami Agency, Miami, Okla.

45. Resolution of Business Committee of the Seneca-Cayuga Tribe of Oklahoma, March 20, 1937; Felix Cohen to H. A. Andrews, March 18, 22, 1937; Harold Ickes to Andrews, April 26, 1937; Ben Dwight to A. C. Monahan, May 10, 1937; Andrews to

Monahan, March 24, 1937, Monahan to Andrews, March 30, 1937; Constitution and By-Laws of Seneca-Cayuga Tribe of Oklahoma, April 26, 1937; File: Seneca-Cayuga — Constitution and By-laws, Miami Agency, Miami, Okla. For the charter, constitution and bylaws of the Seneca-Cayuga Tribe of Oklahoma, see also George E. Fay, comp., *Charters, Constitutions, and By-laws of the Indian Tribes of North America* 6: 73–81.

46. Ben Dwight to A. C. Monahan, May 10, 1937, File: Seneca-Cayuga—Constitution and By-laws, Miami Agency, Miami, Okla.

47. Ibid.; H. A. Andrews, Circulars Sent to "All Adult Members of the Seneca Act and What It Means" (Pamphlet); Andrews to John Collier, April 24, 1937, File: Seneca-Cayuga — Constitution and By-laws, Miami Agency, Miami, Okla.

48. John Collier to H. A. Andrews, April 20, 1937, File: Seneca-Cayuga — Constitution and By-laws, Miami Agency, Miami, Okla.

49. Interview of Ruby Diebold, Aug. 18, 1979. According to Chief James Allen, the Seneca-Cayugas, mostly poor farmers, largely survived the depths of the Great Depression by adopting a barter system of exchange. Interview of Chief James Allen, Aug. 17, 1979.

50. H. A. Andrews to John Collier, April 24, 1937, File: Seneca-Cayuga — Constitution and By-laws, Miami Agency, Miami, Okla. Ben Dwight remarked that no opposition to tribal incorporation "was sensed" at the meetings explaining the constitution and the Oklahoma Indian Welfare Act. Dwight to A. C. Monahan, May 10, 1937, File: Seneca-Cayuga — Constitution and By-laws, Miami Agency, Miami, Okla.

51. Besides Armstrong, the Business Committee included Watson Whitewing, Grover Splitlog, Christopher Bomberry, Chester Hubbard, Tom Peacock, and Hayden Spicer. H. A. Andrews to Thelma Goetting, Dec. 22, 1937 with attached list of Tribal Business Committee, File: Seneca-Cayuga — Constitution and By-laws, Miami Indian Agency, Miami, Okla. The election was held on June 1, 1937 at the ceremonial grounds.

52. Nannie Lee Burns, Field Notes on "The Seneca's Midsummer Festivities," Aug. 25, 1937, (WPA) Indian-Pioneer History, 79: 361, IAD, OHS; H. A. Andrews to commissioner of Indian affairs, Oct. 11, 1940, File: Seneca-Cayuga — Constitution and By-laws, Miami Agency, Miami, Okla.

53. O. D. Hall, "Battle Against Floods and Soil Erosion Waged on Many Fronts," *Harlow's Weekly* 44 (June 15, 1935): 13; Elmer Thomas, "Forty Years of Legislation," (Thomas' unpublished autobiography), pp. 105–111, Elmer Thomas MSS., Unnumbered Box, Western History Collection, University of Oklahoma. For this massive project, see W. R. Holway, *A History of the Grand River Dam Authority, State of Oklahoma, 1935–1968* (Tulsa, Okla., 1968), 2 vols.; William A. Settle, Jr., *The Dawning: A New Day for the Southwest: A History of the United States Army Corps of Engineers, Tulsa District* (Tulsa, Okla., 1975), pp. 39–41.

54. Governor Leon C. Phillips (Oklahoma), "Confidential Preliminary Report, Grand River Dam Authority," Sec. II, p. 2, Governor Leon C. Phillips MSS., Western History Collection, University of Oklahoma; Interview of Chief James Allen, Aug. 17, 1979; Sturtevant, "Oklahoma Seneca-Cayuga," p. 539.

55. Interview of Annie Bumberry, Nov. 4, 1937, (WPA) Indian-Pioneer History, 17: 323, IAD, OHS; "Confidential Preliminary Report, Grand River Dam Authority," Sec. II, p. 2.

56. "Confidential Preliminary Report, Grand River Dam Authority," Sec. II, p. 2. "Quarterly Report of Enrollee Program Activities," Dec. 31, 1939, CCC-Indian Division, Quapaw Agency Records, FRC#351862 Federal Records Center, Fort Worth, Tx. The Indians were responsible for clearing timber along the dam's route.

7 — The Big Deal

1. Philp, *John Collier's Crusade*, pp. 161– 62; Collier, *From Every Zenith*, pp. 216– 26, 345– 51. This experiment has been written about extensively. For the best accounts, see Graham Taylor, "Anthropologists, Reformers, and the Indian New Deal," *Prologue: The Journal of the National Archives* 7 (Fall 1975): 151– 62; D'Arcy McNickle, "Anthropology and the Indian Reorganization Act," in *The Uses of Anthropology*, Walter Goldschmidt, ed. (Washington, D.C., 1979), pp. 51– 60; and Lawrence C. Kelly, "Anthropology and Anthropologists in the Indian New Deal," *Journal of the History of the Behavioral Sciences* 16 (Jan. 1980): 6– 24.

2. William N. Fenton to William Zimmerman, Aug. 18, 1934; Fenton to William Duncan Strong, Oct. 2, 1934; Zimmerman to Fenton, Feb. 9, 1935; and John Collier to Fenton, Feb. 16, 1935, Fenton MSS.

3. Interview of William N. Fenton, June 21, 1978, Albany, N.Y.; Jesse Cornplanter to Joseph Keppler, Sept. 25, 1934, Joseph Keppler MSS., Museum of the American Indian Library; William N. Fenton, "Aboriginally Yours, Jesse J. Cornplanter," in *American Indian Intellectuals*, Margot Liberty, ed. (St. Paul, Minn., 1978), pp. 177– 95; William N. Fenton, "Tonawanda Reservation, 1935: The Way It Was," Speech at the Opening of Ernest Smith Exhibition, July 16, 1976, Rochester Museum and Science Center.

4. William N. Fenton to John Collier, Feb. 11, 1935, Fenton MSS.

5. Interview of William N. Fenton, June 21, 1978.

6. Harrison Ground to John Collier, March 26, 1935, Fenton MSS.

7. John Collier to Harrison Ground, April 20, 1935, Fenton MSS.

8. William N. Fenton to Miss McGair, July 11, 1935, Fenton MSS.

9. William N. Fenton to John Collier, Feb. 11, 1935.

10. William N. Fenton to Miss McGair, July 11, 1935.

11. Ibid.

12. William N. Fenton to John Collier, Feb. 23, 28, March 7, 26, 30, April 12, May 2, 10, 17, June 20, Sept. 10, 17, 23, Oct. 25, Dec. 23, 1935, Aug. 18, 1937; Fenton to William Duncan Strong, Oct. 14– 15, 1935, Fenton MSS; William N. Fenton, "The Tonawanda Indian Library," *Indians at Work* 3 (Oct. 15, 1935): 46– 48.

13. William N. Fenton to John Collier, Sept. 3, Nov. 19, Dec. 23, 1935, Fenton MSS.

14. William N. Fenton to William Duncan Strong, Oct. 14– 15, 1935.

15. William N. Fenton, "Some Social Customs of the Modern Seneca," (New York State) *Social Welfare Bulletin* 7 (Jan.– Feb. 1936): 4– 7.

16. Ibid.; William N. Fenton to John Collier, March 18, April 19, Sept. 23, Oct. 25,

Nov. 23, 1935, Feb. 22, 1936, Aug. 14, 1937; Fenton to Harry Driher (supt., N.Y. State Highway Dept., Genesee County), March 14, 1936, Fenton MSS; Cephas Hill to C. Carleton Perry, Dec. 8, 1935, Indian Arts Project Correspondence, RMSC. William N. Fenton, "Guide Posts on Tonawanda Reservation," *Indians at Work* 3 (Jan. 1, 1936): 31–32; Arthur C. Parker, "A Museum Sponsors an Indian Arts Project," *Social Welfare Bulletin* 7 (Jan.–Feb. 1936): 12; William N. Fenton and Cephas Hill, "Reviving Indian Arts Among the Senecas," *Indians at Work* 2 (June 15, 1935): 13–15; Fenton, "Tonawanda Reservation, 1935"; Jesse Cornplanter to Joseph Keppler, July 30, 1935, Sept. 25, 1934, Joseph Keppler MSS., Museum of the American Indian Library.

17. Fenton, "Some Social Customs of the Modern Seneca," p. 7.

18. William N. Fenton to John Collier, Aug. 14, 1937, April 17, 1938; Fenton to Evelyn Pierce, Aug. 18, 1937, Fenton MSS. Fenton's writings, based on his Tonawanda experiences of the 1930s, include "Masked Medicine Societies of the Iroquois," Smithsonian Institution, *Annual Report* (Washington, D.C., 1940), pp. 397–430; "Tonawanda Longhouse Ceremonies; Ninety Years After Lewis Henry Morgan," Bureau of American Ethnology *Bulletin* 128 (Washington, D.C., 1941), pp. 140–66; "The Iroquois Eagle Dance: An Offshoot of the Calumet Dance," Bureau of American Ethnology, *Bulletin* 156 (Washington, D.C., 1953).

19. For the best treatments of the CCC-ID program, see Donald L. Parman, "The Indian Civilian Conservation Corps," (Ph.D. diss., University of Oklahoma, 1967); and his "The Indian and the Civilian Conservation Corps," *Pacific Historical Review* 40 (Feb. 1971): 39–56.

20. W. K. Harrison to commissioner of Indian affairs, Aug. 10, 1935, Entry 1000, General Records, 1933–44, CCC-Indian Division, New York, RG75, NA.

21. Parman, "The Indian and the Civilian Conservation Corps," pp. 39–42; J. P. Kinney to John Collier, June 21, 1933; Collier to Kinney, June 21, 1933; Clyde Leavitt (acting assistant dean, New York State College of Forestry) to Collier, June 28, 1933; Collier to Leavitt, July 1, 1933, and Percy E. Melis (Forestry Branch, Indian Service) to Kinney, Aug. 8, 1933, J. P. Kinney MSS., Box 29, #1791A, Cornell University. For Kinney's critique of Collier, see his *Facing Indian Facts* (Laurens, N.Y., 1973), pp. 4–7.

22. Parman, "Indian Civilian Conservation Corps," pp. 236–60; J. P. Kinney, "Indian Emergency Conservation Work, April 1933 to June 30, 1939," J. P. Kinney MSS., Box 21, #1791A, Cornell University.

23. John A. Salmond, *The Civilian Conservation Corps 1933–1942* (Durham, N.C., 1967), p. 33; Parman, "The Indian and the Civilian Conservation Corps," pp. 40–41.

24. Parman, "The Indian Civilian Conservation Corps," p. 55.

25. Kinney, "Indian Conservation Work."

26. Parman, "The Indian Civilian Conservation Corps," p. 258; Report on Emergency Conservation Relief Work attached to Letter from W. K. Harrison to John Collier, Aug. 10, 1935; "First Citizens of Syracuse" *Syracuse* (N.Y.) *Herald*, July 27, 1933.

27. Clinton G. Pierce Report, "General Survey of Reservation and Forest Conditions in Relation to Proposed Emergency Conservation Work on the Indian Reservations of the State of New York," attached to Letter from Pierce to W. K. Harrison, Feb. 21, 1935, Entry 1000 General Records, 1933–44, CCC-Indian Division, New York, RG75, NA.

28. *Hearings on S. Res. 79*, 37: 20781.

29. W. K. Harrison to commissioner of Indian affairs, with attached report "Special Problems" by Clinton G. Pierce, Aug. 10, 1935, Entry 1000 General Records, 1933–44, CCC-Indian Division, New York, RG75, NA.

30. Ibid.

31. J. P. Kinney to commissioner of Indian affairs, Nov. 21, 1935, Entry 1000, General Records, 1933–44, CCC-Indian Division, New York, RG75, NA.

32. Joseph F. Tarbell, Report on "St. Regis Drainage Project," May 4, 1938, Entry 1000, General Records, 1933–44, CCC-Indian Division, New York, RG75, NA.

33. Ibid.

34. Clinton G. Pierce, "Drainage Situation on the St. Regis Reservation, Hogansburg, New York" attached to Letter from Harrison to Collier, Aug. 10, 1935.

35. Anne R. Coleman, "Report on New York Indians for the Association on American Indian Affairs, Inc.," (New York, 1939), p. 6, found in General Records Concerning Indian Organization, 1934–56, New York, RG75, NA.

36. Tarbell Report, May 4, 1938.

37. Ibid.

38. James P. Edwards (adjuster of accounts for IECW Projects) to commissioner of Indian affairs, Nov. 25, 1936, Entry 1000, General Records, 1933–34, CCC-Indian Div., New York, RG75, NA.

39. Tarbell Report, May 4, 1938.

40. Frank Terrance to John Collier, Nov. 23, 1935, Entry 1000, General Records, 1933–44, CCC-Indian Div., RG75, NA.

41. Tarbell Report, May 4, 1938.

42. Coleman, Report on New York Indians, p. 6; WPA, *Social and Economic Survey of New York Indian Reservations* (Buffalo, N.Y., 1939), p. 3.

43. Richmond Martin to Joseph Keppler, Dec. 10, 1939, Joseph Keppler MSS., Museum of the American Indian.

44. "Dr. Parker Praises NYA's Indian Program," *Rochester (N.Y.) Democrat and Chronicle*, April 20, 1939, Scrapbook, Rochester Museum and Science Center; Interview of Louis R. Bruce, Jr., Dec. 11, 1980, Washington, D.C. "Indian Youth Train for Camp Service," *New York Times*, April 24, 1938, sec. II, p.4; "Young Indians at Camp Outing," *Niagara Falls (N.Y.) Gazette*, June 15, 1938, Scrapbook, Rochester Museum and Science Center; "Onondaga Indians Cling to Traditions of Ancestors," *Syracuse (N.Y.) Post Standard*, Nov. 30, 1941, sec. II, p. 26; "NYA Dinner to Be Given By Onondagas," *Syracuse Herald*, June 16, 1936, p. 20.

45. Interview of Louis R. Bruce, Jr., Dec. 11, 1980. Bruce is the son of an Indian dentist-missionary (Methodist) on the Onondaga Reservation. He is a graduate of Syracuse University. For Bruce's career see Joseph H. Cash, "Louis Rook Bruce," in *The Commissioners of Indian Affairs, 1924–1977*, Robert M. Kvasnicka and Herman J. Viola, eds. (Lincoln, Nebr., 1979), pp. 333-40. Louis R. Bruce, Jr., "Indian Trail to Success," *Readers' Digest* (Nov. 1949), Reprint of *American Magazine* article (Sept. 1949) found in National Congress of American Indians MSS., Box 17, Series 4, National Anthropological Archives, Smithsonian Institution, Washington, D.C.

46. Louis R. Bruce, Jr., to Governor Herbert H. Lehman, March 18, 1938, Governor Herbert H. Lehman MSS., Microfilm Reel 73, Onondaga Nation of Indians, Columbia University; "Indians Youth Train for Camp Service," *New York Times*, April 24, 1938; Louis R. Bruce, Jr., "Foreword," in (NYA) *Indian Counselor's Handbook of Legends and Information on the Iroquois* (Washington, D.C., 1940), found in NYA Records, Publications File, Series 330, New York, RG119, NA.

47. Interview of Ray Fadden, July 15, 1980, Onchiota, N.Y. Stanley W. Johnson, "The Tuscarora Indian School's Experiment," *New York State Education* 22 (June 1935): 696–736.

48. "Indian Youth Train for Camp Service," *New York Times*, April 24, 1938.

49. Ibid.

50. (NYA) *Indian Counselor's Handbook of Legends and Information on the Iroquois*.

51. Interviews of Chief Corbett Sundown and Ramona Charles (director, Tonawanda Indian Community House), May 22, 1980, Tonawanda Indian Community House, Akron, N.Y.

52. Arthur C. Parker to George W. Kellogg, Aug. 4, 1936, Arthur C. Parker MSS., Box 4, File 19, University of Rochester; David C. Adie (commissioner, N.Y. State Department of Social Welfare), Remarks at the Dedication of the Tonawanda Indian Community House, May 13, 1939, in *Tonawanda Indian Reservation Community House*, pamphlet found in Lieutenant Governor Charles Poletti MSS., File: "Henricks, Mrs. Walter A. and Tonawanda Indians," Columbia University.

53. Interview of Nameé Henricks, May 20, 1980, Penn Yan, N.Y. In appreciation for her help, the Senecas later gave her an Indian name "Sah-nee-weh" and adopted her into the nation.

54. Lester W. Herzog, Remarks at the Dedication of the Tonawanda Community House, May 13, 1939, in *Tonawanda Indian Reservation Community House*.

55. Nameé Henricks to Governor Herbert H. Lehman, Dec. 10, 12, 1937, Jan. 27, Feb. 4, April 16, 1938, Governor Herbert H. Lehman MSS., Microfilm Reel 97, Tonawanda Indian Reservation, Columbia University; Henricks to Lieutenant Governor Charles Poletti, July 24, 1940, April 17, Nov. 12, Nov. 24, 1941, Lieutanant Governor Charles Poletti MSS., File: "Henricks, Mrs. Walter A. and Tonawanda Indians," Columbia University; Henricks to Mrs. Franklin D. Roosevelt, Nov. 19, 1936, Box 1384, Series 100, File: "Mrs. Walter Henricks, 1936"; Jan. 3, 1937, Box 1503, Series 100, File: "Hea-Hen, 1937," Eleanor Roosevelt MSS., Franklin D. Roosevelt Presidential Library, Hyde Park.

56. William N. Fenton to John Collier, Feb. 28, 1935, March 26, March 30, 1935, Fenton MSS. Other active members included Inez Blackchief, Elsina and Peter Doctor, Ira Mitten, Wayman Jemison, Russell Hill, Mrs. Levi Clute, and Mrs. Luther Ground.

57. Arthur C. Parker to John Collier, April 3, 1935, Arthur C. Parker MSS., Box 1, File 6, University of Rochester.

58. John Collier to Arthur C. Parker, April 18, 1935; Elmer Thomas to Parker, April 20, 1935; Parker to Collier, April 22, 1935; William N. Fenton to Mrs. Walter A. Henricks, April 27, 1935, Parker MSS., Box 1, File 6, University of Rochester.

59. Collier to Parker, April 18, 1935.

60. Fenton to Henricks, April 27, 1935, Parker MSS.

61. John Collier to Mrs. Franklin D. Roosevelt, Nov. 1, 1935, Box 1384, (filed with 1936), Eleanor Roosevelt MSS. Collier also cooperated with Henricks in planning sessions in Washington; however, he refused Mrs. Roosevelt's request to appoint her to a post in the Indian Service in New York. Mrs. Walter A. Henricks to Roosevelt, March 4, Dec. 7, 1936, Box 1384; Collier to Roosevelt, Feb. 1, 1937, Box 1503, Eleanor Roosevelt MSS.

62. William N. Fenton to John Collier, April 24, May 10, 1935, Fenton MSS.

63. Interview of Nameé Henricks, May 20, 1980; Mrs. Franklin D. Roosevelt to John Collier, Oct. 30, 1935; Roosevelt to Lester Herzog, Oct. 26, 1935; Mrs. Malvina Scheider (Roosevelt's secretary) to Mrs. Walter A. Henricks, July 13, 1935; Ellen S. Woodward (assistant WPA administrator) to Scheider, July 22, 1935; Henricks to Roosevelt, May 9, Dec. 26, 1935, May 15, Aug. 28, 1936, Box 1384, Eleanor Roosevelt MSS.; Scheider to John E. Harris (P.W.A.), June 4, 1936; Scheider to Richard N. Elliott (acting comptroller general), July 21, 1936; Roosevelt to J. R. McCarl (comptroller general), June 27, 1936, Box 1503, Eleanor Roosevelt MSS.

64. Mrs Walter A. Henricks to Mrs. Franklin D. Roosevelt, Nov. 9, 1935, Box 1384, Eleanor Roosevelt MSS; William N. Fenton to John Collier, March 26, 1935, Fenton MSS; Arthur C. Parker to Council of Councilors, Tonawanda Indian Band, Sept. 16, 1935; Mrs. Hanover Spring to Parker, Aug. 14, Sept. 8, 1935, Parker MSS., Box 4, File 18, University of Rochester.

65. Aaron H. Poodry to A. C. Parker, Nov. 26, 1935, Parker MSS., Box 4, File 18, University of Rochester. The project received formal endorsement from the council on August 13, 1935; however, some remained opposed to the project for another 6 months. Resolution signed by Chief Solon Skye, Tonawanda Nation of Indians, Council of the Chiefs, Aug. 13, 1935, Parker MSS., Box 4, File 18, University of Rochester.

66. Parker to (Tonawanda) Council of Councilors, Sept. 16, 1935, Parker MSS., Box 4, File 18, University of Rochester.

67. Quoted in Wes Gallagher, "Indian Community Center Launched Amid Gala Rites," *Rochester Democrat and Chronicle*, May 11, 1937, Rochester Public Library, Newsclippings File: "WPA."

68. William N. Fenton to John Collier, March 30, 1935, Fenton MSS; Fenton to Mrs. Henricks, March 17, 1936; Mrs. Hanover Spring to Dr. Parker, March 20, 30, 1936; Parker to Mrs. Spring, March 24, 1936, Parker to Harry M. Hirsch (assistant welfare commissioner), May 27, 1936, Parker MSS., Box 4, File 18, University of Rochester; Mrs. Walter A. Henricks to Charles Poletti, April 22, 1940, Charles Poletti MSS., File: "Henricks, Mrs. Walter A. and Tonawanda Indians," Herbert H. Lehman Collection, Columbia University.

69. Mrs. Walter Henricks to Mrs. Franklin D. Roosevelt, Dec. 12, 1935, March 4, 12, April 9, 1936, May 8, 1936, Box 1384, Eleanor Roosevelt MSS.; Henricks to Roosevelt, Jan. 11, 1937, Box 1503, Eleanor Roosevelt MSS; David C. Adie to Clarence Post (WPA deputy administrator), March 2, 1936, Parker MSS., Box 4, File 18, University of Rochester.

70. Clarence Post to Arthur C. Parker, March 5, 1936, Parker MSS., Box 4, File 18, University of Rochester.

71. Arthur C. Parker to Clarence Post, March 4, 16, 1936; Parker to Mrs. Franklin D. Roosevelt, March 5, 1936; Parker to Mrs. Hanover Spring, March 13, 1936; Nameé Henricks to Parker, March 12, 1936 (two letters on same day); David C. Adie to Parker, March 12, 1936; Parker to Adie, March 13, 1936, Parker MSS., Box 4, File 18, University of Rochester. A. S. Weber Memorandum to Governor Lehman, Feb. 10, 1938, Governor Herbert H. Lehman MSS., Microfilm Reel 97, Tonawanda Indian Reservation, Columbia University; Henricks to Roosevelt, March 12, April 9, May 8, May 27, 28, 1936, Box 1384, Eleanor Roosevelt MSS.

72. Mrs. Walter A. Henricks to Mrs. Franklin D. Roosevelt, April 9, May 8, 1936, Eleanor Roosevelt MSS.; David C. Adie to Parker, March 13, 1936, Parker MSS.; New York State Department of Social Welfare, *70th Annual Report of the State Board of Social Welfare* for the year ended June 30, 1936 (Albany, N.Y., 1937), p. 25.

73. New York State Senate, "An Act to provide for the maintenance of the Tonawanda Community House," March 31, 1936, Parker MSS., Box 4, File 18, University of Rochester. Swartz introduced a similar bill in the assembly on April 9, 1936. Assembly Bill No. 2873, April 9, 1936, Box 1384, Eleanor Roosevelt MSS. Parker's wording was incorporated into the bill. He sent two letters to Post on March 16, one describing the project and justifying it for legislative purposes and the other outlining his views as a museum director about the architectural necessities for the community center. Parker to Adie, March 13, 1936; Parker to Post, March 16, 1936, Parker MSS.

74. A. S. Weber Memorandum to Governor Lehman, Feb. 10, 1938, Governor Herbert H. Lehman MSS.; Herzog, Remarks at the Dedication of the Tonawanda Community House, May 13, 1939; Henricks to Roosevelt, Nov. 16, 28, 1936, Box 1384, Eleanor Roosevelt MSS.

75. Nameé Henricks to Governor Herbert H. Lehman, Jan. 27, 1938, Governor Herbert H. Lehman MSS. Eleanor Roosevelt's major concern about the project was this point. According to Mrs. Roosevelt: "We must remember that it cannot be WPA forever! Are your people training for ultimate skills?" Roosevelt to Henricks, Jan. 8, 1937, Box 1503, Eleanor Roosevelt MSS.

76. Henricks to Lehman, Jan. 27, 1938, Lehman MSS.

77. Herzog, Remarks at the Dedication of the Tonawanda Community House, May 13, 1939; Interview of Nameé Henricks, May 20, 1980; Fenton, "The Tonawanda Indian Library"; "Seek to Replace Indian Library," *Rochester* (N.Y.) *Times-Union*, Jan. 8, 1937, p. 31. The cornerstone of the building was laid in ceremonies held on May 10, 1937. "Long House or Indians," *New York Times*, May 9, 1937, Sec. II, p. 3; Gallagher, "Indian Community Center Launched Amid Gala Rites."

78. Interview of Chief Corbett Sundown, May 22, 1980.

79. See, for example, "Indian as an 'Alien' is Barred from WPA," *New York Times*, Sept. 19, 1937, p. 18.

8 – The Seneca Renaissance, 1935 – 41

1. There are two different bands of Seneca Indians living in New York State that have had distinctive political systems and divergent histories since the first half of the nineteenth century. The Seneca Nation of Indians have three reservations — Allegany, Cattaraugus, and Oil Spring. The Tonawanda Band of Senecas occupy a single reservation near Akron, New York. Although there were two programs in reviving Iroquois arts — at Cattaraugus and at Tonawanda — Parker saw them as one project, and hence, the present chapter treats them as one. Indian Arts Project, Inventory Books, 1935 – 41, I and II, RMSC; Indian Arts Project, Work Cards, 1935 – 41, RMSC; Interview of Cephas Hill, July 26, 1978, Tonawanda Indian Reservation; William N. Fenton, "Tonawanda Reservation, 1935: The Way It Was," speech at opening of Ernest Smith exhibition, July 16, 1976, RMSC. Mr. Hill, a Seneca Indian, was the "assistant project supervisor" at Tonawanda.

2. Alfred Haworth Jones, "The Search for a Useable American Past in the New Deal Era," *American Quarterly* 23 (Dec. 1971): 710 – 24.

3. The historical literature on the WPA Federal Arts Project is too voluminous to cite in its entirety. For an excellent recent survey of WPA arts projects in New York State, see Marlene Park and Gerald Moskowitz, *New Deal for Art* (Hamilton, N.Y., 1971), p. xii, 1 – 64, 75, 82, 127.

4. Harry M. Hirsch, "New York State Indians," *Social Welfare Bulletin* 7 (Jan. – Feb. 1936): 1; Interview of Francis Kettle, July 26, 1977; Fenton, "Tonawanda Reservation, 1935"; *Fighting Tuscarora*, pp. 120 – 26.

5. Interview of Cephas Hill, July 26, 1978, Tonawanda Indian Reservation; Interview of David Bartholomew, May 3, 1975, at the opening of the exhibition: "North American Indian Art: The Iroquois," State University College, New Paltz, New York. The late Mr. Bartholomew of Hudson, New York, was a friend of several participants in the Seneca Arts Project, including Jesse Cornplanter. Over the past forty years, he acquired one of the best private collections of Iroquois art in existence and was a recognized authority on the twentieth century art techniques of the Six Nations until his death in 1979.

6. Interview of Arleigh Hill, July 25, 1978, Rochester Museum and Science Center. Mr. Hill was Parker's chauffeur, "man-friday," model for the Rochester Museum's dioramas, confidante, and later custodian of the Arts Project collection until 1972. The best studies of Parker are the following: William N. Fenton, "Introduction," in *Parker on the Iroquois*, William N. Fenton, ed. (Syracuse, N.Y., 1968), pp. 1 – 47; Hazel Hertzberg, *The Search for an American Indian Identity*, pp. 48 – 53; and her "Nationality, Anthropology and Pan-Indianism in the Life of Arthur C. Parker," *Proceedings of the American Philosophical Society* 123 (Feb. 1979): pp. 47 – 72; W. Stephen Thomas, "Arthur Caswell Parker: Anthropologist, Historian and Museum Pioneer, 1881 – 1955," *Rochester History* 17 (July 1955): 1 – 20.

7. Interviews of Arleigh Hill, July 25, 1978; William N. Fenton, June 21, 1978, State University of New York, Albany; W. Sheldon Fisher, July 24, 1978, Valentown Museum, Fishers, N.Y. Mr. Fisher was an assistant archeologist at the Rochester Museum until 1937 and was later associated with the Rochester Historical Society. Parker's flair for

public relations is evident in the enormous amount of news coverage the Rochester Museum received in the Rochester press throughout his tenure as director.

8. The Senecas are matrilineal. Since Parker's mother was a non-Indian, he was not on the tribal rolls and consequently cannot be considered legally Seneca. Both Hazel Hertzberg and William Ritchie claim Parker was one-fourth Seneca, while William N. Fenton maintains that he "was certainly no more than one-fourth Seneca, and probably nearer one-eighth." Hertzberg, *The Search for an American Indian Identity*, p. 49; William Ritchie, "Arthur Caswell Parker," *Dictionary of American Biography*, Supplement 5, 1951– 55 (New York, 1977), p. 533; Fenton, "Introduction," p. 5.

9. Fenton, "Introduction," pp. 4– 6. Parker's pride in his Seneca heritage is evident in his biography of his grand uncle, "The Life of Ely S. Parker," *Buffalo Historical Society Publications* 23 (1919). Arthur C. Parker, "Presentation and Unveiling of the Morgan Tablet at The Morgan Centennial Celebration at Wells College, Aurora, New York," *Proceedings* of the New York State Archaeological Association, Morgan Chapter, (1919), 1: 23– 27.

10. Hertzberg, *The Search for an American Indian Identity*, pp. 49– 50; Fenton, "Introduction," p. 13.

11. Arthur C. Parker, "Museum Motives Behind the New York Arts Project," *Indians at Work* 2 (June 15, 1935): 11.

12. Parker frequently, in romantic fashion, used terms such as "racial genius," in less than social scientific terms to describe the Iroquois. See the conclusion to his "The Amazing Iroquois," *Art and Archaeology* 23 (March 1927): 105– 108.

13. Quoted in Fenton, "Introduction," p. 43.

14. After describing the fire and the destruction of 160 of the 235 articles in the Morgan Collection, Parker asked Joseph Keppler for his own distinguished Iroquois collection (which is housed today at the Museum of the American Indian). Parker to Keppler, March 29, April 11, 1911, Joseph Keppler MSS., Museum of the American Indian Library.

15. Thomas, "Arthur Caswell Parker: Anthropologists, Historian, Museum Pioneer," pp. 8– 9; Personal communication, William A. Ritchie, Oct. 26, 1978. Dr. Ritchie, the former New York State archeologist, was the senior archeologist at the Rochester Museum during Parker's tenure.

16. "The Indian Arts Project," *Museum Service*, 9 (Jan. 15, 1936): 8–9; Arthur C. Parker, "The Indian Arts and Crafts Project of the Rochester Museum of Arts and Sciences," press release for WPA arts and crafts display in Albany, July 29, 1938, Indian Arts Project Correspondence, RMSC; Arthur C. Parker, "A Museum Sponsors an Indian Arts Project," 12. Interestingly, a WPA pamphlet wrote about the project: "Inspired by Morgan's research work, the Rochester Museum of the present day has been deeply interested in Indian exhibits. Consequently, with W.P.A.'s cooperation, it set up an arts and crafts project with Seneca Indian workmen." Empire State's Indian Wards, WPA Women's and Professional Projects (Albany, 1936?), p. 8. Fenton, "Introduction," pp. 1– 25.

17. Arthur C. Parker to John M. Clarke, June 16, 1909, Parker MSS., New York State Cultural Education Center.

18. Parker, "A Museum Sponsors an Arts Project," p. 12.

19. Thomas, "Arthur Caswell Parker: Anthropologist, Historian, Museum Pioneer," p. 8–9; Interview of W. Sheldon Fisher, July 24, 1978. "Museum Budget Cut Held Great Mistake," *Rochester* (N.Y.) *Journal*, Nov. 16, 1931; "Appropriation Slash Held Possibly Fatal to Museum," *Rochester* (N.Y.) *Democrat and Chronicle*, Nov. 14, 1932, Newsclipping Files: "Rochester Museum," Rochester Public Library; "Arthur C. Parker Resigns," *Museum News* 10 (Dec. 1, 1932): 1.

20. Park and Moskowitz, *New Deal for Art*, p. xii; Arthur C. Parker to Dr. Lewis A. Wilson, April 18, 1934, Indian Arts Project Correspondence, RMSC.

21. Proposal: Indian Arts Project, July 30, 1934, Indian Arts Project Correspondence, RMSC.

22. Ibid.

23. C. Carleton Perry to Joseph Leichtner, July 30, 1934, Indian Arts Project Correspondence, RMSC.

24. Arthur C. Parker to John C. Brennan, Jan. 11, 1935, Arthur C. Parker MSS., Box 1, File 6, University of Rochester; Interview of Cephas Hill, July 26, 1978; Interview of Arleigh Hill, July 25, 1978; Interview of David Bartholomew, Aug. 4, 1978, New Paltz, N.Y.

25. Fenton, "Introduction," pp. 14–15. For the best study of Cornplanter, see Fenton, "Aboriginally Yours, Jesse J. Cornplanter," pp. 176–95. Cornplanter had neurasthenia as a result of being gassed during World War I. Jesse Cornplanter to C. Carleton Perry, April 5, 1938, Indian Arts Projects Correspondence, RMSC.

26. Interview of Harrison Ground, July 26, 1978, Tonawanda Indian Reservation; Interview of Cephas Hill, July 26, 1978; Interview of Arleigh Hill, July 25, 1978; Interview of David Bartholomew, Aug. 4, 1978. Cornplanter, a meticulous artist, was the slowest worker on the project and the least productive. Moreover, a drinking problem and occasional orneriness often interfered with his great artistic talent. See Indian Arts Project Inventories, 1935–1941, I and II; C. Carleton Perry to Jesse Cornplanter, April 1, 1938, Indian Arts Project Correspondence, RMSC.

27. Interview of William N. Fenton, June 21, 1978; Fenton, "Tonawanda Reservation, 1935."

28. Interview of Cephas Hill, July 26, 1978; William N. Fenton to John Collier, Oct. 25, 1935, Fenton MSS. See also Arthur C. Parker, "A Museum Sponsors an Indian Arts Project," p. 13. Hill and Fenton, "Reviving Indian Arts Among the Senecas," p. 13. "Making the Basswood Burden Strap," (Everett Parker), WPA film, 1936?, RMSC.

29. Fenton, "Tonawanda Reservation, 1935"; Interview of Arleigh Hill, July 25, 1978; Interview of Cephas Hill, July 26, 1978. Quoted in "Indian's Paintings Reveal His Talent," *Batavia* (N.Y.) *News*, Nov. 17, 1936. See also, "He Lost His Job, But He Replaced it With a Career; Museum Proud of Indian's Art," *Rochester Democrat and Chronicle*, Nov. 16, 1936. Both articles found in Indian Arts Project Correspondence, RMSC.

30. Fenton, "Tonawanda Reservation, 1935." Interview of William N. Fenton, June 21, 1978; Jeanette Collamer, "The Paintings of Ernest Smith," paper presented at the Iroquois Conference, Oct., 1975, Rensselaerville, N.Y. Ms. Collamer spent nearly a month interviewing Smith before his death and helped to organize the major exhibition:

"Images from the Longhouse: Paintings of Iroquois Life by Seneca Artist Ernest Smith, 1907–1975," Rochester Museum and Science Center, July 17–Oct. 17, 1976.

31. Interview of Cephas Hill, July 26, 1978; Personal communication, William A. Ritchie, Oct. 26, 1978; Interview of Arleigh Hill, July 26, 1978.

32. C. Carleton Perry to Cephas Hill, Dec. 18, 1939, Indian Arts Project Correspondence. Perry wrote in 1938: "Considerable care is exercised in securing the correct media from which the objects are made." C. Carleton Perry, "Indian Arts and Crafts Project," *Museum Service* 11 (Oct. 15, 1938): 172.

33. C. Carleton Perry to Walco Bead Co., Sept. 18, Oct. 8, 14, 1935; to Cephas Hill, July 15, 1935; to Peter J. Loeb, May 13, 1935; to A. J. Jeremy, Oct. 9, 1935; to Sanborn White Eagle, Aug. 27, 1935; to A. J. Jeremy, Jan. 29, 1936; to Jesse Cornplanter, April 1, 1938, Indian Arts Project Correspondence, RMSC.

34. C. Carleton Perry to Pawnee Bills Trading Post, Aug. 19, 1937, Indian Arts Project Correspondence, RMSC.

35. Interview of Arleigh Hill, July 25, 1978; Interview of Cephas Hill, July 26, 1978; "Indian Museum to Open," *New York Times*, June 23, 1935; "Indians to Conduct Exhibition of Arts," *Rochester Democrat and Chronicle*, June 23, 1935; "City Aids First Tribal Museum of Indian Arts," *Rochester Journal*, June 23, 1935, Museum Scrapbook, RMSC. Sanford Plummer was one of the finest painters on the project. He was born in 1907 on the Cattaraugus Reservation. He studied at the Beaux Arts School and the Academy of Fine Arts in New York City. In his paintings of Iroquois ceremonial dances, legends, and games, he employed watercolors, pen and ink, and charcoal. His work was exhibited at the Buffalo Museum of Science in Humboldt Park. Charles H. Berry to John Collier, April 22, May 16, 1939; Sanford Plummer to René d'Harnoncourt, April 9, 1939; Harold Tolley and Helen Wayne to Berry, April 17, 1939, Records of Indian Arts and Crafts Board, Exhibits and Expositions, Numbered Files, 1939–40, no. 147, RG435, NA.

36. Sadie and Edith Kennedy to C. Carleton Perry, March 2, 1936; Libbie Pierce to Perry, July 20, 1936, Indian Arts Project Correspondence, RMSC; Arthur C. Parker to Libbie Pierce, April 29, 1936, Parker MSS., Box 4, File 18, University of Rochester; Sarah Hill to C. Carleton Perry, Jan. 29, 1938, Indian Arts Project Correspondence, RMSC; Interview of Cephas Hill, July 26, 1978.

37. Interview of Cephas Hill, July 26, 1978; Interview of William N. Fenton, June 21, 1978; Grandma Shongo to Arthur C. Parker, March 13, 1937, Director's Office Files, RMSC.

38. Jesse Cornplanter to Joseph Keppler, undated (probably 1937), Keppler MSS., Museum of the American Indian.

39. Eric Branham to C. Carleton Perry, Dec. 18, 1935, Indian Arts Project Correspondence, RMSC; *Proceedings* of the City Council of Rochester (Jan. 27, 1936), p. 27; (May 24, 1938), pp. 169–70; (Feb. 11, 1941), p. 34, Rochester Public Library; Eric Branham to Arthur C. Parker, Dec. 14, 1936; W. E. McCarthy to Parker, June 29, 1937; C. Carleton Perry to Branham, June 5, 1938, Indian Arts Project Correspondence, RMSC; Interview of W. Sheldon Fisher, July 24, 1978; Interview of Arleigh Hill, July 25, 1978; C. Carleton Perry to W. H. Roberts, May 5, 1937, Indian Arts Project Correspondence, RMSC.

40. C. Carleton Perry to W. H. Roberts, May 1937, Indian Arts Project Correspondence, RMSC.

41. In 1938, the project received $4,311 from the City of Rochester. Three years later, Rochester's City Council allocated $4,700 for the project. *Proceedings* of the City Council of Rochester (May 24, 1938), pp. 169–70; (Feb. 11, 1941), p. 34. Interestingly, the *Proceedings* also indicate that the WPA funding had decreased from $22,142.40 in 1938, to $14,927.60 before its demise in 1941. Arthur C. Parker to Joseph Keppler, May 1, 1940, Joseph Keppler MSS., Museum of the American Indian Library.

42. "Big Chief Lehman at Fair," *Rochester Democrat and Chonicle*, Sept. 9, 1937; "Herzog Adopted by Indian Tribe," *Buffalo* (N.Y.) *Evening News*, May 11, 1937, Museum Scrapbooks, RMSC. Jesse Cornplanter conducted the adoptions, and, in each case, Parker presided over the welcoming ceremonies. Ruth Atwood, "On the Bank of Cattarauagus," *Rochester Democrat and Chronicle*, Aug. 25, 1935; "Iroquois Arts Revive," *Rochester Democrat and Chronicle*, Sept. 8, 1937; "Indians Revive Ancient Art," *Rochester* (N.Y.) *Times-Union*, Oct. 13, 1939, WPA Newsclipping File: "Indians," Rochester Public Library. "TERA-Sponsored Project Seen as Boom to Indians," *Buffalo* (N.Y.) *Courier Express*, March 31, 1935; "Revival of Ancient Arts and Crafts Aimed to Give State's Indian Independence," *Rochester Democrat and Chronicle*, Jan. 24, 1935; "Early Arts, Crafts of Indians Revived in WPA Project," *Buffalo Courier Express*, Jan. 16, 1938, and James A. Murphy, "Uncle Sam—A Patron of the Arts," *Rochester Democrat and Chronicle*, March 22, 1936; "Indian's Painting Reveals His Talent," *Batavia News*, Nov. 17, 1936; interview of Sheldon Fisher, July 24, 1978.

43. Interview of Cephas Hill, July 26, 1978; Jesse Cornplanter to Joseph Keppler, Dec. 12, 1935, Joseph Keppler MSS., Museum of the American Indian Library.

44. See work cards of Melinda Skye, Everett Parker, Alice Poodry, and Ira Mitten for 1936 and 1937 as examples, RMSC; Park and Moskowitz, *New Deal for Art*, p. 16.

45. C. Carleton Perry to Inez Dane Ross, Jan. 16, 1935, Indian Arts Project Correspondence, RMSC.

46. Jesse Cornplanter to C. Carleton Perry, March 28, 1936, Indian Arts Project Correspondence, RMSC. Jesse Cornplanter took nearly twice as long as other woodcarvers. Jesse Cornplanter, "Mask," Work Card 1683, March 29, 1937 — $32.13 labor, $.40 materials, 68 hours of work; Elon Webster, "Mask," Work Card 1688, March 31, 1937 — $18.43 labor, $.50 materials, 39 hours of work, RMSC.

47. William E. McCarthy to Cephas Hill, Aug. 27, Oct. 23, 1940, Indian Arts Project Correspondence, RMSC. The correspondence in the collection is full of references to the social and family problems that affected the arts project.

48. Arthur C. Parker, "Art Reproductions of the Seneca," *Museum Service* 14 (Nov. 1941): 31; Jesse J. Cornplanter to Merle H. Deardorff, Dec. 9, 1941, Merle H. Deardorff MSS., Box 1, General Correspondence, Pennsylvania Historical and Museum Commission Archives, Harrisburg. The first fire, which also obliterated the reservation library at Tonawanda, destroyed 6,000 books, artists' tools, and several of Ernest Smith's paintings. "Seek to Replace Indian Library," *Rochester Times-Union*, Jan. 8, 1937, Newsclipping File: "WPA," Rochester Public Library; Arthur C. Parker to Joseph Keppler, Feb. 1, 1937; Jesse J. Cornplanter to Joseph Keppler, Feb. 4, 1937, Joseph Keppler MSS., Museum of the American Indian Library. The fires were both mysterious in their origin. According to

Cephas Hill, the fire in the winter of 1937 was caused by the failure to stoke out the fireplace properly, while the second was caused by children playing with matches. Interview of Cephas Hill, July 26, 1978. Parker, it is clear from the Indian Arts Project Correspondence of 1941, believed the second fire to be the work of arsonists.

49. Interview of Arleigh Hill, July 25, 1978; Interview of Cephas Hill, July 26, 1978.

50. Arthur C. Parker to Joseph Keppler, Jan. 28, 1938, Joseph Keppler MSS., Museum of the American Indian.

51. "Parker to Aid Art of Indians," *Rochester Democrat and Chronicle*, May 20, 1935; "Dr. Parker's Work in Reviving Indian Arts to be National Model for Interior Department," *Rochester Democrat and Chronicle*, May 24, 1935; "Hope for the Indians," *Rochester Democrat and Chronicle*, May 25, 1935; "Curator Pleads Indians' Cause with New Deal," Newspaper Unknown, 1935, Rochester Museum Scrapbooks, RMSC. Collier also had published two articles on the Seneca Arts Projects in his Indian Service magazine, *Indians at Work*, on June 15, 1935. Parker, "Museum Motives Behind the New York Arts Project," pp. 11–12; Hill and Fenton, "Reviving Indian Arts Among the Senecas," pp. 13–15. It is important to note that the Indian Arts and Crafts Board was created in August, 1935.

52. "Exhibition of Indian Art: Display Open to Public in WPA Headquarters in Albany P.O.," *Gloversville* (N.Y.) *Leader-Republican*, Aug. 2, 1938; "Seneca Installation of 300 Articles in New York State Exhibit at World's Fair," *Rochester Democrat and Chronicle*, April 7, 1939, found in Rochester Museum Scrapbooks, RMSC; "'Rochester-Made' Indians to Bow Before World's Fair Crowds," *Rochester Democrat and Chronicle*, July 21, 1938, WPA Newsclipping Files: "Indians," Rochester Public Library; "Museum Gets Number 1 Spot at World's Fair," *Rochester Democrat and Chronicle*, March 11, 1938, WPA Newsclipping Files: Rochester Museum, Rochester Public Library.

53. Interview of Cephas Hill, July 26, 1978.

54. Proposal: Indian Arts Project, July 30, 1934, Indian Arts Project Correspondence, RMSC. See also "Indians Interested in Art Project Work," *Pearl River* (N.Y.) *Searchlight*, June 5, 1936, found in Indian Arts Project Correspondence, RMSC. Certain art techniques were lost and could never be revived. Iroquois pottery found in archeological digs could never be recreated, despite the museum staff's efforts. Personal communication, William A. Ritchie, Nov. 1, 1978.

55. Interview of David Bartholomew, Aug. 4, 1978; Interview of W. Sheldon Fisher, July 24, 1978; Thomas, "Arthur Caswell Parker: Anthropologist, Historian and Museum Pioneer," p. 1–20; Fenton, "Introduction," p. 9.

56. Parker, "A Museum Sponsors an Indian Arts Project," p. 13.

9 – The Oneida Language and Folklore Project, 1938–41

1. Interviews of Loretta Webster, Oneida, Wis., Oct. 18, 1978; Clifford Abbott, Oneida, Wis., Oct. 18, 1978; Jack Campisi, New Paltz, N.Y., Feb. 13, 1980. Mrs. Webster is the director of the Oneida project today. Dr. Abbott, assistant professor of anthropology at the University of Wisconsin, Green Bay, and Dr. Jack Campisi, assistant professor

of anthropology at the State University of New York, Albany, are both former students of Dr. Floyd Lounsbury and are two of the major linguists working as teachers and consultants on the project today.

2. The WPA Federal Writers' Project also has been written about extensively. For a recent analysis, see Monty Noam Penkower, *The Federal Writers' Project: A Study in Government Patronage of the Arts* (Urbana, Ill., 1977).

3. Ibid., pp. 17– 18, 146– 54; Elizabeth Williams Cosgrove, "The Grant Foreman Papers: Indian and Pioneer History," *Chronicles of Oklahoma* 37 (Winter 1959– 60): 507– 10.

4. Jerre Mangione, *The Dream and the Deal* (Boston, 1972), pp. 373– 74.

5. Robert Ritzenthaler, "The Oneida Indians of Wisconsin," *Bulletin of the Public Museum of the City of Milwaukee* 19 (Nov. 1950): 25.

6. Morris Swadesh, "Pattern Impact on Phonetics of Bilinguals," in *Language, Culture and Personality: Essays in Memory of Edward Sapir*, Leslie Spier, et al., eds. (Menasha, Wis., 1941), p. 61.

7. Interviews of Anderson Cornelius, Oneida, Wis., Oct. 21, 1978; Melissa Cornelius, Oneida, Wis., Oct. 21, 1978.

8. Quoted in "Tribal Myths Will Be Saved," *Milwaukee* (Wis.) *Journal*, January ?, 1939, found in Robert Ritzenthaler Field Notes, Milwaukee Public Museum.

9. Margaret Szasz, *Education and the American Indian* (Albuquerque, N. Mex., 1974), pp. 71– 76.

10. William N. Fenton to A. C. Monahan (assistant to Commissioner Collier), June 1, 1935, Fenton MSS.

11. W. Duncan Strong to William Fenton, Sept. 26, 1935, Fenton MSS.

12. Interview of Floyd Lounsbury, New Haven, Conn., Nov. 16, 1978.

13. Quoted in C. F. Voegelin and Z. S. Harris, eds., "Index to the Franz Boas Collection of Materials for American Linguistics," *Language Monograph* 22 [Supplement to *Language: Journal of the Linguistic Society of America* 21 (July– Sept. 1945) (Baltimore, Md., 1945)]: 5.

14. Morris Swadesh, "The Internal Economy of the Nootka Word: A Semantic Study of Word Structure in a Polysynthetic Language," (Ph.D. diss., Yale University, 1933).

15. Dell Hymes, "Morris Swadesh: From the First Yale School to World Prehistory," in *The Origin and Diversification of Language*, Joel Sherzer, ed. (Chicago, 1967), p. 244, 244 n 22.

16. Ibid., pp. 230– 31.

17. Ibid., pp. 236– 43. According to Hymes, this "concern for the relation of linguistics to public and practical affairs can be found throughout Swadesh's work" and it appears was influenced in part by Sapir, Swadesh's mentor.

18. "Synopsis of the University of Wisconsin — WPA Social Research Program, March, 1938 to February, 1939," President Clarence A. Dykstra MSS., General Correspondence Files, 1938– 1939, Series no. 4/15/1, Box 40, File: WPA, University of Wisconsin Archives, Madison. The university in 1941– 42 also was to sponsor later the WPA Oneida Ethnological Study under Harry Basehart's direction. See his "Historical

Changes in the Kinship System of the Oneida Indians," (Ph.D. diss., Harvard University, 1952).

19. Ibid.

20. Interview of Floyd Lounsbury, November 16, 1978; Hymes, "Morris Swadesh," p. 243; Franz Boas, "Notes on the Iroquois Language," in *Putnam Anniversary Volume: Anthropological Essays Presented to F. W. Putnam* (New York, 1909), pp. 427–60; Marius Barbeau, "Classification of Iroquoian Radicals with Subjective Pronominal Prefixes," Anthropological Series 7, *Memoirs of the Canadian Geological Survey 46* (Ottawa, 1915).

21. Interview of David Skenandore, DePere, Wis., Oct. 22, 1978; "Tribal Myths Will Be Saved."

22. Interviews of Robert Ritzenthaler, Hales' Corners, Wis., Oct. 23, 1978; Floyd Lounsbury, Nov. 16, 1978; Ruth Baird, Oct. 18, 1978; Gordie McLester, Oneida, Wis., Oct. 17, 1978; Robert W. Venables, Interview with Oscar Archiquette, Shell Lake, Wis., July 9, 1970; and Venables' "A Study of a Twentieth Century Oneida," Paper delivered at the Duquesne History Forum, Oct. 31, 1974, Pittsburgh, Pa.

23. Interviews of David Skenandore, Oct. 22, 1978; Floyd Lounsbury, Nov. 16, 1978; Robert Ritzenthaler, Oct. 23, 1978; "Rules for Separating Prefixes From Body of a Word," Oneida Language and Folklore Project handout (original in Floyd Lounsbury's possession).

24. Interview of Floyd Lounsbury, Nov. 16, 1978.

25. "Tribal Myths Will Be Saved"; Interview of Floyd Lounsbury, Nov. 16, 1978.

26. Szasz, *Education and the American Indian*, p. 73. According to Szasz, this BIA-supported project was a first stab at meeting the needs of the non-English-speaking Indian child. Not all of the pamphlets were in Indian languages, but all were designed to appeal to children. The BIA published works in Pueblo, Sioux, and Navajo. The stories were often translated by tribal members and illustrated by Indian artists.

27. "Oneida Worksheets," Oneida Language and Folklore Project handout (In David Skenandore's possession); Interview of Floyd Lounsbury, Nov. 16, 1978.

28. Interviews of David Skenandore, Oct. 22, 1978; Floyd Lounsbury, Nov. 16, 1978.

29. Mrs. Tom Elm to Tillie Baird, "Home Made Hominy," undated, T-16; Nelson B. Cornelius' wife to Dennison Hill, untitled, no date, D-89; Oscar Archiquette, untitled, Feb. 10, 1939, Z-32; Elizabeth Webster to David Skenandore, "Corn Soup," Feb. 20, 1939, V-1, Story Book, Oneida Language and Folklore Project. The three books of stories are presently on file in the Oneida Language Project office on the second floor of the Sacred Heart Seminary at Oneida, Wis. (Hereafter cited as OLFPB).

30. Elizabeth Haff to Tillie Baird, "Indian Salve," undated, T-32; Tillie Baird, "Medicine for Sprains," undated, T-42; Tillie Baird, "Yellow Salve or Simon Anton Salve," undated, T-20, OLFPB.

31. Mrs. Josephine Webster to Tillie Baird, "Lace Work," undated, T-53, OLFPB. Another WPA program in 1935 attempted but failed to revive beadwork at Oneida. For the origins of Oneida lacemaking, see Kate L. Duncan, "American Indian Lace Making," *American Indian Art* 5 (Summer 1980): 28–35, 80.

32. Jonas Elm to Morris Swadesh translated by Guy Elm, Untitled, ? 1938, Z-10; OLFPB.

33. Moses Elm to Guy Elm, "Football," Sept. 22, 1939, G-64, OLFPB. Moses Elm recalled the famous athletic careers of Oneidas at Carlisle — Jonas Mctoxen, Chauncey Archiquette, and Martin Wheelock.

34. Albert Webster to Guy Elm, "Jubilee Singers," June 16, 1939, G-56, OLFPB.

35. Ida Blackhawk, "When I Went to School," Sept. 28, 1939, S-79, OLFPB.

36. Martin Hill to Oscar Archiquette, "I Went to Carlyle (sic) Penn," Sept. 29, 1939, O-62, OLFPB.

37. Oscar Archiquette, "My Punishment for Being Honest," Sept. 25, 1939, O-60, OLFPB.

38. Andrew Beechtree, untitled, Sept. 22, 1939, A-45, OLFPB.

39. Ida Blackhawk to Floyd Lounsbury, "An Indian and a White Man Were Talking," undated, Z-18, OLFPB.

40. William Skenandore to Andrew Beechtree, untitled, undated, A-30, OLFPB.

41. Jonas Hill to Oscar Archiquette, untitled, Sept. 26, 1939, O-64, OLFPB.

42. Oscar Archiquette, "Indian Reorganization Act," undated, O-49, OLFPB.

43. U.S. Congress Congressional Record, 76th Cong., 1st Sess. (March 27, 1939), 84: 3338–42; (July 17, 1939), 84: 9111–210; 76th Cong., 3rd Sess. (Feb. 19, 1940), 86: 1574; (Aug. 24, 1940), 86: 10862–63.

44. Interview of Floyd Lounsbury, Nov. 16, 1978.

45. Ibid.

46. Ibid.; Morris Swadesh, Floyd Lounsbury, Oscar Archiquette, ONΛYODA?ÁIGA DEYELIHWAHGSÁTA [Oneida Hymnal] (Oneida, Wis., 1941), preface. The preface was written by Swadesh and Lounsbury.

47. Interview of Ruth Baird, Oct. 18, 1978. This author was witness to the skill of the Oneida Singers, who were using the revised hymnal, at a performance at the Lutheran Church of Seymour, Wis., on Oct. 22, 1978. Mrs. Baird is their leader.

48. Interview of Floyd Lounsbury, Nov. 16, 1978; Floyd G. Lounsbury, "Oneida Verb Morphology," Yale University Publications in Anthropology 47 (New Haven, Conn., 1953). For a summary of Lounsbury's Iroquoian work, see his "Iroquoian Languages," in Handbook of North American Indians 15: 334–43.

49. Interview of David Skenandore, Oct. 22, 1978.

50. Ibid.

10 – Conclusion

1. John Collier, Memorandum "to Superintendents, et al.," March 6, 1935, Records Concerning the Wheeler-Howard Act, #4894-34-066 (found after Part 11-A), RG 75, NA.

2. Harold L. Ickes, "Indians Have a Name for Hitler," MSS. copy of article appearing in Collier's, Jan. 15, 1944, Harold L. Ickes MSS., Box 114, "Articles," Library of Congress,

Manuscript Division. The five Seneca-Cayugas were Melvin, John, Shannon, Chester, and Vernon Crow. Ray Fadden (Aren Akweks), *Six Nation Iroquois Confederacy Record (World War II)* (Hogansburg, N.Y., n.d.). Interview of Cephas Hill, July 26, 1978. "Indians to Honor Own Heroic Dead," *Syracuse* (N.Y.) *Post-Standard*, Sept. 30, 1945, p. 23.

BIBLIOGRAPHY

Manuscript Collections

American Civil Liberties Union Papers. Princeton University. Princeton, N.J.

Association on American Indian Affairs Papers. Princeton University. Princeton, N.J.

Erl Bates Papers. Cornell University. Ithaca, N.Y.

William M. Beauchamp Collection. Manuscript Division. New York State Cultural Education Center. Albany, N.Y.

William Borah Papers. Library of Congress. Manuscript Division. Washington, D.C.

Usher L. Burdick Papers. Univeristy of North Dakota. Grand Forks, N.D.

Bureau of Indian Affairs. Record Group 75, National Archives. Washington, D.C.
  1. Central Files, 1907–39.
  2. Civilian Conservation Corps-Indian Division, 1933–42.
  3. General Records Concerning Indian Organization, 1934–56.
  4. Office File of Commissioner John Collier, 1933–45.
  5. Records Concerning the Wheeler-Howard Act, 1933–45.
  6. Records of the New York Agency, 1938–49.

Bureau of American Ethnology. (Smithsonian) National Anthropological Archives. Washington, D.C.

Civil Works Administration. Record Group 69, National Archives. Washington, D.C.

John Collier Papers. Yale University. New Haven, Conn.

Royal S. Copeland Papers. University of Michigan. Ann Arbor, Mich.

Merle Deardorff Papers. Pennsylvania Historical and Museum Commission. Harrisburg, Pa.

Democratic Party National Committee Papers, 1928–48. Franklin D. Roosevelt Library. Hyde Park, N.Y.

Democratic Party Women's Division, National Committee Papers, 1932–44. Franklin D. Roosevelt Library. Hyde Park, N.Y.

Doris Duke American Indian Oral History Project. Western History Collection. University of Oklahoma. Norman, Okla.

Clarence A. Dykstra Papers. University of Wisconsin Archives. Madison, Wis.

Federal Emergency Relief Administration. Record Group 69, National Archives. Washington, D.C.

William N. Fenton Papers. In possession of William N. Fenton, Albany, N.Y.

Grant Foreman Papers. (WPA) Indian-Pioneer History. Oklahoma Historical Society. Oklahoma City, Okla.

Howard Gansworth Collection. Buffalo and Erie County Historical Society. Buffalo, N.Y.

J. N. B. Hewitt Papers. (Smithsonian) National Anthropological Archives. Washington, D.C.

Harry Hopkins Papers. Franklin D. Roosevelt Library. Hyde Park, N.Y.

Harold Ickes Collection. Library of Congress. Manuscript Division. Washington, D.C.

Harold Ickes. Office File of Secretary of the Interior. Record Group 48, National Archives. Washington, D.C.

Indian Arts and Crafts Board Records. Record Group 435, National Archives. Washington, D.C.

Indian (Seneca) Arts Project Collection. Rochester Museum and Science Center. Rochester, N.Y.

Indian Collection. Buffalo and Erie County Historical Society. Buffalo, N.Y.

Indian Rights Association. Historical Society of Pennsylvania. Philadelphia, Pa.

Alice Lee Jemison. FBI Main File. Freedom of Information and Privacy Act, #60,431. Released Aug. 17, 1978.

Joseph Keppler Papers. Heye Foundation, Museum of the American Indian Library. Bronx, N.Y.

J. P. Kinney Papers. Cornell University. Ithaca, N.Y.

Oliver LaFarge Papers. Humanities Research Center. University of Texas. Austin, Tx.

Robert La Follette, Jr. Papers. Library of Congress. Manuscript Division. Washington, D.C.

Fiorello La Guardia Papers. New York City Municipal Archives.

Herbert H. Lehman Papers. Columbia University. New York City.

Herbert H. Lehman Papers. Lieutenant Governor of New York, 1929–32. Franklin D. Roosevelt Library. Hyde Park, N.Y.

Robert Marshall Papers. Franklin D. Roosevelt Library. Hyde Park, N.Y.

Carlos Montezuma Papers. State Historical Society of Wisconsin. Madison, Wis.

Miami Agency Records. Bureau of Indian Affairs. Miami, Okla.

National Congress of American Indian Collection. National Anthropological Archives, Smithsonian Institution. Washington, D.C.

National Youth Administration. Record Group 199, National Archives. Washington, D.C.

George Norris Papers. Library of Congress. Manuscript Division. Washington, D.C.

Oneida Language and Folklore Project. Storybooks. Oneida Language Project Office. Sacred Heart Seminary. Oneida, Wis.

Oneida Tribe of Wisconsin. Minutes of the Tribal Business Committee, 1937–42. Oneida Indian Historical Society. Oneida, Wis. (Xerox copies in possession of Dr. Jack Campisi, State University of New York at Albany).

Arthur C. Parker Collection. Manuscript Division. New York State Cultural Education Center. Albany, N.Y.

Arthur C. Parker Papers. University of Rochester. Rochester, N.Y.

Leon C. Phillips Papers. Western History Collection. University of Oklahoma. Norman, Okla.

Charles Poletti Papers. Herbert H. Lehman Collection. Columbia University. New York City.

Public Works Administration. Record Group 135, National Archives. Washington, D.C.

Quapaw Agency Records. Federal Records Center. Fort Worth, Tx.

Quapaw Agency Records. Oklahoma Historical Society (Microfilm publication). Oklahoma City, Okla.

Robert Ritzenthaler Field Notes. Milwaukee Public Museum. Milwaukee, Wis.

Henry Roe Cloud Papers (with Papers of Haskell Institute). Federal Records Center. Kansas City, Mo.

Eleanor Roosevelt Papers. Franklin D. Roosevelt Library. Hyde Park, N.Y.

Franklin D. Roosevelt Papers. Franklin D. Roosevelt Library.

1. Papers as Governor of New York, 1929–32.
2. Papers as President, Alphabetical File.
3. Papers as President, Official File.
4. Papers as President, President's Personal File.

5. Papers as President, President's Secretary's File.

Smiley Family papers. Haverford College. Haverford, Pa.

Alfred E. Smith Collection. New York State Archives. New York State Cultural Education Center. Albany, N.Y.

Elbert D. Thomas Papers. Franklin D. Roosevelt Library. Hyde Park, N.Y.

Elmer Thomas Papers. Western History Collection. University of Oklahoma. Norman, Okla.

Rexford Tugwell Papers. Franklin D. Roosevelt Library. Hyde Park, N.Y.

James J. Wadsworth Papers. Library of Congress. Manuscript Division. Washington, D.C.

Robert F. Wagner, Sr., Papers. Georgetown University. Washington, D.C.

Paul A. W. Wallace Papers. Pennsylvania Historical and Museum Commission. Harrisburg, Pa.

Aubrey W. Williams Papers. Franklin D. Roosevelt Library. Hyde Park, N.Y.

Works Progress Administration. Record Group 69, National Archives. Washington, D.C.

Interviews

Chief James Allen, Aug. 17, 1979, Miami, Okla.

Oscar Archiquette, Oct. 20, 1978, Shell Lake, Wis. Interview conducted and transcribed by Dr. Robert W. Venables, Museum of the American Indian.

Ruth Baird, Oct. 20, 22, 1978, Green Bay, Seymour, Wis.

David Bartholomew, May 3, 1975, Aug. 4, 1978, New Paltz, N.Y.

Catherine Bauer, April 6, 1978, Cherokee Indian Reservation, Cherokee, N.C.

Louis R. Bruce, Jr., Dec. 11, 1980, Washington, D.C.

Ramona Charles, May 22, 1980, Tonawanda Indian Reservation.

Anderson Cornelius, Oct. 21, 1978, Oneida, Wis.

Melissa Cornelius, Oct. 21, 1978, Oneida, Wis.

Rupert Costo, April 20–21, 1979, Geneva, N.Y.

Frank Danforth, Oct. 20, 1978, Oneida, Wis.

Ruby Diebold, Aug. 18, 1979, Bassett Springs, Okla.

Ray Fadden, July 14–16, 1980, Onchiota, N.Y.

William N. Fenton, Sept. 28, 1977, June 21, 1978, Albany, N.Y.

W. Sheldon Fisher, July 24, 1978, Fishers, N.Y.

Robert Galloway, June 3, 1978, Silver Creek, N.Y.

Harrison Ground, July 25, 1978, Tonawanda Indian Reservation.

Nameé Henricks, May 20, 1980, Penn Yan, N.Y.

Arleigh Hill, July 25, 1978, Rochester, N.Y.

Cephas Hill, July 26, 1978, Tonawanda Indian Reservation.

Norbert Hill, Sr., Oct. 17, 1978, Oneida, Wis.

Jeanne Marie Jemison, Aug. 26, 1977, May 2–4, Aug. 23, 1978, Herndon, Va., New Paltz, N.Y., and Tyson's Corners, Va.

Francis Kettle, July 27, 1977, June 4, 1978, Cattaraugus Indian Reservation.

Winifred Kettle, July 27, 1977, May 2–4, 1978, Cattaraugus Indian Reservation and New Paltz, N.Y.

Florence Lay, June 4, 1978, Cattaraugus Indian Reservation.

Beulah Rickard Lillvick, June 6, 1978, Tuscarora Indian Reservation.

Floyd Lounsbury, Nov. 16, 1978, New Haven, Conn.

Gordie McLester, Oct. 17–22, 1978, Oneida, Wis.

Velma Nieberding, Aug. 17, 1979, Miami, Okla.

W. David Owl, July 28, 1977, Versailles, N.Y.

William H. Parcell, Aug. 17, 1979, Miami, Okla.

Edna Parker, June 4, 1977, Cattaraugus Indian Reservation.

Genevieve Plummer, July 28, 1977, Allegany Indian Reservation.

Chief Irving Powless, Sr., May 15, 1979, Onondaga Indian Reservation.

Robert Ritzenthaler, Oct. 23, 1978, Hales' Corners, Wis.

Jim Schuyler, Oct. 20, 1978, Oneida, Wis.

Pauline Seneca, June 4, 1978, Cattaraugus Indian Reservation.

Chief Leon Shenandoah (Tadodaho), May 15, 1979, Onondaga Indian Reservation.

David Skenandore, Oct. 22, 1978, Oneida, Wis.

Chief Corbett Sundown, May 22, 1980, Tonawanda Indian Reservation.

Loretta Webster, Oct. 18, 1978, Oneida, Wis.

Charles Banks Wilson, Aug. 18, 1979, Miami, Okla.

Government Publications

American Indian Policy Review Commission. *Final Report.* 2 vols. Washington, D.C., 1977.

Annual Reports of the Board of Indian Commissioners, 1869–1930. Washington, D.C.

Annual Reports of the Commissioner of Indian Affairs, 1875–1945. Washington, D.C.

Annual Reports of the Secretary of the Interior, 1933–42. Washington, D.C.

Birdseye, Ruth A. *Indian Education in New York State, 1846–1953–1954*. Albany, N.Y., 1954.

Donaldson, Thomas, comp. *The Six Nations in New York*. Special Supplement Prepared by the Interior Department for the Eleventh Census, 1890. Washington, D.C., 1894.

Haas, Theodore H. *Ten Years of Tribal Government Under IRA*. Washington, D.C., 1947.

Kappler, Charles J., comp. *Indian Affairs: Laws and Treaties*. 5 vols. Washington, D.C., 1904–1941. (Volume 2 has been reprinted as Indian Treaties, 1778–1883, New York, 1972).

New York State. *Annual Reports of the New York State Board of Charities, 1868–1929*. Albany.

———. *Annual Reports of the New York State Board of Social Welfare, 1929–1936*. Albany, N.Y.

———. *Annual Reports of the New York State Department of Social Welfare, 1936–1942*. Albany, N.Y.

———. *Annual Reports of the New York State Interdepartmental Committee on Indian Affairs, 1959–1974*. Albany, N.Y.

———. *Annual Reports of the New York State Superintendent of Public Instruction, 1887–1941*. Albany, N.Y.

———. Assembly. Legislative Document 51: *Report of the Special Committee Appointed by the Assembly of 1888 to Investigate the "Indian Problem" of the State*. Albany, N.Y., 1889.

———. Assembly. Legislative Document 40: *Report of the Special Committee to Investigate and Ascertain the Extent of the Powers Possessed by the State to Regulate and Control the Affairs and Property Rights of the Indians*. Albany, N.Y., 1906.

———. Assembly. *Report of the New York State Indian Commission, 1922*. (Everett Report).

———. Governor's Commission on Unemployment Relief. *Work Relief in the State of New York*. Albany, N.Y., 1936.

———. *Public Papers of Herbert H. Lehman, Forty-ninth Governor of the State of New York*. 10 vols. Albany, N.Y., 1934–47.

———. Temporary Emergency Relief Administration. *Administration of Public Employment Relief in New York State: It's Scope, Accomplishments and Cost, April 1, 1934–March 31, 1935*. Albany, N.Y., 1935.

(Smithsonian) *Handbook of North American Indians*. Vol. 15 Bruce G. Trigger and William C. Sturtevant, eds. Washington, D.C., 1978.

United States Congress. *Congressional Record*, 1875–1945.

———. House. Committee on Indian Affairs. Hearings on H.R. 9720: *Indians of New York*. 71st Congress. 1st Session. Washington, D.C., 1930.

———. House. Committee on Indian Affairs. Hearings on H.R. 7902: *Readjustment of Indian Affairs*. 73rd Congress. 2nd Session. Washington, D.C., 1934.

———. House. Committee on Indian Affairs. Hearings on S. 2045: *A Bill to Promote the General Welfare of the Indians of Oklahoma*. 74th Congress. 1st Session. Washington, D.C., 1935.

———. House. Committee on Indian Affairs. Hearings on H.R. 6234: *A Bill to Promote the General Welfare of the Indians of the State of Oklahoma and for Other Purposes*. 74th Congress. 1st Session. Washington, D.C., 1935.

———. House. Committee on Indian Affairs. Hearings on H.R. 7781 and other matters: *Indian Conditions and Affairs*. 74th Congress. 1st Session. Washington, D.C., 1935.

———. House. Committee on Indian Affairs. Hearings on S. 2103: *Wheeler-Howard Act—Exempt Certain Indians*. 76th Congress. 3rd Session. Washington, D.C., 1940.

———. Senate Subcommittee of the Committee on Indian Affairs. Hearings on S. Res. 79: *Survey of Conditions of the Indians in the United States*. 43 parts. 70th–76th Congress. Washington, D.C., 1928–43.

———. Senate. Committee on Indian Affairs. Hearings on S. 5302: *Fish and Game Within the Allegany, Cattaraugus, and Oil Spring Reservations*. 72nd Congress. 2nd Session. Washington, D.C., 1933.

———. Senate. Committee on Indian Affairs. Hearings on S. 2755 and S. 3645: *To Grant to Indians Living Under Federal Tutelage the Freedom to Organize*. Washington, D.C., 1934.

———. Senate. Subcommittee of the Committee of the Interior and Insular Affairs. Hearings ... *New York Indians*. 80th Congress. 2nd Session. Washington, D.C., 1948.

United States. National Resources Board. Land Planning Committee. *Indian Land Tenure, Economic Status and Population Trends*. Washington, D.C., 1935.

Court Cases

Deere et al. v. State of New York et al. 22 F 2d. 851 (1927).

Ex Parte Green. 123F2d.862 (1941).

Richard Isaac v. Ackland Davey. 2RCS 897 (1977).

Lonewolf v. Hitchcock. 187 U.S.553 (1903).

McCandless, Commissioner of Immigration v. United States ex. rel. Diabo. 18 F2d862, 25F2d71 (1927).

Oneida Indian Nation v. County of Oneida. 414 U.S.661 (1974).

People v. Redeye. 358NYS 2d632 (1974).

United States v. Boylan. 265F165 (1920).

United States v. Forness. 125F 2d932 (1942).

Woodin v. Seeley. 252 NYS818 (1931).

Newspapers and Periodicals

Akwesasne Notes

Albany Knickerbocker News

Albany Knickerbocker Press

Albany Times-Union

American Indian

Auburn Citizen Advertiser

Baltimore Sun

Batavia News (N.Y.)

Brooklyn Daily Eagle

Buffalo Courier-Express

Buffalo Evening News

Daily Oklahoman

De Pere Journal Democrat

The First American

Harlow's Weekly

Indian Education

Indians at Work

Indian Truth

Miami Daily News-Record (Okla.)

Milwaukee Journal

Milwaukee Sentinel

The Nation

New York State Education

New Republic

New York Herald Tribune

New York Times

Niagara Falls Gazette

Progressive Education

Rochester Democrat and Chronicle

(Rochester) *Museum Service*

Rochester Times-Union

Salamanca Republican-Press (N.Y.)

The Six Nations

Sunset

Survey

Syracuse Herald

Syracuse Post Standard

Social Welfare Bulletin
(New York State)

Southern Workman
  (Hampton Institute)

Tulsa Daily World
Tulsa Tribune

Washington Post
Wassaja (Chicago)
Wassaja (San Francisco)
Wisconsin State Journal (Madison)

Books and Pamphlets

Abrams, George H. J. *The Seneca People*. Phoenix, Ariz., 1976.

Akwesasne Notes. *A Basic Call to Consciousness: The Hau De No Sau Nee Address to the Western World, Geneva, Switzerland, Autumn, 1977*. Rooseveltown, N.Y., 1978.

Armstrong, William H. *Warrior in Two Camps: Ely S. Parker, Union General and Seneca Chief*. Syracuse, N.Y., 1978.

Baird, W. David. *The Quapaw Indians*. Norman, Okla., 1980.

Bauer, Fred B. *Land of the Cherokees*. Brevard, N.C., 1971.

Beauchamp, William M. *A History of the New York Iroquois*. New York State Museum Bulletin 78. Albany, N.Y., 1905.

Bellush, Bernard. *Franklin D. Roosevelt as Governor of New York*. New York, 1955.

Berkhofer, Robert F., Jr. *The White Man's Indian*. New York, 1978.

Bowers, C. A. *The Progressive Educator and the Depression: The Radical Years*. New York, 1969.

Boyce, George A. *When the Navajos Had Too Many Sheep: The 1940's*. San Francisco, Calif., 1974.

Burner, David. *Herbert Hoover: A Public Life*. New York, 1979.

———. *The Politics of Provincialism: The Democratic Party in Transition, 1918–1932*. New York, 1968.

Burnette, Robert and John Koster. *The Road to Wounded Knee*. New York, 1974.

Burns, James MacGregor. *Roosevelt: The Lion and the Fox*. New York, 1956.

———. *Roosevelt: The Soldier of Freedom*. New York, 1970.

Carlson, John Roy (pseud. of Arthur Derounian). *Under Cover: My Four Years in the Nazi Underworld of America*. New York, 1943.

Carmer, Carl. *Dark Trees to the Wind*. New York, 1949.

———. *Listen for a Lonesome Drum*. New York, 1936.

Chambers, Clarke A. *Seedtime of Reform: American Social Service and Social Action, 1918–1938*. Minneapolis, Minn., 1963.

Chazanof, William. *Joseph Ellicott and the Holland Land Company: The Opening of Western New York*. Syracuse, N.Y., 1970.

Collier, John. *From Every Zenith*. Denver, Colo., 1963.

————. *Indians of the Americas*. New York, 1947.

————. *On the Gleaming Way*. Denver, Colo., 1962.

Congdon, Charles E. *Allegany Ox-Box*. Little Valley, N.Y., 1967.

Conkin, Paul K. *Tomorrow a New World: The New Deal Community Program*. Ithaca, N.Y., 1959.

Cornplanter, Jesse J. *Legends of the Longhouse*. Philadelphia, Pa., 1938.

Cremin, Lawrence A. *The Transformation of the School: Progressivism in American Education, 1876–1957*. New York, 1961.

Davis, Allen. *Spearheads for Reform: the Social Settlements and the Progressive Movement, 1890–1914*. New York, 1967.

Davis, Kenneth S. *FDR: The Beckoning of Destiny, 1882–1928*. New York, 1972.

Debo, Angie. *And Still the Waters Run: The Betrayal of the Five Civilized Tribes*. Princeton, N.J., 1940.

Diamond, Sandor. *The Nazi Movement in the United States, 1924–1941*. Ithaca, N.Y., 1974.

Dies, Martin. *The Trojan Horse in America*. New York, 1940.

Edmunds, R. David, ed. *American Indian Leaders: Studies in Diversity*. Lincoln, Nebr., 1980.

Fausold, Martin L. *James W. Wadsworth, Jr.: The Gentleman from New York*. Syracuse, N.Y., 1975.

————, ed. *The Hoover Presidency: A Reappraisal*. Albany, N.Y., 1974.

Fenton, William N. *An Outline of Seneca Ceremonies at Coldspring Longhouse*. Yale University Publications in Anthropology, 9. New Haven, Conn.

————. *The Iroquois Eagle Dance, An Offshoot of the Calumet Dance*. Bureau of American Ethnology Bulletin 156. Washington, D.C., 1953.

————, and John Gulick, eds. *Symposium on Cherokee and Iroquois Culture*. Bureau of American Ethnology Bulletin 156. Washington, D.C., 1961.

————, ed. *Symposium on Local Diversity in Iroquois Culture*. Bureau of American Ethnology Bulletin 149. Washington, D.C., 1951.

Foreman, Grant. *The Last Trek of the Indians*. Chicago, Ill., 1946.

Freidel, Frank. *Franklin D. Roosevelt: The Apprenticeship*. Boston, Mass., 1952.

————. *Franklin D. Roosevelt: The Ordeal*. Boston, Mass., 1954.

————. *Franklin D. Roosevelt: The Triumph*. Boston, Mass., 1956.

————. *Franklin D. Roosevelt: Launching the New Deal*. Boston, Mass., 1973.

Fritz, Henry E. *The Movement for Indian Assimilation, 1860–1890*. Philadelphia, Pa., 1963.

Gates, Paul Wallace. *Fifty Million Acres: Conflicts Over Kansas Land Policy, 1854–1890*. Ithaca, N.Y., 1954.

Gibson, Arell, ed. *America's Exiles: Indian Colonization in Oklahoma*. Oklahoma City, Okla., 1976.

————. *Wilderness Bonanza: The Tri-State District of Missouri, Kansas, and Oklahoma*. Norman, Okla., 1972.

Goldschmidt, Walter. *The Uses of Anthropology*. Washington, D.C., 1979.

Graham, Otis. *An Encore for Reform: The Old Progressives and the New Deal*. New York, 1967.

Graymont, Barbara. *The Iroquois in the American Revolution*. Syracuse, N.Y., 1972.

————, ed. *Fighting Tuscarora: The Autobiography of Chief Clinton Rickard*. Syracuse, N.Y., 1973.

Hagan, William T. *American Indians*. 2nd ed. Chicago, Ill., 1979.

Hale, Horatio. *The Iroquois Book of Rites*. William N. Fenton, ed. Toronto, 1963.

Hertzberg, Hazel. *The Search for an American Indian Identity: Modern Pan-Indian Movements*. Syracuse, N.Y., 1971.

Hewitt, J. N. B. *Iroquoian Cosmology*. Part I 21st Annual Report of the Bureau of American Ethnology. Washington, D.C., 1928.

Holway, W. R. *A History of the Grand River Dam Authority, State of Oklahoma, 1935–1968*. 2 vols. Tulsa, Okla., 1968.

Hoover, Herbert. *The Memoirs of Herbert Hoover*. 3 vols. New York, 1952.

Hubbard, Jeremiah. *Forty Years Among the Indians*. Miami, Okla., 1913.

Huthmacher, J. Joseph. *Senator Robert F. Wagner and the Rise of Urban Liberalism*. New York, 1968.

Ickes, Harold L. *The Autobiography of a Curmudgeon*. New York, 1943.

————. *The Secret Diary of Harold L. Ickes*. 3 vols. New York, 1954.

Ingalls, Robert P. *Herbert H. Lehman and New York's Little New Deal*. New York, 1975.

Jemison, Alice Lee, and O. K. Chandler. *Now Who's Un-American? An Exposé of Communism in the United States Government*. Washington, D.C., 1937?

Kellogg, Laura Cornelius. *Our Democracy and the American Indian*. Kansas City, Mo., 1920.

Kelly, Lawrence C. *The Navajo Indians and Federal Indian Policy, 1900—1935*. Tucson, Ariz., 1968.

Kelley, William H., ed. *Indian Affairs and the Indian Reorganization Act: The Twenty Year Record*. Tucson, Ariz., 1954.

Kinney, J. P. *A Continent Lost—A Civilization Won: Indian Land Tenure in America*. Baltimore, Md., 1937.

———. *Facing Indian Facts*. Laurens, N.Y., 1973.

———. *Indian Forest and Range: A History of the Administration and Conservation of the Redman's Heritage*. Washington, D.C., 1950.

———. *My First Ninety-Five Years*. Hartwick, N.Y., 1972.

Kvasnicka, Robert M., and Herman J. Viola, eds. *The Commissioner of Indian Affairs, 1824—1977*. Lincoln, Nebr., 1979.

LaFarge, Oliver, ed. *The Changing Indian*. Norman, Okla., 1942.

Lawson, R. Alan. *The Failure of Independent Liberalism, 1930—1941*. New York, 1971.

Leuchtenburg, William E. *Franklin D. Roosevelt and the New Deal, 1932—1940*. New York, 1963.

———. *The Perils of Prosperity, 1914—1932*. Chicago, Ill., 1958.

Lindquist, G. E. *Red Man in the United States*. New York, 1923.

Lounsbury, Floyd G. *Oneida Verb Morphology*. Yale University Publications in Anthropology 48. New Haven, Conn., 1953.

Lubove, Roy. *The Professional Altruist: The Emergence of Social Work as a Career, 1880—1930*. New York, 1969.

———. *The Progressives and the Slums: Tenement House Reform in New York City, 1890—1917*. Pittsburgh, Pa., 1962.

McCoy, Donald R. *Calvin Coolidge: The Quiet President*. New York, 1967.

McDonald, William F. *Federal Relief Administration and the Arts*. Columbus, Ohio, 1969.

McKelvey, Blake. *Rochester: An Emerging Metropolis, 1925—1961*. Rochester, N.Y., 1961.

McKinzie, Richard D. *The New Deal for Artists*. Princeton, N.J., 1973.

McNickle, D'Arcy. *Indian Man: A Life of Oliver LaFarge*. Bloomington, Ind., 1971.

———. *They Came Here First*. Rev. ed. New York, 1975.

Mangione, Jerre. *The Dream and the Deal; the Federal Writers' Project, 1935—1943*. Boston, Mass., 1972.

Mardock, Robert Winston. *The Reformers and the American Indian*. Columbia, Mo., 1971.

Meriam, Lewis, et al. *The Problem of Indian Administration*. Baltimore, Md., 1928.

Miner, H. Craig. *The Corporation and the Indian: Tribal Sovereignty and Industrial Civilization in Indian Territory, 1865–1907.* Columbia, Mo., 1976.

———, and William E. Unrau. *The End of Indian Kansas: A Study of Cultural Revolution, 1854–1871.* Lawrence, Kan., 1978.

Morgan, Arthur E. *Dams and Other Disasters.* Boston, Mass., 1971.

Morgan, Lewis Henry. *The League of the Ho-de-no-sau-nee or Iroquois.* Rochester, N.Y., 1851.

Murray, Robert K. *The Harding Era.* Minneapolis, Minn., 1969.

Nevins, Allan. *Herbert H. Lehman and His Era.* New York, 1963.

Nieberding, Velma. *The Quapaws.* Miami, Okla., 1976.

O'Connor, Francis. *Art for the Millions.* Greenwich, Conn., 1973.

———, ed. *The New Deal Arts Projects: An Anthology of Memoirs.* Washington, D.C., 1972.

Onondaga Historical Association. *Official Record of the Indian Conference Called to Determine the Status of the Indians of the Six Nations*, March 6–7, 1919. Syracuse, N.Y., 1919.

Otis, D. S. *The Dawes Act and the Allotment of Indian Lands.* Francis Paul Prucha, ed. Norman, Okla., 1973.

Park, Marlene, and Gerald Moskowitz. *New Deal for Art.* Hamilton, N.Y., 1971.

Parker, Arthur C. *Parker on the Iroquois.* William N. Fenton, ed. Syracuse, N.Y., 1968.

Patterson, James T. *Congressional Conservatism and the New Deal: The Growth of the Conservative Coalition in Congress, 1933–1939.* Lexington, Ky., 1967.

———. *The New Deal and the States: Federalism in Transition.* Princeton, N.J., 1969.

Pelley, William Dudley. *Indians Aren't Red: The Inside Story of Administration Attempts to Make Communists of the North Carolina Cherokees.* Asheville, N.C., 1939.

Pells, Richard H. *Radical Visions and American Dreams: Culture and Social Thought in the Depression Years.* New York, 1973.

Penkower, Monty Noam. *The Federal Writers' Project: A Study in Government Patronage of the Arts.* Urbana, Ill., 1977.

Philp, Kenneth R. *John Collier's Crusade for Indian Reform, 1920–1954.* Tucson, Ariz., 1977.

Priest, Loring Benson. *Uncle Sam's Stepchildren: The Reformation of United States Indian Policy, 1865–1887.* New Brunswick, N.J., 1942.

Prucha, Francis Paul. *American Indian Policy in Crisis: Christian Reformers and the Indian, 1865–1900.* Norman, Okla., 1976.

Radomski, Alexander L. *Work Relief in New York State, 1931–1935*. New York, 1947.

Richards, Cara E. *The Oneida People*. Phoenix, Ariz., 1974.

Ritzenthaler, Robert. *The Oneida Indians of Wisconsin*. Bulletin of the Public Museum of the City of Milwaukee, 19. Milwaukee, Wis., 1950.

Rogge, John O. *The Official German Report: Nazi Penetration, 1924–1942: Pan-Arabism, 1939–Today*. New York, 1961.

Romasco, Albert U. *The Poverty of Abundance: Hoover, the Nation, the Depression*. New York, 1965.

Rosen, Elliot A. *Hoover, Roosevelt and the Brains Trust: From Depression to New Deal*. New York, 1977.

Salmond, John A. *The Civilian Conservation Corps, 1933–1942: A New Deal Case Study*. Durham, N.C., 1967.

Schlesinger, Arthur M., Jr. *The Crisis of the Old Order, 1919–1933*. Boston, Mass., 1957.

———. *The Coming of the New Deal*. Boston, Mass., 1959.

———. *The Politics of Upheaval*. Boston, Mass., 1960.

Schneider, David M., and Deutsch, Albert. *The History of Public Welfare in New York State, 1867–1940*. Chicago, Ill., 1941.

Schwartz, Jordan A. *The Interregnum of Despair: Hoover, Congress, and the Depression*. Urbana, Ill., 1970.

Searle, Charles F. *Minister of Relief: Harry Hopkins and the Depression*. Syracuse, N.Y., 1963.

Settle, William A., Jr. *The Dawning: A New Day for the Southwest: A History of the United States Army Corps of Engineers, Tulsa District*. Tulsa, Okla., 1975.

Shimony, Annemarie. *Conservatism Among the Iroquois at the Six Nations Reserve*. Yale University Publications in Anthropology, 65. New Haven, Conn., 1961.

Smith, Geoffrey S. *To Save a Nation: American Countersubversives, the New Deal and the Coming of World War II*. New York, 1973.

Smith, James F. and Robert M. Kvasnicka, eds. *Indian-White Relations: A Persistent Paradox*. Washington, D.C., 1976.

Spier, Leslie, et al., eds. *Language, Culture and Personality: Essays in Memory of Edward Sapir*. Menasha, Wis., 1941.

Swadesh, Morris. *The Origin and Diversification of Language*. Joel Sherzer, ed. Chicago, 1967.

Szasz, Margaret. *Education and the American Indian: The Road to Self-Determination, 1928–1973*. Albuquerque, N. Mex., 1974.

Taylor, Graham D. *The New Deal and American Indian Tribalism: The Administration of the Indian Reorganization Act, 1934–1945*. Lincoln, Nebr., 1980.

Terkel, Studs. *Hard Times: An Oral History of the Great Depression*. New York, 1970.

Tooker, Elisabeth. *The Iroquois Ceremonial of Midwinter*. Syracuse, N.Y., 1970.

————, ed. *Iroquois Culture, History and Prehistory: Proceedings of the 1965 Conference on Iroquois Research*. Albany, N.Y., 1967.

Trani, Eugene P., and David L. Wilson. *The Presidency of Warren G. Harding*. Lawrence, Kan., 1977.

Tyler, Daniel, ed. *Red Men and Hat Wearers: Viewpoints in Indian History*. Boulder, Colo., 1976.

Upton, Helen M. *The Everett Report in Historical Perspective: The Indians of New York State*. Albany, N.Y., 1980.

Wallace, Anthony F. C. *The Death and Rebirth of the Seneca*. New York, 1970.

Washburn, Wilcomb E. *The Assault on Tribalism: The General Allotment Law (Dawes Act) of 1887*. Philadelphia, Pa., 1975.

————. *The Indian in America*. New York, 1975.

————. *Red Man's Land/White Man's Law: A Study of the Past and Present Status of the American Indian*. New York, 1971.

Warren, Harris Gaylord. *Herbert Hoover and the Great Depression*. New York, 1959.

Wheeler, Burton K. *Yankee From the West*. Garden City, N.Y., 1962.

Wilbur, Ray Lyman, and Arthur M. Hyde, eds. *The Hoover Policies*. New York, 1937.

————. *The Memoirs of Ray Lyman Wilbur, 1875–1949*. Edgar Eugene Robinson and Paul Carroll Edwards, eds. Stanford, Calif., 1960.

Williams, Ted C. *The Reservation*. Syracuse, N.Y., 1976.

Wilson, Charles Banks, ed. *The Quapaw Agency Indians*. Miami, Okla., 1947.

Wilson, Edmund. *Apologies to the Iroquois*. New York, 1959.

Wilson, Joan Hoff. *Herbert Hoover: Forgotten Progressive*. Boston, Mass., 1975.

Wolfskill, George, and John A. Hudson. *All But the People: Franklin D. Roosevelt and His Critics, 1933–1939*. New York, 1969.

————. *The Revolt of the Conservatives: A History of the American Liberty League, 1934–1940*. Boston, Mass., 1962.

Zinn, Howard, ed. *New Deal Thought*. Indianapolis, Ind., 1966.

Articles

Abler, Thomas S. "Friends, Factions, and the Seneca Nation Revolution of 1848." *Niagara Frontier* 21 (Winter 1974): 74–79.

Barbeau, Marius. "Classification of Iroquoian Radicals with Subjective Pronominal Prefixes." Anthropological Series 7, *Memoirs of the Canadian Geological Survey* 46. Ottawa, Ontario, 1915.

Berkhofer, Robert F., Jr. "The Political Context of a New Indian History." *Pacific Historical Review* 40 (Aug. 1971): 363–82.

Billington, Ray Allen. "Government and the Arts: The WPA Experience." *American Quarterly* 13 (Winter 1961): 466–71.

Boas, Franz. "Notes on the Iroquois Language." In *Putnam Anniversary Volume: Anthropological Essays presented to F. W. Putnam*. New York, 1909.

Bromert, Roger. "The Sioux and the Indian CCC." *South Dakota History* 7 (Fall 1978): 340–56.

Campisi, Jack. "New York-Oneida Treaty of 1795: A Finding of Fact." *American Indian Law Review* 4 (1976): 71–82.

Chernow, Barbara A. "Robert Morris: Genesee Land Speculator." *New York History* 58 (April 1977): 195–220.

Cohn, Bernard S. "History and Anthropology: The State of Play." *Comparative Studies in Society and History* 22 (April 1980): 198–221.

Clute, James W. "The New York Indians' Rights to Self-Determination." *Buffalo Law Review* 22 (Spring 1973): 985–1019.

Downes, Randolph C. "A Crusade for Indian Reform, 1922–1934." *Mississippi Valley Historical Review* 32 (December 1945): 331–54.

Duncan, Kate L. "American Indian Lace Making." *American Indian Art* 5 (Summer 1980): 28–35, 80.

Fenton, William N. "Aboriginally Yours, Jesse J. Cornplanter." In *American Indian Intellectuals*. Margot Liberty, ed. St. Paul, Minn., 1978.

———. "Asher Wright's Seneca Mission." *Proceedings* of the American Philosophical Society, 100 (1956): 567–81.

———, ed. "Seneca Indians by Asher Wright (1959)." *Ethnohistory* 4 (1957): 302–321.

———. "The Iroquois Confederacy in the Twentieth Century: A Case Study of the Theory of Lewis Henry Morgan in 'Ancient Society.'" *Ethnology* 4 (July 1965): 251–65.

————. "The Iroquois in History." In *North American Indians in Historical Perspective*, Eleanor B. Leacock and Nancy O. Lurie, eds. New York, 1971.

————. "Problems Arising From the Historic Northeastern Position of the Iroquois." In *Essays in Historical Anthropology of North America*. *Smithsonian Institution Miscellaneous Collections* 100 (1940): 159–251.

————. "This Island, the World on the Turtle's Back." *Journal of American Folklore* 75 (Oct.–Dec. 1962): 283–300.

Fox, Daniel. "The Achievement of the Federal Writers' Project." *American Quarterly* 12 (Spring 1961): 3–19.

Gower, Calvin W. "The CCC Indian Division: Aid for Depressed Americans, 1933–1942." *Minnesota History* 43 (Spring 1972): 3–13.

Graymont, Barbara. "New York State Indian Policy After the Revolution." *New York History* 57 (Oct. 1976): 438–74.

Gunther, Gerald. "Governmental Power and New York Indian Lands — A Reassessment of a Persistent Problem of Federal-State Relations." *Buffalo Law Review* 7 (Fall 1958): 1–14.

Hauptman, Laurence M. "Alice Lee Jemison." In *Notable American Women: The Modern Period*. Barbara Sicherman and Carol Hurd Green, eds. Cambridge, Mass., 1980.

————. "Alice Lee Jemison: Seneca Political Activist, 1901–1964." *Indian Historian* 12 (June 1979): 15–22.

————. "Governor Theodore Roosevelt and the Indians of New York State." *Proceedings* of the American Philosophical Society, 119 (Feb. 1975): 1–7.

————. "The Iroquois School of Art: Arthur C. Parker and the Seneca Arts Project, 1935–1941." *New York History* 60 (July 1979): 282–312.

————. "Raw Deal: The Iroquois View the Indian Reorganization Act of 1934." In *Studies on Iroquoian Culture*. Nancy Bonvillain, ed. (Rindge, N.H., 1980), pp. 15–24.

————. "Senecas and Subdividers: The Resistance to Allotment of Indian Lands in New York, 1875–1906." *Prologue: The Journal of the National Archives* 9 (Summer 1977): 105–116.

Hertzberg, Hazel. "Arthur C. Parker, Seneca, 1881–1955." In *American Indian Intellectuals*. Margot Liberty, ed. St. Paul, Minn., 1979.

————. "Nationality, Anthropology and Pan-Indianism in the Life of Arthur C. Parker." *Proceedings* of the American Philosophical Society, 123 (Feb. 1979): 47–72.

Hogan, Thomas E. "City in a Quandary: Salamanca and the Allegany Leases." *New York History* 55 (Jan. 1974): 79–101.

Howard, James H. "Cultural Persistence and Cultural Changes as Reflected in Oklahoma Seneca-Cayuga Ceremonialism." *Plains Anthropologist* 6 (1961): 21–30.

———. "Environment and Culture: The Case of the Oklahoma Seneca-Cayuga." Oklahoma *Anthropological Society Newsletter* 18 (Sept. 1970): 5–13; (Oct. 1970): 5–19.

Hymes, Dell. "Morris Swadesh: From the First Yale School to World Prehistory." In *Morris Swadesh, The Origin and Diversification of Language*. Joel Sherzer, ed. Chicago, Ill., 1967.

Jacobsen, Peter Maxwell. "Who Rules the Valley of the Six Nations?" *McGill Law Journal* 22 (1976): 130–47.

Jones, Alfred H. "The Search for a Useable American Past in the New Deal Era." *American Quarterly* 23 (Dec. 1971): 710–24.

Kelly, Lawrence C. "Anthropology and Anthropologists in the Indian New Deal." *Journal of the History of the Behavioral Sciences* 16 (Jan. 1980): 6–24.

———. "Choosing the New Deal Indian Commissioner: Ickes versus Collier." *New Mexico Historical Review* 46 (Oct. 1974): 269–88.

———. "The Indian Reorganization Act: The Dream and the Reality." *Pacific Historical Review* 44 (Aug. 1975): 391–412.

Koppes, Clayton R. "From New Deal to Termination: Liberalism and Indian Policy, 1933–1953." *Pacific Historical Review* 46 (Nov. 1977): 543–66.

Kunitz, Stephen J. "The Social Philosophy of John Collier." *Ethnohistory* 18 (Summer 1971): 213–19.

Lounsbury, Floyd G. "One Hundred Years of Anthropological Linguistics." In *One Hundred Years of Anthropology*. J. O. Brew, ed. Cambridge, Mass., 1968.

McNickle, D'Arcy. "Anthropology and the Indian Reorganization Act." In *The Uses of Anthropology*. Walter Goldschmidt, ed. Washington, D.C., 1979.

Manley, Henry S. "Buying Buffalo from the Indians." *New York History* 28 (July 1947): 313–29.

Mathews, Jane De Hart. "Arts and the People: The New Deal Quest for a Cultural Democracy." *Journal of American History* 62 (Sept. 1975): 316–39.

Mathur, Mary E. Fleming. "The Jay Treaty and the Boundary Line." *Indian Historian* 3 (Winter 1970): 37–40.

MeKeel, Scudder. "An Appraisal of the Indian Reorganization Act." *American Anthropologist* 46 (April–June 1944): 209–217.

Parman, Donald L. "The Indian and the Civilian Conservation Corps." *Pacific Historical Review* 40 (Feb. 1971): 39–57.

————. "J. C. Morgan: Navajo Apostle of Assimilation." *Prologue: The Journal of the National Archives* 4 (Summer 1972): 83–98.

Philp, Kenneth R. "Albert B. Fall and the Protest from the Pueblos, 1921–1923." *Arizona and the West* 12 (Autumn 1970): 237–54.

————. "Herbert Hoover's New Era: A False Dawn for the American Indian." *Rocky Mountain Social Science Journal* 9 (April 1972): 53–60.

————. "John Collier and the Crusade to Protect Indian Religious Freedom, 1920–1926." *Journal of Ethnic Studies* 1 (Spring 1973): 22–38.

————. "John Collier and the Indians of the Americas: The Dream and the Reality." *Prologue: The Journal of the National Archives* 11 (Spring 1979): 4–21.

Quinten, B. T. "Oklahoma Tribes, the Great Depression and the Indian Bureau." *Mid-America* 49 (January 1967): 29–43.

Ritchie, William A. "Arthur Caswell Parker, 1881–1955." *American Antiquity* 21 (1956): 293–98.

Smith, Michael T. "The History of Indian Citizenship." *Great Plains Journal* 10 (Fall 1970): 25–35.

————. "The Wheeler-Howard Act of 1934: The Indian New Deal." *Journal of the West* 10 (July 1971): 521–34.

Stein, Gary C. "The Indian Citizenship Act of 1924." *New Mexico Historical Review* 48 (July 1972): 257–74.

Szasz, Margaret G. "Indian Reform in a Decade of Prosperity." *Montana, the Magazine of Western History* 20 (Winter 1970): 16–27.

Taylor, Graham. "Anthropologists, Reformers, and the Indian New Deal." *Prologue: The Journal of the National Archives* 7 (Fall 1975): 151–62.

————. "The Tribal Alternative to Bureaucracy: The Indian's New Deal, 1933–1945." *Journal of the West* 13 (Jan. 1974): 128–42.

Thomas, W. Stephen. "Arthur Caswell Parker: Anthropologist, Historian, Museum Pioneer, 1881–1955." *Rochester History* 18 (July 1955): 1–20.

Trani, Eugene. "Hubert Work and the Department of the Interior, 1923–1928." *Pacific Northwest Quarterly* 61 (Jan. 1970): 31–40.

Vernon, Howard. "The Cayuga Claims: A Background Study." *American Indian Culture and Research Journal* 4 (Fall 1980): 21–35.

Weeks, Charles. "The Eastern Cherokee and the New Deal." *North Carolina Historical Review* 43 (July 1976): 303–319.

Wilkinson, Norman B. "Robert Morris and the Treaty of Big Tree." *Mississippi Valley Historical Review* 60 (Sept. 1953): 257–78.

Wright, Peter M. "John Collier and the Oklahoma Indian Welfare Act of 1936." *Chronicles of Oklahoma* 50 (Autumn 1972): 347–71.

Dissertations

Abler, Thomas S. "Factional Dispute and Party Conflict in the Political System of the Seneca Nation." Ph.D. diss., University of Toronto, 1969.

Bach, Arthur L. "The Administration of Indian Resources in the United States, 1933–1941." Ph.D. diss., University of Iowa, 1942.

Basehart, Harry W. "Historical Changes in the Kinship System of the Oneida Indians." Ph.D. diss., Harvard University, 1952.

Campisi, Jack. "Ethnic Identity and Boundary Maintenance in Three Oneida Communities." Ph.D. diss., State University of New York, Albany, 1974.

Freeman, John L., Jr. "The New Deal for Indians: A Study in Bureau-Committee Relations in American Government." Ph.D. diss., Princeton University, 1952.

McKinzie, Kathleen O'Connor. "Writers on Relief: 1935–1942." Ph.D. diss., Indiana University, 1970.

Parman, Donald L., "The Indian and the Civilian Conservation Corps." Ph.D. diss., University of Oklahoma, 1967.

Philp, Kenneth R. "John Collier and the American Indian, 1920–1945." Ph.D. diss., Michigan State University, 1968.

Rawick, George P. "The New Deal and Youth: The Civilian Conservation Corps, the National Youth Administration, the American Youth Congress." Ph.D. diss., University of Wisconsin, 1957.

Ruetten, Richard T. "Burton K. Wheeler of Montana: A Progressive Between the Wars." Ph.D. diss., University of Oregon, 1961.

Swadesh, Morris. "The Internal Economy of the Nootka Word; a Semantic Study of Word Structure in a Polysynthetic Language." Ph.D. diss., Yale University, 1933.

INDEX

THE IROQUOIS AND THE NEW DEAL

was composed in 12-point VIP Cloister Old Style and leaded one point,
with display type also in VIP Cloister Old Style,
by Utica Typesetting Company, Inc.;
printed by sheet-fed offset on 50-pound, acid-free Glatfelter Antique Cream,
Smythe-sewn and bound over boards in Joanna Arrestox,
by Maple-Vail Book Manufacturing Group, Inc.;
and published by

SYRACUSE UNIVERSITY PRESS

Syracuse, New York 13210

Date Due

NOV 2